Western
Australia
as it is today
1906

Also published by
University of Western Australia Press for
the Charles and Joy Staples
South West Region Publications Fund:

A Tribute to the Group Settlers
by P.E.M. Blond

For Their Own Good
by A. Haebich

Dearest Isabella
by P. Joske

Portraits of the South West
edited by B.K. de Garis

A Guide to Sources for the History of South Western Australia
compiled by Ronald Richards

Jardee: The Mill that Cheated Time
by Doreen Owens

Blacklegs: The Scottish Colliery Strike of 1911
by Bill Latter

Barefoot in the Creek
by L.C. Burton

The Charles and Joy Staples South West Region Publications Fund was
established in 1984 on the basis of a generous donation made to The University
of Western Australia by Charles and Joy Staples.

The purpose of the fund was to make the results of research on the South
West region of Western Australia widely available so as to assist the people of
the region and those in government and private organizations concerned with
South West projects to appreciate the needs and possibilities of the region in
the widest possible historical perspective.

The fund is administered by a committee whose aims are to make possible
the publication (either by full or part funding), by the University of Western
Australia Press, of scholarly research in any discipline relevant to the South
West region.

Western Australia
as it is today
1906

Leopoldo Zunini
Royal Consul of Italy

Edited and translated by
Margot Melia and Richard Bosworth

The Charles and Joy Staples
South West Region Publications Fund

University of Western Australia Press

This edition first published in 1997 by
University of Western Australia Press
Nedlands, Western Australia 6907
for the Charles and Joy Staples
South West Region Publications Fund

Originally published as *L'Australia attuale:
usi e costumi—agricoltura, industria e commercio,*
by Società Tipografico—Editrice Nazionale,
Torino, 1910

COVER PHOTOGRAPH: A group of
prospective settlers inspecting land,
Battye Library, 4045B/19
INSET PHOTOGRAPH: Motoring party,
Battye Library, 23714P

National Library of Australia
Cataloguing-in-Publication entry:

Zunini, Leopoldo
    [L'Australia attuale. English]
    Western Australia as it is today, 1906.

    ISBN 1 875560 97 1.

    1. Agriculture - Western Australia. 2. Italians
    - Western Australia. 3. Western Australia -
    Economic conditions - 1901–1914. I.
    Title. II. Title: L'Australia attuale. English.
    (Series: Staples South West Region
    publication series).

630.9941

Production by
Benchmark Publications Management, Melbourne
Consultant editor: Janet Blagg
Designed by Derrick I Stone Design, Melbourne
Typeset in 10/11 Meridian
Printed by Scott Four Colour Print, Perth

In memory of
A.C. 'Charlie' Staples,
died 23 April 1997.

Lover of the South West,
history, knowledge and
humankind.

Foreword

I have enjoyed this translation of Leopoldo Zunini's *L'Australia attuale* and believe that anyone concerned about problems of environmental degradation in Western Australia will find much of interest here. Zunini's report presents a broad-ranging account of agricultural developments in Western Australia in the years immediately following Federation. Of course Zunini's conclusions regarding the practicality of those developments should be examined with care: for instance, he and his delegates reflected biases from their Italian experience. Were they, perhaps, too critical of one-crop farms in the wheat belt?

More importantly, Zunini was inevitably influenced by those sections of Western Australian society with which he had most contact. James Mitchell, with his determination to clear the forest eastwards of the Darling Range, believing this to be the 'fast track to civilization' regardless of what we now know to be the environmental costs, was one who helped Zunini to 'see' Western Australia. However, despite the pressure of Mitchell and others in the Perth business community, Zunini and the delegates preferred the Upper Blackwood with its possibilities for a mixed farming more like that practised in Northern Italy. Mitchell might guide them, but they retained minds of their own.

Of course, in the end no 'Victor' or 'Emmanuel' settlements were founded and only a scattering of Italians—prominent names, mentioned by Zunini, are the Pollettis of Tambellup, and the Tiraboschis, Ferraris and Abbadinis of Kojonup and district—made their individual way to the South West before the First World War. (Giuseppe Torrisi, having heard of the delegation's visit, reached

Fremantle in 1909 and, by way of Wellington Mill, moved to Donnybrook in 1913.) A more numerous Italian presence in the South West would grow only slowly in the interwar period and then more rapidly with the commencement of mass Italian migration to Australia after the Second World War.

Nonetheless, the issues raised by Zunini in the first decade of the century are still with us. In the Upper Blackwood district today, farmers continue to debate which parts of their land are best suited to a single crop and which would be most productive if worked with garden, orchard and pasture crops. Similarly we go on discussing the homogeneity of our heritage, and thus we need all the reminders we can get on the varied origins of our peoples—English and Irish, Italian and Greek, and most recently, Vietnamese and Chinese, and many others. I congratulate Margot Melia and Richard Bosworth on producing this translated edition of Zunini's book and recommend it to all those Western Australians who are interested in hearing the views on their state of an intelligent and diligent Italian almost a century ago.

A.C. Staples
March 1997

Contents

Foreword by A.C. Staples   vii
Preface   xiii
Leopoldo Zunini in Western Australia by Margot Melia   1
Leopoldo Zunini and Liberal Italy by Richard Bosworth   12
Translators' Note   26
To the Reader   27
Map of the South West   28

Chapter One
*My First Journey to Western Australia—Albany—Perth—The Italian
Community—The Labour Question.*   29

Chapter Two
*I Return to Italy—How to Establish our Settlers in Australia?—Mission to
London—Second Journey to Western Australia—I Accompany the
Agricultural Delegates—The Norddeutscher Lloyd—The Straits of
Messina—Port Said—Aden—Colombo—Fremantle—The Immigration
Restriction Act.*   40

Chapter Three
*Arrival in Perth—Democracy and Railways—Hotels—Newspapers and
Journalists—The Midland Company.*   53

Chapter Four
*Australian Agriculture—Tours to the Harvey River and Kalamunda—
The Arduino Farm—Fruit Cultivation.*   60

Chapter Five
The Main Inspection Tour Begins—Some Geographical Notes about Western Australia—Its Agricultural Areas—Settlers and Squatters—Northam—Drinking Habits in Australia—The Flora of Western Australia—Agricultural Shows—Competitions.　　71

Chapter Six
Goomalling—The Battle against Rabbits—The Rabbitproof Fence—Agricultural Machinery—Intensive Pasturing and its Profits—Cereal Cultivation.　　83

Chapter Seven
Return to Northam—The Robustelli Farm—The Spencer Farm—Chaff—The Chinese in Australia—The Extreme South of Western Australia—The Minister for Agriculture—Mr Throssel—Catholics and Protestants—Car Trips—Mount Dick.　　91

Chapter Eight
Trip to Kellerberrin—Artesian Wells—The Water Pipeline to Coolgardie—The Leake Farm—Granite Outcrops—Aborigines—The Mitchell Farm—The Wheat Belt—The Harvest—Wool and Sheep Shearing.　　102

Chapter Nine
The Northam Agricultural Show—Banquet and Speeches—Beverley—Sandy Soils—Narrogin—The Official Reception—Mr Brown and his Opinions—The Clayton Farm—The State Experimental Farm.　　115

Chapter Ten
Wagin—Minister Piesse—His Properties—Information on Sheep Farming—A New Cincinnatus—Katanning—Piesse the Member of Parliament—Vines and Fruit Trees—Wine Production.　　126

Chapter Eleven
Tenterden—Country Hotels—The Climie Farm—More about Intensive Pasturing—Unexpected Farmers—Mount Barker—The Sounness Orchard and Apple Production.　　134

Chapter Twelve
Albany—The Millars Company—Denmark—A Ghost Town—The Impenetrable Forest—Good Fishing—Denmark's Resources—Millars' Intentions.　　141

Chapter Thirteen
Tambellup—The Polletti Farm—A Socialist Senator—Travelling in the Bush—An Australian Hyde Park—The Effect of Cultivation on the

Climate—Kojonup—'Poison Land'—A Farming Mayor—The Stephens'
Farm—Paddocks and Blackboys—Land for Italians—A Zoological
Garden—The Blackwood—Lost in the Forest?—Bridgetown.   149

Chapter Fourteen
The Balbarrup District—The Giant Forest Continues—The South-West
Corner of the State—The Timber Industry—Tree Oils—The Bridgetown
District—Greenbushes—Sardinian Type Railways—Balingup—
Donnybrook—An Australian 'Emilia'—The Settlement of Hamel—
Arrival in Perth after the Great Inspection Tour.   165

Chapter Fifteen
Journey to Moora—Gingin and the Cultivation of Oranges—
The Midland Railway Company Land—Berkshire Valley—
The Benedictine Abbey—An Automobile Adventure—An Ideal
Pasture—The Advantage of a Special Train—Return to Perth.   174

Chapter Sixteen
The Delegates' Impressions—Where to put our Settlements?—
The Departure of the Delegates For Italy—The Beginning of Negotiations
with the Western Australian Government—The Blackwood Region—My
Arrival in Kojonup—English Society—On the Balgarrup—Journey into
the Unknown—The Swamps—Aboriginal Camp—An Unfortunate
Hunter—A Wonderful Country—The Dinninup River.   186

Chapter Seventeen
Along the Blackwood—The Stewart Property—Ants and Ant-hills—
The Bush Maze—Norrish's Resourcefulness—The Popularity of the
Italian Consul—The Agricultural Development of Western Australia. 200

Chapter Eighteen
Journey to Geraldton—Its Surroundings—The Government Farm at
Chapman—Erin Farm—Paradise—Newmaracarra—Glengarry—
Dongara—The Phillips Farm—An Australian Sunset—The Salt Lake—
Arrival in Perth.   209

Conclusions   225

Appendix:
Western Australian Commerce with Notes Concerning Australasian
trade—Report by Cavaliere L. Zunini, Royal Consul at Perth   237

Bibliography   263

A Party of selectors in search of land, Kojonup 1906. H.S. Ranford, the official guide for the delegation, on far left and Italian Consul, Leopoldo Zunini, second from left.
Battye Library 4045B/25

Preface

I was working peacefully one day in the Biblioteca Nazionale in Rome when I found reference to a book written by a certain Leopoldo Zunini. It was entitled *L'Australia attuale: usi e costumi* (a literal translation would be 'Australia as it is today: customs and behaviour') and published in Turin in 1910. When a copy was produced for me to read, it turned out that the title was something of a misnomer and the book in fact was an account of Zunini's travels around Western Australia in 1906–07, in his capacity as local representative of the Italian government.

When I returned to Western Australia I looked for a copy at the Reid and Battye libraries. None was to be found, though eventually I did locate a copy in the Mitchell Library in Sydney, perhaps the only one still in Australia. I also talked to Margot Melia about the matter. She was finishing a Ph.D. on American history but she had long had an interest in the Italian presence in Western Australia. She began to do some research on Zunini, which she published in the 1991 issue of *Studies in Western Australian History* which we jointly edited.

Zunini's *L'Australia attuale* was a very rare book, a non-English language account by an intelligent and observant foreigner of Western Australia, at a time when people here began, in the first years after Federation, finally to believe that the state had a future. Zunini was trying to further a migration scheme for Italian settlers and, in pursuit of ideal land, he travelled the state from Geraldton to Denmark but with special attention directed at the south-west. As he went, he recorded land usage and productivity, his reception by local settlers, and the nature of the environment. Zunini was sympathetic, optimistic, expansive and probably, on occasion, somewhat misled by those he met—certainly his statistics should be read as his and not as the definitive word. Zunini became a great fan of Western Australia and thought his account important enough to publish even after he had been transferred to another posting and his migration plan had collapsed.

In any case, given the book's unavailability and its unique nature, Margot Melia and I decided to edit it and translate it into English. We convinced Bill Latter and Charlie Staples that the translation should be made available to those interested in the early history of Western Australia and who like to read an authentic period piece. We are especially grateful to Charlie and to the committee of the Charles and Joy Staples South West Region Publications Fund for assisting UWA Press in the publication of this book. It goes without saying that Western Australia is a tiny market and that serious works like that of Zunini will only be published here through subsidy. We are also grateful to Janine and Ian Drakeford and others at UWA Press for again preserving the highest publication standards, despite perennially working under the economic fundamentalist axe. We were lucky, too, in drawing on the excellent editorial advice of Janet Blagg in her work on our text. We thank Joanna Sassoon and others on the staff of the Battye Library, especially for their help in tracing those of the photographs in the Zunini original which we have reproduced here. We are in debt, too, to Judy Bolton of the UWA history department, who did so much work in typing and formatting the book in its early stages. As ever, we acknowledge the contribution to our lives of Bruno and Michal. In sum, it has been fun for both Margot Melia and Richard Bosworth to engage with Leopoldo Zunini. We wish our readers similar enjoyment as they meet a lover of Western Australia or, to be more accurate, a lover and admirer of one of those many Western Australias the histories of which eddy through our lives.

Margot Melia and Richard Bosworth

Leopoldo Zunini in Western Australia

Margot Melia

Leopoldo Zunini greeted his new appointment to serve as Italian Vice-Consul in Albany, Western Australia, in November 1902, with enthusiasm. The posting coincided with his elevation to the rank of Vice-Consul First Class following seven years service in the field and appealed to what he termed his innate Ligurian sense of adventure.[1] Born in Savona on 20 December 1868, he graduated in jurisprudence at the University of Turin in 1890 before entering the diplomatic service in 1896. He remains, however, a somewhat enigmatic figure. His writings provide few clues to his private life, although it is clear from an entry in a volume of diplomatic biographies that he moved steadily up through the ranks.[2] His reminiscences of his first tour of duty in Western Australia, which appear early in the diary, suggest that he relished the opportunity to live and work in Australia.[3] It was a new nation, he observed, markedly different from those which he had known in the Old World or the Americas; its unique flora, fauna and distinctive landscape awaited discovery and he was keen to observe at first hand its people, their society and the political system in place in the newly federated nation.

These high hopes plummeted on reaching Albany when it became abundantly clear that headquarters in Rome had but a hazy idea of Australian geography. Perhaps they had as their guide earlier sailing charts which designated the settlement as first and last port of call on the Australian continent for European shipping, and consequently, a place of importance. By 1902 however, Albany's position had declined, overtaken by the new harbour at Fremantle adjacent to the state capital Perth. Zunini, who had stayed briefly in Perth upon arrival from Italy and been charmed by its setting on the Swan River, quickly realised the absurdity of maintaining a consulate far from the social, political and economic centre of the state. Urgent representations to his superiors pointing out their error and requesting that the office be transferred to the city ensued and three months later the consulate opened in Perth.

Details of Zunini's first tour of duty in Western Australia are sketchy. He found Perth a pleasant and attractive enough place in which to live but he was dismayed by the overt anti-Italian attitudes of the majority of Anglo-Australians. Italians, he realised, occupied a lowly position on the social scale and, indeed, were deemed to belong to an incorrigibly inferior race. One reason for this, he observed, was the belief among Australian workers that Italian immigrants were willing to work for below-award wages. They were said to be flooding the market with cheap labour, to the detriment of the locals. The ethnocentric press of the day, scenting a popular cause, took up the refrain avidly, creating and fomenting further antipathy through their pages. Zunini spent much of his time refuting allegations of Italian knavishness of one sort or another and trying to improve the image of Italy and Italians.

The situation deteriorated rapidly in 1904 and a number of violent confrontations between Italian and Australian workers took place. The government of the day, led by Walter James, did what it could to quell the disturbances and established a Royal Commission to investigate the vexed question of so-called southern European immigration.[4] Evidence was taken in the goldfields and elsewhere and Italians and other 'southern Europeans' were exonerated from charges that they were contract workers or had worked for below-award wages. Zunini found James to be a sympathetic official ally in a difficult situation as well as something of an Italophile. They struck up a warm professional and personal relationship which carried over into their later negotiations on Italian immigration to Western Australia.

According to Zunini, James advocated reform of Australia's restrictive immigration policy which, at the time, largely excluded non-British immigrants. It was agreed that some restraint on those foreigners who used Australia only as a place to make quick money and then return home was warranted, but genuine immigrants, particularly those who were prepared to go on the land, should be encouraged.[5] James had in mind the industrious farmers he had seen at work in Europe whom he believed would make excellent settlers. Zunini thoroughly approved the idea, coinciding as it did with one dear to his heart.

As early as 1890, in a work which may have been part of a university thesis, the young Zunini had shown a keen interest in the emigration question.[6] The treatise foreshadowed Zunini's later emigration philosophy and informed his eventual role as Italian government negotiator in the scheme to establish group settlements of Italian peasant farmers in Western Australia. He firmly believed that, if properly funded and organised, family groups of peasants, well versed in all aspects of agriculture, made the best emigrants. They would undoubtedly flourish in Western Australia, bring honour to the name of Italy, and, incidentally, stimulate trade. When James confided his own quite similar views to Zunini the stage was set for serious deliberations.

Zunini returned to Italy on leave in September 1905 and lost no time in presenting his views about group settlement to Admiral Reynaudi, the Italian Commissioner for Emigration. Reynaudi appears to have been generally well disposed to the project, although he did express some reservations about the necessity for, and availability of, the required initial capital. Zunini agreed that the question regarding who would finance the project clouded the otherwise promising discussions; ideally, the chosen emigrants would fund themselves, or, alternatively, private enterprise might be pressed to underwrite the scheme. Both options, however, were impractical at that time; peasant farmers, given the nature of their husbandry, were unlikely to have cash available and the idea of a privately funded settlement, Zunini contended, was anathema to what he described as the 'almost socialist' government in Australia.[7] Zunini was nonetheless confident that these obstacles would eventually be overcome by further negotiations between the interested parties and his reassurances seem to have eased initial Italian disquiet about the scheme. Preliminary discussions were held in London in December 1905 between Zunini and James, by then superannuated to the post of Western Australia's Agent-General there.

The meetings were essentially informal. James told Zunini that he was 'personally most anxious to see a flow to Australia of Italians from the northern portions of your country,'[8] and promised them 'a home beneath the Southern Cross not less prosperous and free than that offered by South America.'[9] The rhetoric was encouraging, but the question of how the scheme would be funded loomed large. The Western Australian government, while seeking to liberalise its immigration policies, was restricted in the implementation of any reforms, particularly those which might entail financial assistance, by the weight of public opinion which was generally suspicious of immigrants who had no initial capital. The theory prevailed that English slum dwellers or inmates of the 'work house' would flood the country if emigration were subsidised. There was, Zunini observed, a pervasive culture of 'self-help' abroad in the country which governments could not afford to ignore.[10]

In an effort to overcome the problem Zunini presented James with a plan, formulated by Reynaudi, under which the Italian government would agree to institute a scheme of financial arrangements, in the form of guarantees, which would assist the emigrants during the early, most critical, phase of their settlement. It was more an expression of intent than a firm financial commitment and was limited in extent. It would be called upon in the event, said to be unlikely, that settlers failed to meet their financial obligations to the state's Agricultural Bank. Nevertheless, the plan served to smooth over any nagging doubts about the financial aspects of the scheme and negotiations were able to proceed.

Inconclusive as the London talks were, the two governments did agree on one important point. It would be useful to have representatives, from the area most likely to furnish prospective emigrants, visit Western Australia to assess its potential and suitability as a destination for the proposed immigrants. Three delegates from the region of Emilia in north-central Italy were chosen to make the journey: Giuseppe Ricci of Portomaggiore, Guido Ruozi of Reggio Emilia and Romano Bottoni of Molinella. Zunini, as one of the architects of the scheme and because of his familiarity with Western Australia, would lead the group and act as its interpreter. The Western Australian government, if a little uncertain how to respond to the prospect of Italian immigration, did agree to underwrite all expenses for the mission and to organise an itinerary which would allow the delegates to evaluate the different farming areas of the state.

Zunini met the three men for the first time in Genoa in August 1906, prior to the group's departure for Australia. He was impressed by their enthusiasm and the way in which they had already identified with the task in hand. It augured well for the success of the mission; they would be travelling together for some months and it was essential that they quickly establish an atmosphere of mutual respect and congeniality despite the obvious class differences between Zunini, the lettered diplomat, and the three peasant farmers.

The voyage was largely uneventful. Zunini, the more experienced traveller, steered his charges safely past the wily hawkers who plied their trade in Red Sea ports and warned against the shady deals proposed by precious stone merchants in Colombo. The delegates were both fascinated and repelled by the lands and peoples of the Middle East and Asia and, as the voyage dragged on, they longed to make landfall in Western Australia.

The unprepossessing sand dunes which greet the voyager at Fremantle failed to cast a pall over the warm welcome extended to Zunini and the delegates by representatives of the state government. The farmers were soon installed in an 'Italian' hotel, owned by Giuseppe Oldrini, a leading figure in the city's small Italian community. Zunini, who had some harsh words to say about Australian hostelries in general, was accommodated, as befitted his status as consul, at the Palace Hotel on St George's Terrace.[11]

The government had appointed Henry S. Ranford, a functionary of the Lands Department, as guide and mentor to the group. He knew the country outside Perth well, was an efficient organiser and enthusiastic about the project. He proved to be an excellent choice and quickly established a good working relationship with Zunini and the delegates. He was a stickler for punctuality and insisted the group keep to the pre-arranged itinerary even when Zunini and the delegates would have liked to tarry at some congenial spot. If he came in for some good-natured ribbing from time to time about his clock-watching, snoring and fear of the motor car, it was all in fun and he was held in the highest esteem by the Italians. That was just as well because the journey on which they were venturing together was long and sometimes tedious; communication, relayed through an interpreter, was difficult and time consuming, and the accommodation and meals in some country towns left much to be desired. Yet there is no hint of disappointment or discontent in the narrative. The tour appears to have been a remarkably harmonious undertaking in every way. If the group was subjected to any anti-Italian slurs or jibes along the way, Zunini was far too diplomatic to mention them.

The itinerary drawn up by the Western Australian government took the delegation to the major agricultural areas of the south-west, especially those adjacent to the Great Southern Railway. Spring 1906 was a perfect time for the visit. Fat cattle grazed in lush green pastures; wheat, ripening to perfection under cloudless skies, waved in the breeze, while fruit and vegetables added their bounty to what seemed like a terrestrial paradise to the enthusiastic visitors. If the bush loomed dark, dense, mysterious, and not a little frightening, on the horizon the wildflowers, birds and animals were enchanting.

The delegation found Western Australians, on the whole, to be friendly and hospitable. They welcomed the group into their homes and plied them with tea and cakes, almost hourly it seemed; they took them driving through the bush at breakneck speed in newfangled automobiles or in four-in-hand buggies. They proudly exhibited the fruits of their labour, the cleared land, the crops, the numberless herds of sheep and cattle, the endless fences, and their isolated homesteads where they struggled to establish and observe the niceties of another world. Zunini, the urbane diplomat, and his more rustic companions, appear to have relished the situation. They were, after all, traversing the New World. It was increasingly apparent to the delegation that, in the antipodes, transplanted English mores and values grew differently from the parent stock and a seemingly more egalitarian society had evolved. Zunini noted that working-class men and women in Western Australia, unlike their European counterparts, displayed little deference to, and, in terms of dress and manners, were indistinguishable from, their social betters. Equally, politicians had few delusions of grandeur; they did not give themselves airs but dressed like men in the street and mingled unselfconsciously with the public. If the ladies' nail-hammering competition at the Shamrock Hotel in Northam was a strange antipodean rite of passage and the widespread and—to their European eyes—excessive, consumption of beer and spirits, not to mention the ubiquitous tea, betokened a certain malaise, there was, nonetheless, a vigour and general belief in the future of the state which was infectious.

Of course it was a white Europeanised Western Australia that appealed. The indigenous people whom the group encountered along the route appeared as shadowy, sickly figures, ravaged by alcohol and surviving on the fringe of society. Zunini remarked on their parlous condition, made reference to contemporary anthropological opinion concerning their origins and recorded the extent of government policy and assistance. He was sympathetic towards the Aboriginals' obvious distress, although he was a man of his time and viewed their plight in Darwinian terms, as very likely presaging their eventual extinction. The Italian settlers who might be attracted to Western Australia, would, by contrast, he thought, be healthy, robust family groups, already well-versed in agriculture and imbued with a desire and will to make good.

Zunini worked conscientiously to fulfil the terms of the brief entrusted him by both governments. The delegation took meticulous notes about land forms, soil condition, crops, weather, rainfall and the myriad other factors a would-be successful farmer needs to consider before selecting their land. The group did extensive field work, consulted the locals and carefully weighed the evidence. They were pleased by all they saw, but they were also realists and understood and respected the limit to the prospects confronting a settler. Although they were impressed by the wheat-growing regions in the north and would have been happy to see a settlement in that area, they realised that the establishment costs were considerable. Eventually, two areas were chosen; one in the Kojonup district and the other in the extreme south-west, the area favoured by the Western Australian government. The delegates were also favourably impressed with the land they saw around Denmark on the south coast. The mill-town, owned by Millars and abandoned to the bush by its inhabitants when the timber cutting lease expired, was of considerable interest. They reasoned that if the land could be bought from the company at a fair price, the immigrant families would have a ready-made village to live in while they got their bearings.

Zunini was appointed to conduct the final round of negotiations in Perth on behalf of the Italian government. Discussions were already well advanced and a Memorandum of Agreement, drawn up by Walter James and James Mitchell, had been sent to Italy for approval. The agreement provided for the establishment of two reserves; one, designated the Victor Reserve, would be established in the south-west coastal area of the state and the other, not surprisingly, called the Emmanuel Reserve would be in the vicinity of the Great Southern Railway.[12]

It seemed as if the project was at last to come to fruition. There remained two or three minor points of difference but, as Zunini pointed out, these could be resolved at a meeting scheduled to be held in London later in the year. He returned to Italy in June 1907 convinced that matters were proceeding smoothly and reported accordingly to the Commission for Emigration. Zunini concluded his treatise at this point by reiterating his views, and those of the delegates, concerning the suitability of Western Australia as a destination for Italian peasant farming families.

His confidence about a successful outcome of these last-minute negotiations was ill-founded. The matter appears to have dragged on inconclusively through the latter part of 1907 until early March 1908, when it became clear that the scheme had encountered insurmountable problems and would not proceed. The sequence of events which lead to the abandonment of the project are not altogether clear. Brief entries in the Western Australian government Cabinet minutes of the time suggest that the question of Italian immigration was discussed, although there is little indication as to the nature of the deliberations. The scheme had never enjoyed the complete support of the government, despite the very public approbation of prominent politicians like Walter James and James Mitchell. The premier of the day, Newton-Moore, had earlier, as minister for Lands and Agriculture, given only tepid approval to the scheme when it was first mooted. Italians, he conceded, 'would make excellent settlers,' but, he had warned, it must be kept in mind that, 'if our ideals are to be realised it is certain that British blood must flow through the veins of the generations yet unborn in Australia,' and he had urged that 'first consideration be given to the British immigrants.'[13]

Any misgivings about the enterprise harboured by those opposed to the scheme among government ranks were seemingly confirmed when strong public opposition to the project emerged early in the new year as details concerning the negotiations became generally known. The *Morning Herald*, in its News of the Day column, suggested that the government had not fully disclosed the actual terms of the proposed agreement. The writer warned against the scheme and the folly of transplanting people from 'the land of the olive and the fig,' and hoped that the 'experiment . . . will not be lightly proceeded with.'[14] The unemployed also added their voice to the opposition. In January a group met to ask the government to suspend negotiations,[15] and in February numbers of the unemployed marched through the streets of Perth behind an unequivocal banner which read 'Australia for the Australians—No Dagoes Wanted.'[16] Other meetings of the unemployed followed at which the Labour Party, then in opposition, made capital of the mounting disquiet about Italian immigration, emphasising that the people had only themselves to blame for returning such an inept government.[17] No doubt an increasingly disenchanted electorate gave the government cause for some concern but, by March, a much more serious problem of a political nature with its origins far from the sandy shores of Western Australia loomed unexpectedly.

It was Colonial Secretary J.D. Connolly who first alerted the government to the danger of accepting Italian immigrants whose political leanings were suspect. He had received a letter from Father Timothy O'Brien, the parish priest of St Brigid's in West Perth, expressing regret that the families to be selected would come from around Ferrara. O'Brien, quoting an unnamed Italian 'friend' in Perth, asserted that the immigrants would be 'families of socialists, lawless and irreligious who are continually harassing the Italian government with their strikes.'[18] His informant had suggested instead that 'good honest families from Piedmont and Lombardy might be selected.'[19] Plainly there was also opposition of a regional and political nature to the scheme within the fledgling Italian community in Perth. This was an ominous development. It raised the spectre of socialism and anarchy. Foreign dissidents would surely bring their fiendish ideas to this tranquil British outpost. Connolly must get in touch with the Bishop of Perth as soon as possible in order 'that he may use his influence to prevent this low class from landing in Western Australia.'[20]

Whether the colonial secretary discussed the matter with the bishop is not known. However, Connolly lost little time in forwarding O'Brien's letter to the premier with an accompanying memo suggesting that the matters raised in the letter 'should receive very careful consideration.'[21] He noted that a 'very excellent class of settler' might be obtained from the regions referred to by O'Brien, and he urged the government to be 'very careful to avoid the other classes namely, the socialists and anarchists, as they would certainly be a great nuisance in any country.'[22] The immediate reaction of the premier to the news is not known. The three delegates did, indeed, hail from the Emilia region, a major centre of early agrarian socialism in Italy, although there is no indication in the text of their political affiliations. Zunini did remark on the strength of the labour movement in Australia but did not compare its militancy with that of its Italian counterpart.

Whether from the fear of transplanted European political ideologies taking root in Western Australia or, more pragmatically, from the fear of voter backlash in the face of rising unemployment, the government, by 1 May 1908, had decided to abandon the scheme. A telegram from Rason, the state's Agent-General in London, stating that he had 'declined to negotiate' further on the question of Italian immigration put an end to the high hopes which had sustained the promoters of the scheme over the months of complex negotiations. Earlier Rason, while perhaps playing up to his British audience, had foreshadowed the end of the state's brief flirtation with the group settlement of foreigners. In an address to the Anglo-Saxon Club in London in April 1908, he enshrined the British-first policy which would characterise Australia's immigration laws until after the Second World War. 'They wanted as he wanted,' he told those assembled, '[that] Australia be the home of the Anglo-Saxon race. Or, if they could not be purely Anglo-Saxon as near as they could get it.'[23]

Zunini's response to the failure of his cherished scheme is not known. His report of the fact-finding mission, entitled L'Australia

Attuale, was published in Italy in 1910, by which time Zunini, who had been promoted to Consul First Class, was serving in Baghdad. He would go on to enjoy a distinguished career in the consular service in Europe, Africa, England and the United States, rising to the rank of Consul-General First Class. On his retirement in 1928 he was designated a Special Envoy and Minister Plenipotentiary. He lived to see his country transformed and all but destroyed by Fascism and war, and died in Sassello in his native Liguria in June 1944.

The unbridled xenophobia of the day effectively scuttled the scheme in official circles. But, as Richard Bosworth has observed, the story of immigration to Australia is often one of government policy being derailed by the flow of events in the real world.[24] Italians increasingly found their way to Western Australia, despite the best efforts of the ethnocentric press and politicians to prevent this eventuality. Some, like Sicilian Giuseppe Torrisi, had been inspired by Zunini's glowing reports of the country and its potential for those willing to work hard. He made the bold decision to up stakes and move his entire family to Western Australia. Tentatively they put down roots, survived and, in time, prospered. As Zunini had predicted, they became the catalyst for others, the first link in what, in the Donnybrook district, became a classic example of chain migration.

Zunini's narrative traces a journey that began with high hopes; a social experiment that was radical, ahead of its time, seemingly and strangely untainted by prejudice. It foundered, not because it was ill-conceived, but because it called for a world view of immigration which looked beyond narrow local interest and challenged the country's entrenched traditions of racial and national superiority.

---

1   Leopoldo Zunini, *L'Australia Attuale*, Turin, 1910, p. 1. The region of Liguria in north–west Italy flanks the Ligurian Sea between the French border and La Spezia. Genoa, its main city and port, jealously guards its historical reputation as a great maritime power and home of famed navigators and explorers. Zunini evidently identified closely with the tradition, perhaps seeing himself as something of a latter-day Christopher Columbus sallying forth to conquer new worlds.

2   *La Formazione della Diplomazia Nazionale (1867–1915)*, Rome, 1987, pp. 765–6.

3   Zunini, *L'Australia Attuale*, p. 1. Zunini's apparent enthusiasm for his Australian posting may have been influenced by an earlier work, *Il Continente Nuovissimo ossia L'Australasia Britannica*, written by the Italian Consul-General in Melbourne, Paolo Corte, and published in Turin in 1898. The work, which is wide ranging, examines the history, geography, flora and fauna of the different colonies, refers to the way in which European society has been transplanted in the antipodes, and goes on to make some interesting and quite detailed observations about Aboriginal life, languages and customs.

4   See Report of Royal Commission on the Immigration of non-British Labour, Minutes, Votes and Proceedings of Parliament, 1st Session, 5th Parliament, 1904, Vol. II, pp. 1123–223.

5 Ibid., p. 12–13.
6 Leopoldo Zunini, *Emigrazione*, Savona, 1890.
7 Ibid., p. 20.
8 Like many Anglo-Saxons, James seems to have been at pains to make a distinction between northern and southern Italians. The fairer, more 'nordic' northerners, usually from the Lombardy and Veneto regions, were preferred as immigrants, probably because they most closely resembled the English in physical terms.
9 Walter James to Leopoldo Zunini, London, 18 December 1905. James Papers, Battye Library State Archives of Western Australia, BLSA.
10 Ibid.
11 Zunini declared that the only hotels in Perth worthy of consideration were the Palace and the Esplanade, judging the former the superior of the two.
12 The Victor Reserve, suited to root crops, fruit, dairying etc., would comprise 320 acres, whereas the Emmanuel Reserve, set aside for cereals and mixed farming, would comprise 640 acres. See Memorandum, Italian Immigration File, 1496/1908, BLSA.
13 Departmental Memo, 9 February 1906, 5 March 1906. Italian Immigration File 1496/1908, BLSA.
14 *Morning Herald*, 2 January 1908.
15 *West Australian*, 15 January 1908.
16 Ibid., 24 February 1908.
17 Ibid., 2 March 1908.
18 T. O'Brien to Colonial Secretary, 7 March 1908, Italian Immigration File 1495/1908 BLSA. See also P. Corner, *Fascism in Ferrara, 1915–1925*, Oxford, 1975, pp. 1–27.
19 Ibid.
20 Ibid.
21 Connolly to Newton-Moore, Departmental Memo 10 March 1908, Italian Immigration File 1495/1908, BLSA.
22 Ibid.
23 *West Australian*, 9 May 1908.
24 See R. Bosworth & M. Melia, 'The Italian feste of Western Australia and the Myth of the Universal Church', in R. Bosworth & M. Melia (eds), *Aspects of Ethnicity, Studies in Western Australian History*, Vol. XII, p. 71.

Leopoldo Zunini and Liberal Italy

Richard Bosworth

Leopoldo Zunini reached Western Australia from Liberal Italy. Given that, like all authors, he would, even as he contemplated a 'foreign' world, write at least partially about himself, it becomes important to ask what was Italy like as a polity and a society in the decade before the First World War? What did it share with Western Australia and how were the two places diverse? What cultural baggage from Old Europe did Zunini carry with him as he reached Fremantle?

Italy had come into its somewhat equivocal existence as a modern nation state in the decades from 1848 to 1870 through the processes of its so-called Risorgimento or 'rising again' (though no state had ever existed before with the borders which this new Italy would possess). The regime which established itself in this political revolution called itself liberal and would continue to govern the peninsula until the Fascist accession to power in 1922.

In the first decades of its existence, Liberal Italy was fraught with insecurities and fragilities. Unification had given Italy the international role of 'Least of the Great Powers' and most liberal politicians agreed that Italy must behave as the Greater Powers did, even if that involved the expense of participating in an arms race or in imperialist conquest in Africa, and the danger of joining the Alliance System (from 1882 Italy, at least while peace survived, was a member of the Triple Alliance with Germany and Austria-Hungary). Nor were domestic politics any more settled and happy. Regional divisions, most notoriously between north and south, and in part reflecting the 'real' history of the disunification of the peninsula, were reflected in every social index and influenced every political action. Ideology, too, could occasion dispute. Though a 'Catholic country' (even if the practice of religion varied greatly from region to region, class to class and gender to gender), Liberal Italy had been united in spite of the Vatican, and the national state remained technically at war with the Church until the Lateran Pacts signed by Mussolini and Pope Pius XI in 1929.

Other divisions abounded. For centuries the Italian peninsula, and especially that part of it north of Rome, had been a place of cities—in 1800 there was a higher concentration there of centres with a population above 50,000 than anywhere else in Europe. In Milan, Bologna, Florence, Perugia and the rest, the *città* was a bastion of *civiltà*, at least in the eyes of local intellectuals. The definition of this last category was always rather vague—in Messina, for example, a poor person in 1908 remarked disarmingly to a visiting journalist that, here, 'we address all members of the bourgeoisie with the title *professore*.'[1] These cities were, of course, not modern industrial ones, with economies based on factories. Rather, still part of the early modern world, life in each *città*, with its (promise of) urbanity, was nourished by an agrarian hinterland. *Civiltà* was constructed on the backs of the peasantry who, well into the twentieth century, constituted the majority of the 'Italian' population, though they were more likely to identify themselves as *paesani* (inhabitants of their local village or *paese*) or *cristiani* than as nationalised citizens of the Italian state. A chasm—at best of incomprehension and, only too frequently, of fear and loathing—separated peasant and urban Italy, popular culture and national or regional *civiltà*.

Nor were peasants naturally united. Rather, one peasant habitually differed from another in their relation to the land. Small landowners had little in common with share-croppers. Both types of landholding peasants distinguished themselves from day-labourers, a group which was becoming markedly more numerous just before the outbreak of the First World War as agricultural capitalism ousted older forms of production, notably in those parts of the Po Valley from which Zunini's delegates came.[2] A male peasant and a female peasant; a peasant at forty and one at twenty; peasants with particular positions in the family (both natural and as extended by godparenting arrangements): all possessed individual histories and identities. The most certain thing about the subjects of Liberal Italy, be they peasants or workers, large landowners or urban bourgeoisie, was that they were not reliably 'Italian' (and could scarcely agree on what liberal might mean).

As if to demonstrate these divisions, in the 1890s the Risorgimento settlement was tested and, in most ways, seemed drastically to fail. In 1892–94 Sicilian peasant socialists, organised in so-called *fasci* (a word without its later connotations, meaning united groups), revolted in demand of social justice—in Catania at that time it was estimated that even an employed city worker earned a wage 20 per cent below subsistence level.[3] The government reacted to what it perceived as a threat of social revolution with condign brutality. In early 1894 Prime Minister Francesco Crispi, himself a Sicilian, dispatched 40,000 troops to the island, and the *fasci* leaders, their civic rights peremptorily suspended, were tried and condemned by court martial.

While a social crisis afflicted Sicily, in Rome the banking system all but collapsed, amid clear evidence of corruption in the highest places—Crispi, King Umberto I and Giovanni Giolitti, the most promising administrator among the new generation of liberal politicians, all had to combat allegations that they were personally implicated in the financial misdeeds of the moment. With not always disinterested advice and aid from Germany, the banks survived but, in March 1896, Italy suffered a humiliating imperial defeat at Adowa in Ethiopia. Urged on by Crispi, who with blatant cynicism was hoping that a victory in Africa would divert attention from the parlous political and social situation at home, an Italian army was cut to pieces by the forces of the Ethiopian Emperor Menelik II. In one battle as many Italian soldiers died as had been casualties for unification in the wars of the Risorgimento. As a result Italy, for the time being, withdrew from Africa (except for its residual and unrewarding, even costly, holdings in Eritrea and the Somaliland). A leading political diarist predicted that any further international humiliation would be 'lethal' to the whole Liberal system.[4]

In the next years political and social crises continued to dog Liberal Italy. In 1898, there were widespread demonstrations against the social order, with the epicentre not this time in 'backward' Sicily but in Milan, the site of the national Stock Market and, in most senses, the economic capital of the country. The motive on this occasion could not be ascribed to peasant rebelliousness, rather, it demonstrated that socialism, with its agenda of political revolution, had taken root in Italy (though some more traditionally anticlerical Liberals believed that an anti-Italian Catholic conspiracy was as much to blame). Now King Umberto gave the prime ministership to a general, Luigi Pelloux, and Italy's pretensions to a Liberal political system seemed hollow indeed. In July 1900 what might well be defined as a *decennium horribilem* closed with the assassination of the hapless king by an anarchist returned from a period of emigration in Paterson, New Jersey. Forty years of political unification seemed to have brought few gains to the peoples of the Italian peninsula and the Risorgimento political order seemed liable to imminent collapse.

Yet times were changing. The decade before the First World War would, for many Italians, be the best years in their history, until those prosperous ones which would succeed the economic miracle of the 1950s. It is a period known to Italians as *l'età giolittiana*, the Giolittian era, after the politician who emerged from his difficulties in the *Banca Romana* scandal to be Prime Minister for most of the time between 1903 and 1914. The economy began to grow with industrialisation—however much serious industrial development was regionally confined to the Turin–Milan–Genoa triangle. In 1911–12, Italy even won an imperial war and, with whatever doubtful utility, added Libya and the Dodecanese islands to its possessions. In those same months, Giolitti's fourth government legislated a minimal national insurance scheme on the 'progressive' German model and passed a franchise reform which gave some 65 per cent of adult males the vote in the 1913 elections. Giolitti's policy of 'holding the ring' in disputes between unionised workers and industrialists and, with less scrupulousness, between peasants and landowners, offered a greater possibility of social justice than ever before and even seemed to portend a flexibility of admin-istrative method which might justify for Liberal Italy the appellation 'a democracy in the making.'[5]

In practice, many problems lingered. Once the decision was made in 1915 to enter the First World War, the institutions of Liberal Italy were set on a course which would lead to their collapse, in the war's aftermath, into the tyranny of Fascism. But those who lived in Giolittian Italy, naturally, did not know of this sad fate, and it is possible to find an optimism in Giolittian discourse and a belief that Italy was at last becoming both genuinely Liberal and genuinely 'Italian.' In the Italian version of the *belle époque*, it could indeed be surmised that Italy's middle classes, perhaps its workers, and maybe even some of its peasantry, were 'turning into Italians' and therefore bringing, however belatedly, also to Italy that twentieth century process of state construction known as 'the nationalisation of the masses.' Many a Giolittian discerned no contradiction between the great ideals of 'power and the pursuit of peace.'[6]

Certainly Leopoldo Zunini was an archetypal citizen of Liberal Italy in this regard. Though he was well aware of being a Ligurian, he was simultaneously proud of what he deemed his nation's progress and was anxious to urge Italy on to further development and to further international success. Italians, he repeatedly advised, must cast aside both their sense of inferiority—towards the British Empire, for example—and their reluctance to accept the most modern commercial and business practices. Zunini, then, was that classic variety of late nineteenth and early twentieth century liberal, who believed both in progress and in social Darwinian competition, and felt no need to privilege one over the other. He was too much an optimist to contemplate the sort of authoritarianism adopted under Fascism, an authoritarianism the lineaments of which were already being sketched out by intellectuals less convinced by the 'gains' being won for the nation during Giolitti's term in office.[7]

These anti-Giolittians were often nationalists, but ones who thought that a nation could be constructed only through discipline and order (and a proper respect for their own views and social position). The Nationalist Association would be founded in Florence in 1910 and, with its refining of an ideology of authoritarianism, would provide a crucial training ground for many later Fascists. By contrast to these Italian practitioners of the 'politics of cultural despair,' Zunini was a sort of democrat. In Western Australia, he genuinely approved what he perceived to be the democracy of the bush or frontier and, at least while out of Italy, could hope that he was seeing a viable future. A headlong motor car ride into Moora, improvements in crop productivity on this farm or that, the 'openness' and 'genuineness' of Western Australian politicians, all to Zunini portended that happy future awaiting a humankind which, through science and the application of its intelligence, was mastering more and more of the world. For Zunini, the lamps of (European) civilization had certainly not yet been extinguished and no unbridgeable fissure separated the great ideals of liberty, equality and fraternity.

To what extent, however, it must be asked in our own post-modern society, is Zunini's text, in its optimism and 'democracy,' being 'constructed for him,' given the existence of a certain Italian discourse about Australia. How original, how independent and how profound an analyst of Western Australia is the author of *L'Australia attuale*?

I have written elsewhere about early Italian commentators on Australia and do not propose to repeat that detail here.[8] Suffice it to say that the Italian literature on Australia was usually composed after a relatively short visit, and by a journalist, a priest or, perhaps, an 'expert' on migration issues. Typical conclusions were that Australia was vastly wealthy—as Attilio Brunialti wrote in 1888, the colonies of the southern continent were among *'le coming nations;'*[9] that its working class had wonderfully good pay and conditions—for Giovanni Battista Belangero in 1898 workers were 'the real sovereign bosses' of the country;[10] and that Australia offered a pleasing model of applied (national) socialism—for the director of the Establishment fortnightly *Nuova Antologia*, Maggiorino Ferraris, whose ideas prefigured those of the Nationalist Association, newly federated Australia exemplified the 'most absolute negation of the doctrine of free trade.' If Italy was to be properly concerned with national development, he averred, what it needed was 'a Government of the Australian type.'[11]

If much commentary was enthusiastic, other Italian visitors saw some disadvantages in this democratic or protectionist paradise. At least one socialist doubted the clichés about 'King Working Man,' and detected instead rampant capitalism and a drastic popular ignorance of socialist theory.[12] A missionary priest was disturbed by the thought that local women were out of control and had made themselves 'the absolute family heads.'[13] Other visitors noticed that 'aborigines and kangaroos were not very different in the eyes' of colonial Australians, and philosophised on the way in which the whole Aboriginal 'race,' now so 'degenerate,' might well be destined to disappear.[14] And, almost all Italian travellers agreed, since white Australians had been in occupation of the continent for too short a time to possess a 'real history,' in the 'newest continent' materialism reigned and 'culture' could scarcely be given voice.[15]

When they turned to Western Australia, the Italian writers were brief indeed. Nineteenth century arrivals were inclined to remark that Perth was 'a city as yet hardly born,' and move on in some haste to the bright lights of Sydney or Melbourne.[16] The Salesian priest, Giuseppe Capra, did notice that the inhabitants of 'Fremantle's Italy' were 'rather indifferent' in regard to religious belief and practice.[17] Later, a Fascist journalist, Mario Miserocchi, with some evident geographical confusion, moralised on the seductive comfort of the local lifestyle: 'Whoever sees Perth, has seen all of Australia: thousands of bungalows, thousands of little beaver houses erected on stumps, one after another, set in a landscape like that of terrestrial paradise, each with its own aviary covered with flowers and all for a mass-produced people without a future.'[18] But the most common reaction was ignorance or bewilderment. In 1940, Miserocchi spoke about Western Australia as a state so vast that 'even if two people greet each other by megaphone, they still hear nothing.'[19] Forty-five years earlier, Paolo

Corte, the Italian Consul-General in Melbourne, and thus to be Zunini's immediate boss, admitted that he simply could not find out how many 'Italians' lived in Western Australia, given his fellow citizens' mobility and the limitless size of the territory.[20]

Corte was himself something of an exception to the rule that Italian commentators on Australia confined themselves to the superficial and clichéd and, like many a traveller, saw only what they wanted to see and learned only what they had known beforehand. In a number of publications, before and after Federation, he made a considerable attempt to inform Italians about Australia. At the same time, perhaps because the political events of Federation gave Australia a profile which it usually did not possess, Corte preached the need for an augmentation in Italian migration to Australia. As he wrote in 1903: 'To such a place we can and must with happy heart entrust a part of our proletariat in the certainty that they will soon become well-off property owners thanks to the huge amount of fertile and unoccupied land which exists there.' Australians, he reported, had an annual meat consumption of 276 pounds per annum. That total was more than ten times the Italian average.[21]

Perhaps Corte's work encouraged Zunini in his own writing. And yet, in most ways, Zunini's book is unique. In its breadth of information (however sometimes mistaken), in its focus on the single state of Western Australia[22] (with however much occasional gullibility towards locals with interests of their own to peddle), in its *serietà* and in the enthusiasm of its feel for place and society, Zunini's book has no equal in Italian-language literature on Australia.

As Margot Melia has already noted, Zunini joined the consular service of the Italian Ministry of Foreign Affairs in 1896. After short-term appointments to Marseilles, Berne, Tunis, Montevideo and Lima (and a period of sick leave in Rome), he reached Western Australia or, rather, Albany, as Vice-Consul (First Class) in 1902. No doubt he savoured his new status as a fully fledged Vice-Consul but, for those who represented Italy abroad, the port on King George's Sound must have been just about the least prestigious posting in the world.

Some other problems hovered over Zunini's ambitions to make a name for himself. The consular service was separate from the higher status diplomatic career, and consular reports were regularly ignored by that part of the bureaucracy which remained in Rome—the consuls, it was there assumed, were too incorrigibly bourgeois or too ill-prepared intellectually to understand the great world of high politics.[23] Both consular and diplomatic officials were especially notorious for their indifference to anything concerned with emigration.[24] Historians of Italy have frequently agreed with Antonio Gramsci that one of the most evident features of national history was the gap which separated the administration (the *paese legale*, 'legal' Italy) and the people (the *paese reale*, 'real' Italy). Generally speaking, nowhere was this division more evident than in emigration.

Here again, however, Zunini was an exception. While consular officials normally might be expected to publish light *belle-lettrist* pieces of local colour about their current station, and would habitually reinforce them with apposite quotations from Dante and Carducci, Zunini, by contrast, had already written a brief analysis of emigration, the result of his university studies, in 1890. Therein, Zunini argued some theses characteristic of his time. Emigration was one of the most important and longstanding of human activities. The ancients had practised and managed it. In more modern eras, however, Italians had been slow to reap its benefits. Their intellectual zest had, for example, led to the discovery of the Americas which, however, were thereafter 'occupied by other peoples to the detriment and humiliation of Italy.' Post Risorgimento emigration—which Zunini asserted with a sturdy parochialism had originated in Liguria—had begun in a spirit of some entrepreneurship and with the clear intention among most emigrants of only limited sojourn before a return home. But the process had gradually embraced poorer social groups whose departures had become so numerous that the attention and concern of government was aroused. Commentators, Zunini admitted, divided over whether or not state intervention was necessary, and too easily lapsed into 'schematism.' Nevertheless, since emigration was clearly '*di massa*,' there was now no doubt that governments had a duty and right of supervision. The consular service, Zunini maintained, was the logical body both generously to provide welfare and scientifically to assess the whole emigrant experience. Primed to such activity, consuls would do well to foster local committees of 'prosperous, honourable and forward thinking' emigrants. Generally, the young Zunini concluded, 'the State [through such actions] must take on the very delicate and crucial task of making Italians abroad feel that the *patria* diligently oversees and safeguards their interests.' Britain had an empire on which the sun never set; Germany was constructing one; 'it is time that Italy, [too], comes alive and takes that place in the world which is its due.'[25]

If, before Adowa, such Crispian nationalism had seemed but logical, the defeat in Ethiopia did not end national discussion of emigration problems. Rather, in the Giolittian decade, polemics about an appropriate national policy increased and the emigration debate became one of the great issues of the time.[26] The dispute was all the more urgent because the numbers of those departing from Italy spiralled ever upwards. In 1890 some 216,000 left; emigration in 1913 totalled almost 873,000, about one-fortieth of the national population. Only the First World War would curb what the more extreme nationalists, in a metaphor replete with *fin de siècle* concerns over 'degeneration' and the 'survival of the fittest,' had become accustomed to call a 'haemorrhage of Italy's best blood.'

These same nationalists generally went on to argue that this draining away could only be arrested by the creation of a modern Italian empire, to which emigrants could be directed and thus retain their Italian nationality. The invasion of Libya in 1911 was partially prompted by such rhetoric. More sober political commentators wondered, justly, whether, with the onset of the twentieth century, imperial adventures were really the answer, and quite a number continued to see emigration as a 'safety valve' by which the steam being generated by economic change and social conflict within Italy could be dispersed.[27]

Nonetheless, almost everyone agreed that a policy of pure *laissez-faire* towards emigration could not prevail. The Giolittian press frequently published horrendous tales of the exploitation of emigrants on their voyage out or in their place of work in a new society. Zunini was not the only Italian well aware of a racist Italophobia eddying not far below the surface in Anglo-Saxon and other parts of the world. Already in the 1890s there had been cases of murder and pillage of Italian immigrants at Aigues Mortes in southern France and of lynchings at New Orleans in the USA. From Latin America came more frequent tales of exploitation, illness and death. As one contemporary noted, along the paths of emigration to that continent was located 'a filthy mechanism of infamy which can only really be understood by one who has seen and studied the whole environment; there flourish the agent, the sub-agent, the porter, the publican, the money-changer, the restaurateur, each of whom wants to suck the very blood of his victims.'[28] Of course, there were also success stories of Italian emigration to South America[29] but it is notable in *L'Australia attuale* how anxious Zunini is that colonies in Western Australia should not replicate the misadventures which, he believed, had occurred in Brazil and Argentina.

While governments were properly preoccupied with the welfare of their departing citizens, official Italy was engaged financially with emigration in a more direct sense. Emigrants, though doubtless thinking more of their families than of the Italian *patria*, had begun to remit home considerable sums, and economists postulated that these remittances, along with the sums expended by foreign tourists in Italy, were crucial 'invisible assets' to the national economy. Indeed, they concluded, it was unimaginable that the state budget could be balanced without this aid from abroad. The emigrants were accumulating for the nation the capital which it needed to industrialise and 'progress.' Without the regular repatriation of emigrant monies Italy might have to forfeit its pretensions to be a Great Power.

In these circumstances it was natural that a bureaucracy of emigration should start to grow. The most important new agency of the period was the *Commissariato dell'Emigrazione* (Emigration Commission), established in 1901 and headed by that Admiral Reynaudi to whom Zunini from time to time reported.[30] Though Giolitti himself was a model of financial caution and detested that sort of showy external adventurism indulged in by Crispi, his governments did pay more attention to emigration questions than had any of their predecessors. Zunini would thus find Rome unwilling to spend money carelessly, but the idea of some government assistance for the hypothetical Victor and Emmanuel reserves[31] was not by definition an absurd one to put before a Giolittian administration.

What happened to Zunini after his time in Western Australia? Once the emigration negotiations were concluded, in 1908 he was transferred to a newly opened office in Baghdad and there, two years later, promoted Consul. In this new posting he seems typically to have tried very hard to be busy, favouring schemes for the teaching of Italian and for hydraulic works, as well as for railway, road and hotel development, and generally searching out means to enhance the feeble Italian presence in Mesopotamia.[32] Once again circumstances did not greatly favour him and he thereafter pursued an orthodox and rather low key consular career, culminating in appointments to Liverpool in 1920 and Chicago in 1922, where, in 1924, he reached the pinnacle of status as Consul-General First Class. His views on the Fascist dictatorship then taking over his country are unknown but it seems unlikely that he greatly sympathised with Mussolini. In 1926, he was recalled to work in the Ministry of Foreign Affairs and he retired, aged sixty, in 1928.[33] There was a certain nice, if sad, irony in the fact that, as Zunini left diplomatic work, he was in a sense replaced by the Fascist, Renato Citarelli, an official who would have an unhappy career when he became Vice-Consul in Perth in the early 1930s.[34]

In the latter stages of his career, Zunini also does not seem to have continued writing. When he published *L'Australia attuale* in 1910, the emigration scheme to Western Australia was dead. Though in July 1911 his book did receive at least one long and favourable review,[35] by that time the imminence of the Libyan War made it unlikely that much Italian attention could be directed back to Perth or Kojonup—in his own account of the visit, delegate Ricci had spoken of Western Australia as the 'Promised Land,' if one occupied already by 'Anglo-Saxons;'[36] now nationalists repeatedly boasted that Tripoli was the *Terra Promessa* in which Italians themselves at last could settle.

In Perth and in those areas through which he had travelled with so much appreciation and with such attention to detail, Zunini was forgotten, too. Western Australian historiography has been, by tradition, doggedly monolingual and the Battye library is not a place readily to find foreign language texts. No copy of the original edition of *L'Australia attuale* has been traced in Western Australia.

Such oblivion is undeserved. In translating and editing this English-language edition of Zunini's work, Margot Melia and I hope that readers will get the same pleasure we did—and that Zunini himself seems to have gained—from his descriptions of matters as diverse as watching female nail-hammering contests at the Northam Show, traversing the paths of the abandoned timber town of Denmark, being all but lost in the bush out of Bridgetown, and drinking refreshingly cold beer on return to Kojonup. We also hope our readers will savour Zunini's rueful pain at dismal Australian Sundays, at habitual local drunkenness, at inedible Irish-Australian cuisine and at too many bush cups of tea, and note his surprise that Australians could afford the time and expense of consuming six meals per day.[37] It is true that there are occasional patches of laboriousness in Zunini's prose, in the early pages, for example, where he is somewhat obsessive in preparing himself to avoid what he fears will be a racist response from the locals to any Italian initiative, or in some of his reiteration of the details of agricultural production and productivity. Perhaps he can be forgiven these moments of dullness, however, since his words are so evidently prompted by what he saw as his patriotic and official duty. And, of course, Zunini's very reiteration of his worries about Australian Italophobia reveals how recurrent and deep-seated was the Italian fear of being regarded as 'inferior' in the Anglo-Saxon world.

Margot Melia and I are thus delighted to present Zunini's work to Australian readers. Here is an Italian account of Western Australia composed shortly after Federation and of an exemplary seriousness and sensitivity. Of course, in many ways, it is a 'period piece.' But Zunini, in his optimism, his rationality, his openness, and, indeed, his zest for new things and new experiences, is a person for (the best of) our times as well. When, at a Northam which did not yet know of its post-1945 future as a first base for arriving European immigrants, he was called on to give an impromptu speech and concluded by saying that, had he not been born an Italian, he would like to have been a Western Australian, doubtless, in large part, he was merely being a good diplomat. But, in some part, he was also speaking the truth. The Zunini who recalled that, during their journeying, he became accustomed to dine at the same table as his delegates, even though he was a Vice-Consul First Class and they were but peasant farmers, and that he had had to overcome the doubts of the delegates, who themselves initially believed that they should not so nearly deal with an *Eccellenza*,[38] was a man who took to (a version of) democracy. In his own flesh, as it were, he embodied that hope, which we must retain, that meetings between Australia and Italy will continue to prove to the benefit of a democratic humankind.

1 See R.J.B. Bosworth, 'The Messina earthquake of 28 December 1908', *European Studies Review*, 11, 1981, pp. 189–206 for the context of this remark.
2 For a very useful English-language introduction to the deepening social crisis in the region, see P. Corner, *Fascism in Ferrara 1915–1925*, Oxford, 1975. Throughout Zunini's account the delegates, whose exact social position is unclear but who plainly were not *braccianti* (day-labourers), are called by us 'peasant farmers' in order to make the point about the complexity and variability of Italian peasant life.
3 S.F. Romano, *Storia dei Fasci Siciliani*, Bari, 1959, pp. 65–6.
4 D. Farini, *Diario di fine secolo* (ed. E. Morelli), Rome, 1961, p. 865.
5 For this viewpoint, see the classic study by A.W. Salomone, *Italy in the Giolittian era: Italian democracy in the making 1900–1914*, rev. ed., Philadelphia, 1960. For a more muted interpretation, cf. R. Bosworth, *Italy and the approach of the First World War*, London, 1983.
6 For the resonance, see F.H. Hinsley, *Power and the pursuit of peace: theory and practice in the history of relations between states*, Cambridge, 1967.
7 For examples, see A. Lyttelton (ed.), *Italian Fascisms from Pareto to Gentile*, London, 1973.
8 R. Bosworth, 'L'Italia d'Australia' in R. Ugolini (ed.), *Italia–Australia 1788–1988*, Rome, 1991, pp. 27–43.
9 A. Brunialti, 'L'Australia, il suo sviluppo e il suo avvenire fra le nazioni', *Nuova Antologia*, f 501, 1 September 1888, p. 85.
10 G.B. Balangero, *Australia e Ceylon: studi e ricordi di tredici anni di missione*, Turin, [1924], p. 126.
11 M. Ferraris, 'Lo stato e le industrie agrarie in Australia', *Nuova Antologia*, f 754, 16 May 1903, p. 303; 'La crisi degli agrumi: di un consorzio agrumario nazionale', *Nuova Antologia*, f 756, 16 June 1903, p. 655; cf. also his 'Il credito agrario di Stato in Australia', *Nuova Antologia*, f 747, 1 February 1903, pp. 532–44.
12 M.R. Bentivoglio and G. Di Leonardo, *Quintino Ercole*, S. Gabriele, 1984, pp. 47–8; 53–5.
13 G. Capra, *Relazione del viaggio-missione a pro degli italiani emigrati nell'Australia, Tasmania e Nuova Zelanda compiuto nel 1908–1909 dal sacerdote Giuseppe Capra della Pia Società di S. Francesco di Sales*, nd, np (copy in the Vatican Library).

14 A. Brunialti, op. cit., p. 90; G. Capra, 'Una razza destinata a scomparire? Aborigeni d'Australia', *Le Vie d'Italia e del Mondo*, 6, June 1936.

15 e.g. G.B. Balangero, op. cit., pp. 119–20 opining that 'the principal thought and aim of all Australians is to make money and, with money, to live a life of ease' and that this ambition meant that Australians were 'a people without a History and without Heroes.' For the latest manifestation of such views, see J. Gentilli, 'Gli Italiani nell' Australia Occidentale: una comunità isolata in fase di invecchiamento', *Studi Emigrazione*, XXX, 1993. Gentilli there opines that 'the Australian public, given its very brief history and almost total lack of regionalism, understands very little' of Italy's 'real' culture.

16 G. Branchi, 'Da Suez a Melbourne (Australia)—(impressioni del viaggio)', *Nuova Antologia*, XIX, April 1872, p. 872. Branchi, a nineteenth century man, decided from viewing aborigines near Albany that he would rather be related to a gorilla.

17 G. Capra, *Relazione del viaggio-missione*; for more information, see R. and M. Bosworth, *Fremantle's Italy*, Rome, 1993; for still more superficial and derivative contemporary accounts, see, e.g., G. Cora, 'Esplorazioni nell'Australia Occidentale e di mezzo: rilievo di J. Forrest tra i fiumi Ashburton e De Grey', *Cosmos*, VI, 1880, pp. 81–3; Anon., 'L'Australia occidentale', *Rivista Geografica Italiana*, VI, 1900, pp. 289–91. Cf. also the comments of one of the delegates that he had tried to prepare himself for the trip by reading relevant material but had been able to find little except for basic geographical information. G. Ricci, 'Note di un viaggio nell'Australia Occidentale', *Bollettino dell'Emigrazione*, 9, 1907, pp. 3–4. Ricci, in a prose reflecting something of Italian popular culture, then listed ten tasks he set himself, rather like the ten commandments, to be completed by the end of his journey.

18 M. Miserocchi, *Australia: continente minorenne*, Milan, 1940, p. 24; delegate Ricci, on one occasion, remarked enviously that Western Australians did not get up till 9 a.m. G. Ricci, op. cit., p. 41.

19 Ibid., p. 22.

20 P. Corte, *Il continente nuovissimo ossia L'Australasia britannica*, Turin, 1898, pp. 166–7.

21 Ibid., p. 240; P. Corte, 'Nel paese dei kanguroo e degli opossum', *Rivista d'Italia*, VI, 1903, p. 1001; cf. also his 'Gli italiani nell'Australia e nella Nuova Zelanda', *Emigrazione e Colonie, Vol II Asia-Africa-Oceania*, Rome, 1906, pp. 513–37.

22 cf., for example, the much more superficial efforts of Giuseppe Capra, *Il Queensland: terra della Regina (Australia): studio descrittivo per gli italiani*, Milan, 1912; *La Nuova Zelanda: il paese dei Maori*, S. Benigno Canavese, 1913.

23 For some English-language introduction to the Italian Ministry of Foreign Affairs, see R.J.B. Bosworth, *Italy, the Least of the Great Powers: Italian foreign policy before the First World War*, Cambridge, 1979, pp. 95–126.

24 For a classic period description of this division, see L. Villari, *Gli Stati Uniti d'America e l'emigrazione italiana*, Milan, 1912.

25 L. Zunini, *Emigrazione*, Savona, 1890, pp. 2–18.

26 The history of Italian emigration is very poorly served in the historiography. Local studies abound but there is no English-language synthesis. In Italian, the best introductions are Z. Ciuffoletti and M. Degl'Innocenti (eds), *L'Emigrazione nella storia d'Italia: studi e documenti* (2 vols.), Florence, 1978; G. Rosoli (ed.), *Un secolo di emigrazione italiana 1876–1976*, Rome, 1978; E. Sori, *L'Emigrazione italiana dall'Unità alla seconda guerra mondiale*, Bologna, 1979.

27 For an account of the debate, see F. Manzotti, *La polemica sull'emigrazione nell'Italia unita fino alla prima guerra mondiale*, Milan, 1962. It would indeed be true that those regions from which there was massive emigration, then and later, tended to remain politically conservative.

28 L.A. De Boni and R. Costa, 'Gli italiani del Rio Grande do Sul', in M. Pacini (ed.), *Euroamericani Vol. III La popolazione di origine italiana in Brasile*, Turin, 1987, p. 49.

29 e.g. the young economist Luigi Einaudi thought, in 1898, that Argentina might well be destined to play the role for Italians which the United States had played for the Anglo-Saxon people. See G. Dore, *La democrazia italiana e l'emigrazione in America*, Brescia, 1964, p. 200. Recent scholarship has also indicated that social mobility was much easier for emigrants to obtain in the South compared with those who went to North America. For an introduction, see S.L.

Baily, 'The adjustment of Italian immigrants in Buenos Aires and New York, 1870–1914', *American Historical Review*, 88, 1983, pp. 281–305.

30 A recent historian reports, however, that it did not always function with maximum efficiency nor did it resolve the tendency for emigration issues to be waylaid in inter-ministerial conflict. Perhaps Zunini's own scheme was damaged in this way. See E. Sori, op. cit., pp. 268–70.

31 They were, of course, named after Umberto's son and successor, Victor Emmanuel III (1900–1946). For a rather glib, English-language introduction to the history of the Italian monarchy, see D. Mack Smith, *Italy and its monarchy*, New Haven, 1989.

32 D.J. Grange, *L'Italie et la Méditerranée (1896–1911): les fondements d'une politique étrangère*, Rome, 1994, Vol. I, pp. 810; 863–4; Vol. II, pp. 1166, 1186, 1277.

33 Zunini was thus a victim of the so-called 'massacre of the innocents' in which the new regime began to 'fascistise' the ministry (i.e. the time when Fascists overtly brought their own clients into the diplomatic and consular services). For the whole context, see R.J.B. Bosworth, *Italy and the wider world 1860–1960,* London, 1996, pp. 94–136.

34 For his career in Western Australia, see R. Bosworth, 'Luigi Mistrorigo and *La Stampa:* the strange story of a Fascist journalist in Perth', in R. Bosworth and M. Melia (eds), *Aspects of Ethnicity: Studies in Western Australian History XII*, Nedlands, 1991, pp. 61–5; cf. his article 'Il valore del Partito Fascista nel regime', *Economia Nazionale*, XIX, December 1927, pp. 5–6. Citarelli moved into the consular service from a position as head of the Fascist Party Press Office.

35 E. Dipietro, 'Per una colonia agricola italiana in Australia', *Rassegna Nazionale*, XXXIII, 16 July 1911, pp. 269–78.

36 G. Ricci, op. cit., p. 7.

37 It would not be long before Nationalist and Fascist propagandists would seek enviously to define the English as an effete people who partook of five meals a day.

38 In his account Ricci recalls with pleasure that he got to travel in 'first class compartments' on the W.A. railways. G. Ricci, op. cit., p. 6.

25

Translators' Note

As translators our aims were to ensure that the text be easily understood while preserving as much as possible of the flavour, structure and tone of the original.

For the sake of overall clarity and comprehension, the punctuation and paragraph format used in the Italian text has been modified, although Zunini's stylistic idiosyncrasies and textual inconsistencies have largely been retained. His use of *contadino, agricoltore, colono,* as well as 'farmer' and 'settler,' interchangeably throughout the text posed some problems. Both the English equivalents of the Italian terms and the simple English words give little sense of the complexities of land ownership in rural Italy of the period. It was decided, in the interests of clarity and consistency, to use the more generic terms 'farmer,' 'peasant farmer,' and 'settler.'

Zunini wrote for an Italian readership, and his shifts from imperial to metric measurement and Italian lire to sterling—and occasionally, even, to francs—have not been standardised. (Pounds, shillings and pence are represented £.s.d.)

Reader's will note that the current spelling of the Australian Labor Party had yet to be adopted when Zunini wrote.

The original text of *L'Australia Attuale* was lavishly illustrated with photographs depicting various aspects of Western Australian life. Relatively few of these eighty plates have been located however, and, of these, only an emblematic selection has been included in this version.

To the Reader

In writing this book I am resolved not so much to make known to my fellow Italians a country, of which we have but a very hazy idea, as to persuade them of the importance, in economic terms, of establishing relations. Is it not possible that the southern continent, and particularly its western half, might become as fertile a field of activity for our fellow countrymen as America is at this moment? I have asked myself this question many times and I believe the answer is yes. Certainly the difficulties involved are neither few nor trivial; but success all depends on knowing how to get off to a good start and in using the means best suited to the task.

However, I would not like readers to assume that they have at hand the definitive work on [Western] Australia. Instead, my very modest effort is but the result of my assignment from the Emigration Commission to investigate these areas with regard to the possible establishment of settlements of Italian peasant farmers and, at the same time, to seek out a basis of agreement with the local government.

Notwithstanding this rather dry premise, I plan to put together as interesting as possible a description of the physical, social and economic aspects of the country. I must point out, however, that I have excerpted from this volume what I call the diplomatic and legal section, except, naturally, where such references are appropriate and better inform the narrative. The negotiations with the Western Australian government, the relative documents, the in-depth examination of the proposed accord, and the history of the matter will be the subject of a special issue of the *Bollettino dell'Emigrazione*.

Leopoldo Zunini

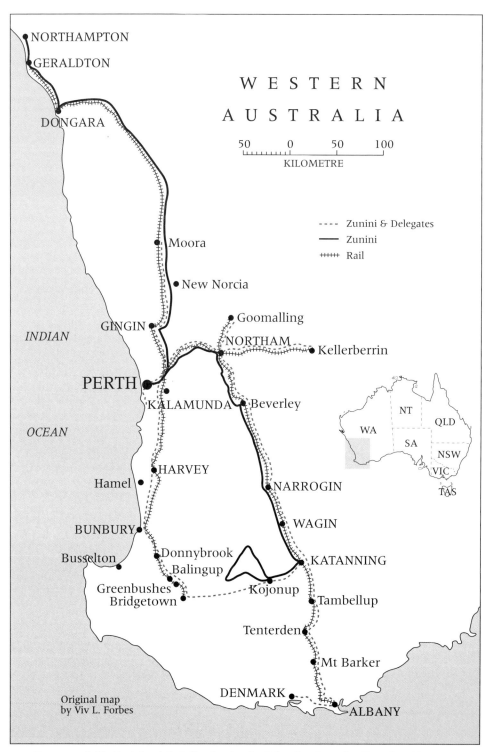

NORTHAMPTON
GERALDTON
DONGARA

WESTERN

AUSTRALIA

50   0   50   100
KILOMETRE

- - - - Zunini & Delegates
———— Zunini
+++++ Rail

Moora

New Norcia

Goomalling

GINGIN

NORTHAM

Kellerberrin

PERTH

KALAMUNDA

Beverley

INDIAN

OCEAN

NT

QLD

WA

SA

NSW

VIC

TAS

HARVEY

Hamel

NARROGIN

WAGIN

BUNBURY

Busselton

Donnybrook
Balingup

KATANNING

Greenbushes
Bridgetown

Kojonup

Tambellup

Tenterden

Mt Barker

DENMARK

ALBANY

Original map
by Viv L. Forbes

Routes travelled by Zunini and the Italian Immigration Delegation, September–November 1906

Chapter One

My First Journey to Western Australia—Albany—Perth—The Italian Community—The Labour Question.

In 1902 the Italian government instituted a Vice-Consulate in Albany with jurisdiction over all Western Australia. I was asked if I wished to take up the position and I accepted the offer with much pleasure. In my seven years in the diplomatic service I had had the opportunity to learn about many different countries; but there is also something naturally adventurous in the Ligurian character which finds us always travelling over the world. Australia had a special attraction for me. Its climate, soil, flora and fauna, and its people, were all so different from those of the Old World and America. It was similarly an interesting country from a social and political point of view: colonies, now states, that had gained self-government were slowly and surely moving towards complete independence; Australia's legislation had conferred great advantages upon the working class and for the most part put into practice those socialist ideals which emancipate women and endow them with civil and political rights. Furthermore, though few vast individual fortunes have been made in Western Australia, a general, almost universal, well-being exists there and poverty is restricted to a small minority. Australia has a social and political structure which, while not perfect in every aspect, has made giant strides along the path of progress.

Yet, so fascinating a country is almost unknown in Italy. With the exception of Melbourne and Sydney, where from time to time, some Italian traveller has penned a line or two, what do we know of the vast Australian continent? The western portion in particular is *terra incognita* in every sense of the word. And yet this section constitutes an area of some one million square miles, blessed with immense mineral and agricultural resources, ideal climatic conditions and a brilliant future.

I sailed from Genoa on 10 February 1903 aboard the steamer *Rhein* of the Norddeutscher Lloyd line and arrived at Fremantle, the state's most important port, on 10 March.

It must be admitted that, at first, Western Australia does not make the best impression upon the traveller, irrespective of where one makes landfall. Both Albany and Fremantle, the principal ports, have been constructed on sand plains which extend many miles inland. Perth, the capital city, situated some twelve miles inland is also built on sandy soil. For this reason, it is hardly surprising that Western Australia has been long neglected by the British government and avoided by its emigrants. It is still said jokingly that this is the land of the three Ss— sand, sorrow and sore eyes. It is true that, until fifteen years ago, the colony, despite its vast size, was of trifling importance, possessing fewer than 50,000 inhabitants. It took the discovery of gold in the Kalgoorlie region to put the place on the map and clarify its true worth. A short distance from the coast there are thousands of kilometres of very fertile land which only await the hand of man to enable them to bear their fruits. Everything—cereals, vegetables and fruit—grows abundantly there. These last in particular have a flavour and aroma unequalled in any other country. The sand when irrigated produces excellent crops; nor does irrigation present any problem, there being abundant supplies of good fresh water only a few metres underground which can be easily pumped to the surface by wind-mills. The lush green semi-tropical growth on the flat plain around Perth bears eloquent testimony to this fact.

I stayed in Fremantle for a few days before transferring to Perth and thence to Albany. I quickly realized that this place was completely unsuitable as the seat of a consular office. Until 1901, it had been the principal port of call for all the major British, German and French shipping companies. With the discovery of gold inland and the rapid increase in population in the goldfields and in the areas adjacent to the capital, the centre of commercial interest shifted to Fremantle, which quickly overtook its rivals to become, in 1902, the main disembarkation port for all the more important international lines.

The few months I spent in Albany I consider to have been among the saddest and most tiresome of my life. It is a hamlet of just over one thousand inhabitants, devoid of any amenities, social life or pastimes. There were no Italians in the district and it was impractical to establish the consulate there so far from the capital and from the Italian community. Except for the three summer months, the climate is the worst in Western Australia because of the incessant rain and howling winds. I was therefore delighted when the government agreed to my proposal that the consulate be transferred to Perth which, for obvious reasons, appeared the best place from which to undertake my assignment.

The capital of the state is a charming little city which, at the time of writing, numbers some 50,000 citizens. Its setting is enchanting and I would say without hesitation that, after Sydney, it is the most picturesque city in Australia. It is situated on the Swan River which, at its mouth, is more an arm of the sea, being two or three miles wide in certain places. The city is overlooked by Mount Eliza which, on one side, slopes gently towards the built-up area and on the other drops away sharply towards the river. The homes of the well-to-do have been raised on its slopes while the summit is graced by an expansive area of some 2000 acres known as Kings Park. The view from up there is unforgettable; one should be there at sunset when, under a cloudless sky, the range of colours is such that even the most varied palette would find it difficult to reproduce.

As a proud Italian, my first sojourn in Australia was less than satisfying. Italians were not held in high esteem at that time. According to public opinion we were classed somewhere between the Chinese and the blacks. I am not exaggerating when I say that we were often dubbed 'black fellows.' The story of the Irish woman who married an Italian and then refused to accompany him to Italy was typical. To the judge who asked the reason for her refusal she replied with astonishment and indignation: 'But, your Honour, do you believe that a British woman could reside happily in a black fellow's country?' (I record her literal words.)

In these circumstances, I realized that my first task would be to try to modify public opinion and present our nation, against which there was so much prejudice, in its true light. I was convinced that closer relations between the two nations would be impossible without each knowing something of the other and developing reciprocal esteem. As long as Australia considered Italy to be a nation on the verge of political and economic collapse and Italians to be a race of beggars, it was pointless to expect that I could fulfil the mission entrusted me by the government of enhancing links between the two countries. It would take interviews, articles in newspapers, speeches, in fact any sort of public or private propaganda, to lead to a better understanding and appreciation of Italy, and to highlight the progress made since

View of Perth in 1908
FROM: *Western Australia, Its Agricultural and Mining Interests, 1909*, Battye Library

Saturday afternoon on the Swan River, South Perth
FROM: *Western Australia, Its Agricultural and Mining Interests, 1909*. Battye Library

unification in 1860. Anyone going to Western Australia and studying the situation and the state of public opinion now would have to say that my efforts have not been in vain.

The Italian colony in Western Australia numbers some two thousand persons, for the most part miners and woodcutters. The hostile feelings towards us seem incomprehensible at first glance, given that our community has, almost always, been composed of the best, most hard-working and industrious sons of the Alpine regions, mainly strong-armed miners from the Valtellina. One needs to look closely at the matter to understand fully the reason for Australians' habitual mixture of antipathy and contempt. Italians were discriminated against because they were Italian and they were not welcome because they were workers. They were scorned because of an ill-founded racial prejudice. What occurred in Western Australia was the same as that which crops up everywhere in the Anglo-Saxon world, namely that the foreigner is held to be an inferior being. And, in Australia, it was we Italians who enjoyed the dubious privilege of being classified among the lowest on the scale of peoples.

Italy was always considered to be a negative entity and, unfortunately, appearances had in large part confirmed that opinion. The fact that only workers had emigrated, that no company with investment capital had opened up a business, and that no steamer flying the Italian flag had been seen in port, had led to the inevitable conclusion that Italy was a nation of beggars. Despite my citing facts and figures, what a labour of Sisyphus it was to refute such deeply ingrained misapprehensions. Even educated persons hesitated to believe my assertions because they flew in the face of appearances.

The ignorance about our culture, and all that might bring honour to the name of the Italian, was downright amazing. Generally speaking, our country was judged in terms of what it was a century ago. For the majority of Australians the period between our being a nonentity in political and economic terms and the present was a blank which served only further to fuel their ingrained prejudices.

The ideas about us which circulated were largely based on English literature (especially novels and travel books) of some decades ago, full to the brim with extravagant accounts of our ways. They were, almost always, the works of persons who had found Italy an awful place in which everything was badly done and inferior to that existing in their own country. And, while it is true that more recent accounts have at least changed their tone, the legend created earlier endures.

The local press did little to produce a favourable atmosphere, although I should distinguish between one paper and another. There were some respectable and honest newspapers, in fact the majority, which were in general little concerned with us and limited themselves to the odd item of political news or other relevant report; hardly ever did they inform the public about anything to do with our social or economic life, since plainly such items would have been of little interest to their readers. But, if these papers ignored or sometimes looked askance at us, they were nevertheless prepared to recognize the truth when it was pointed out to them. These papers, in fact, were very helpful to me in my campaign to raise the image of Italy in the public domain. However, there were also rags, decked out under the guise of the popular press (when in fact they should be called purveyors of libel), whose circulation depended upon regaling their readers with gossip and daily scandal, and which pandered to the basest desires and prejudices of the masses. In their pages attacks against foreigners in general and against Italians in particular had become a real art. The working class in Western Australia, afraid of competition on the labour market, were already suspicious of and hostile to our workers. Thus these papers set out to rouse prejudice and hostility whenever possible against the hated 'Dago,' painting him in even blacker colours.[1] Their attacks were not limited to Italians living in Australia but were extended, quite violently, towards our nation as a whole. The damage their campaign has done, and continues to do, is immense, because rancour and envy were combined with ignorance.

I have noted earlier that our emigration was at first viewed without enthusiasm because it was composed mainly of workers. Unfortunately this adverse attitude remained very much alive and I found combatting it very unpleasant. It was not just a case of trying to raise the image of our fellow countrymen in terms of public opinion by showing with facts and figures that Italy could hold its own with any other nation on earth; rather I had to endeavour to make our workers welcome by the mass of the populace and by Australian workers. It was thus necessary once and for all for me to solve this social question, although, as anybody could see, it would be no easy task. The hostile feelings nurtured here were the result of circumstances peculiar to the Australian working class.

---

1 This is the nickname given to Latin emigrants, particularly Italians, in Anglo-Saxon countries. Its origin lies in the common Castilian name Diego which, since the time of colonization in North America, the British have used to describe Spaniards living in their territory.

The Labour Party, which has a very developed organisation and political practice in this country, has been able to effect legislation very favourable to workers. High wages have been the most significant of Labour's victories. Let us take the case of Western Australia in particular where one can say, without fear of contradiction, that the worker is better paid than anywhere else in the world. It remains to be seen if this land of milk and honey will last for long because one must not forget that the wealth down there depends in large measure upon the gold mines and these are certainly not infinite. Indeed, as elsewhere, the richest mines have begun to peter out and the miners have moved on to the less fruitful; in this situation wages must eventually go down because no capitalist I know wants to tie up his money in a losing enterprise. Nevertheless, the boom continues and, even though there are some less than reassuring signs, the worker does not yet have to worry too much about falling wages. Rather the greatest present danger is competition from foreign labour. But this peril is largely offset by the very strict provisions of the Immigration Restriction Act which puts every sort of obstacle in the path of the immigrant. In fact, the law if applied to the letter could have the effect of hermetically sealing Australia off from the foreigner. However, both for international reasons and in the best interests of the country, Australians cannot adopt such a radical policy, and so a certain number of foreign workers are allowed to enter the country and of these the majority are Italian.

Now it is a fact that Italians who migrate to Australia are excellent, disciplined, intelligent and sober workers, and, consequently, are preferred by the mine owners to local Australians who, although they are skilled, are very frequently given to drink and are somewhat lazy. In turn, however, such preference stimulates a high degree of hostility towards our immigrants among local workers. Two or three times in the last five years violent agitation has broken out against them, particularly in April 1904 when matters reached a point where it appeared there would be bloodshed at any minute. Every imaginable accusation has been hurled against Italians. One had only to read the so-called popular press to see the level this paroxysm of hatred had reached. Finally, the government had to intervene and established a Royal Commission to investigate whether there was any truth in the accusations. It was proved beyond a shadow of a doubt that none of the charges was sustainable and, citing just one example of an economic nature, that our workers had never worked for lower wages than those paid to Australians and had, therefore, never caused wages to drop, nor had they ever come to Australia as contract workers (which is absolutely prohibited by law), and that they had never bribed the foremen to secure employment etc. At the same time it was implicitly admitted that Italians worked harder than the locals and were, therefore, preferred by the bosses. Obviously the Labour Party, on these grounds, could not demand their expulsion, but a resentment against our workers survives which, while partly allayed, is not yet dead.

I have digressed somewhat in this matter but I believe it was necessary to do so because the question of labour is at the heart of Australian politics; not least among the reasons for mooting the idea of an Italian agricultural settlement, which has been well-received throughout the southern continent, was the hope that these problems could thus be resolved.

I had already raised this matter with Walter James who was then premier, when more serious disturbances had occurred. I found him to be an intelligent and more than capable and enlightened statesman. He tried everything to reduce the agitation but, at the same time, made me realize that, besides police action, the situation required additional, more radical, means in order to effect a complete change in immigration policy. His ideas were definite. Like it or not, the Italian worker was in competition with the local worker, if not because they worked for lower pay then because they were more industrious; therefore, it was difficult, given the present state of the labour market, to hope that good relations could be established between the workers of both nations. From the point of view Australia's national interest it should be said that while it was true that our migrants helped generate wealth, they did not go to Australia with the idea of settling down; rather, to stay a year or so and to save as much as possible of their high wages and send their savings home. They arrived alone, without their families. But Western Australia, immense as it was, needed people to exploit its limitless resources, especially those in the agricultural sector. Thus, the state could expect to benefit little from the Italians who came as sojourners.

On the other hand, in a complex situation like this, one must never forget the very particular circumstances which apply to the local labour market. Western Australia, at present, is essentially a mining centre, with few or no other industries. Now the mines represent a steady, if fixed, source of employment for a certain term. In round numbers there are about 20,000 employed there. Supposing that several thousand miners arrived from Europe and were unable to find work, they would constitute a danger and a liability for the government that sponsored them. They might obtain jobs but local workers would have to be retrenched. Obviously the mine owners would agree to keep the old hands and take on the new only if there were a proportional decrease in wages, something to which the Labour Party would never agree; not to mention that the wage scale in Australia is rigid and leaves the individual little room to negotiate.

Thus, Italian emigration to Western Australia needed to follow a completely different path from that which had previously been pursued. While once it had been assumed that immigrant groups had been comprised entirely of workers who went to work as employees for cut-rate wages, now it was opportune to replace them with a different class of person, namely farmers who would work for themselves and, profiting from the liberal agricultural laws of the country, would become landowners to their own benefit and to that of their new country. Nor did such arrangements have anything to fear from the immigration law. It sought to damp down competition on the labour market, but certainly was not opposed to the entry of immigrants who would not arouse local prejudices. In fact, indirectly, an increase in agricultural productivity could actually be to the advantage of Western Australian workers, leading to a reduction in the price of consumer goods. Thus, in a practical sense, there would be no opposition to Italians coming, not even from the Labour Party; indeed it was worth noting that the few Italian farmers who have already settled in the country were the only ones of our people to be well received.

Mr James, who concurred with the above ideas, had always been of the opinion—indeed it was a plank of his electoral platform—that it was time for Australia to abandon its policy of isolationism in order to attract the best type of agriculturalist from different European countries. He seemed convinced that the population of the country, relative to its area, was too small to ensure progress. With its vast stretches of exceedingly fertile land the country could hope to achieve primacy in the field of agriculture similar to that which it now enjoyed in terms of its mineral wealth. Only by the implementation of a wise immigration policy, he maintained, would it be possible to bring these ideas to fruition. His own personal experience, together with our frequent discussions, convinced me of his sympathy towards Italy. I was very happy about this because, for some time, I had been of the opinion that it would be useful for us to have an agricultural settlement in Australia.

In fact, soon after my arrival, I had had cause to appraise the immense resources of this country, or as they say here the *possibilities*, and I was convinced that Western Australia offered tremendous scope to our farmers. I had travelled by train from Perth to Albany through most of the so-called agricultural sector and had been amazed by the endless fertile plains, almost entirely uninhabited and awaiting only the hand of dedicated settlers to realize their real worth. I had also been in Northam with the Premier during the course of his election campaign and had been able to appreciate the worth of the district and its splendid climate and soil.

As a result of my observations a report was presented to my superior, the Consul-General in Melbourne, at the end of 1904, drawing the attention of the Australian government to the possibility of bringing our farmers here. But neither I nor Mr James hid the serious difficulties, be they moral or material, which might hamper the realization of this scheme. At the moral level there was widespread hostility against us. However, as I explained, such hostility, which exists in many other countries besides Australia, was largely the product of ignorance or trade protection; the first had to be overcome by means of effective propaganda and I had already registered some significant and very satisfying progress in that area, notably among the more educated class. Secondly, with the gradual substitution of the aforementioned workers by those belonging to the agricultural sector, the majority of future settlers would be owner-farmers, already respected in the community, and no threat to the labour market.

The material, or rather the financial, obstacles to the project were more serious. All Australia is covered by uninterrupted bush which requires time and money to clear; thus, under normal circumstances, only the farmer who has sufficient capital to meet these initial costs and keep going until the first harvest, which sometimes can be held up for some two years, has the possibility of establishing himself in the country. At present few Italian, or for that matter other European, farmers have such means at their disposal; small landowners generally own their farm and possess no capital. For them, emigration means selling their farm, and the reluctance of that type of person to take such a step is well known.

The need of primary capital, which is officially estimated to be between £100 and £150, is obviously a major stumbling block to agricultural development in the southern continent. What happens is that the majority of those who acquire land do not possess the necessary technical, theoretical and practical knowledge, but are individuals who have been in the country for some time and have managed, by working at other jobs, to scrape together some funds and, attracted by the security and high returns of the investment, turn themselves into farmers. Obviously this kind of person is not well-suited to farming, particularly on virgin land.

Strong and robust farmers, used to country life and who know their business, are the best settlers for a place like Western Australia. Italy has an abundance of such people; but, as already noted, almost all lack the necessary means; how then might they be transplanted in Australia?

Chapter Two

I Return to Italy—How to Establish our Settlers in Australia?—Mission to London—Second Journey to Western Australia—I Accompany the Agricultural Delegates—The Norddeutscher Lloyd—The Straits of Messina—Port Said—Aden—Colombo— Fremantle—The Immigration Restriction Act.

In September 1905, after a stay of almost three years in Australia, I was granted leave by the government to return home. I took advantage of the occasion to express my views, in person, to the Commissioner-General for Emigration, about the timeliness of establishing an agricultural settlement in Australia. I found Admiral Reynaudi decidedly in favour. The benefit to our country resulting from a careful policy of immigration in vast, fertile and largely unpopulated lands was not lost on him. The settlement of groups of our peasants would serve not only the interests of the peasants themselves, who could not fail to prosper given the excellent soil and climatic conditions and the country's liberal land laws,[1] but also those of the mother country herself which might, in a similar fashion, activate, or rather create commercial contacts with the newest continent which, unfortunately, were singularly lacking at present. It could happen in Australia as it had in America where business men, following in the footsteps of their countrymen, had gradually established themselves.

The Commissioner-General agreed, however, that there were a number of difficult hurdles particularly with respect to the not inconsiderable initial capital required by the prospective settler. Obviously, the scheme would be easier to implement if one were able to choose persons who had their own capital. Such a group, once

---

1   According to official information furnished by Mr Walter James, of 4000 farming families settled in Western Australia since 1894 (the date of the foundation of the Agricultural Bank), only about ten had failed. None of them were Italians.

40

settled in Australia, would bring out their relatives and friends who, because they would be supported by those who were already settled, would have no need of initial capital. Thus natural forces would control and propel the migrant flow. But, as I have already said, the main difficulty lies in finding families in such a flourishing condition, the more so at present given that their numbers are so few. It is clear that a few individuals scattered about a large area would not be able to function as a point of reference which might give rise to a settlement of any importance. In Western Australia there are only five or six of our farmers. They went there by their own means some years ago and though they find themselves in good economic condition, their number has nevertheless remained stationary. One seemingly obvious solution would have been to encourage a private company to buy up large tracts of land and have it organize the settlements. However, such a system would have confronted insurmountable difficulties in a country with virtually a socialist system, where the state is everything, and wants to do everything.

In due course, I conveyed Mr James' views on the matter, as he had expressed them to me earlier, to Admiral Reynaudi. The task of clearing the land, the Premier had suggested, should be considered a public service and as such be paid at the going daily rate. Thus the immigrant would be able to support himself until the first harvest, or at least until he had fulfilled the legal requirements which in turn allowed the State Agricultural Bank to lend money to farmers. Mr James had also mooted the idea of allotting us land that had already been cleared by the government. However, it was debatable if this measure would suffice, given that travelling expenses as well as establishment and maintenance costs in the first days after arrival were not to be covered.

I have made mention of the State Agricultural Bank which has shown itself to be an important factor in the development of agriculture in Western Australia. But, given its nature and the strict regulations on which it is based, it is evident that *alone* it would not be able to eliminate the more serious difficulties, that is, the initial costs. It would seem, at first glance, that the Western Australian government, which would have stood to gain much from such a settlement, in its own interests, should have been more than willing to underwrite the project. But, before pronouncing judgement, one must understand the exact situation. Public opinion, until recently, has been extremely hostile towards immigration; only agricultural immigrants with capital were admitted and then under strict regulation.

The government is now adopting a more liberal line; but it has to do so with great caution in order not to clash with the many prejudices and suspicions. And this, more than anything else, has limited the extent to which it can help the peasant farmer with little capital to establish himself.

There has always been an entrenched dislike in Australia of schemes which encourage those without means to immigrate, albeit they were British. This is largely the result of the spirit of self-help which is typically Anglo-Saxon but also stems from the fear that the wretched and impoverished class left behind in the old country would flood the new. In Australia a poor immigrant is immediately suspected, whether it be true or not, of coming from the slums or the work-house. Instead, the perception of a farmer is of one who enjoys a certain well-being, who owns or leases land, and is never, in the true sense of the word, indigent. The rejection of a scheme proposed by General Booth, the much admired founder of the Salvation Army, which would have seen a mixed bag of individuals sent to Australia, clearly showed the feelings of the Australian populace in this matter.

Given a similar set of circumstances it would have been difficult, if not impossible, for the Western Australian government, in the face of public opinion, to have been seen offering advantages to *poor Italians* that had not been offered to *Englishmen* in similar conditions (despite the fact that the government was now persuaded of the excellence of our albeit not well-to-do farmers). In Australia such an event would be hailed as an invasion of ne'er-do-wells [*lazzaroni*] and, even when viewed benevolently, a threat to the labour market.

Bearing in mind these many difficulties related to place as well as substance that stood in the way of settling Italian farmers in Australia, it was Admiral Reynaudi who came up with what was the only solution to the basic problem. The Western Australian government would allot land and advance the cost of fares, accommodation, equipment and subsistence funds which the settler would repay by instalment. The Emigration Commission would proceed with the selection of families and institute a financial arrangement up to a fixed amount, in the form of a guarantee and subject to certain conditions. The main aim of such an arrangement, as already noted, was to assist the immigrant during the period between settlement on the property and the first harvest or at least until he was eligible for the subsidy from the Agricultural Bank.

Given that the arrangement would apply only to the first group (set at no more than one hundred families), the burden on the Commission would have been fairly light. Thus, with relatively little sacrifice, significant progress could have been made towards opening up a hitherto hermetically sealed country to our agrarian emigrants and towards laying down a firm foundation for the development of our trade with these vast and rich areas. (In the direct negotiations with the Western Australian government which ensued, the strict limitations imposed on the concept of a guarantee reduced it, more or less, to an absurdity. Almost certainly, even in the worst case scenario, the Commission would not have been responsible for more than a few tens of thousands of lire. However, I must say that up to now the Western Australian government has not set much store on keeping to its announced financing plans, judging it more prudent to hide its salient features to offset prejudice, particularly that from the extremist faction of the Labour Party.)

Moreover, the fact that the selection of the families, upon which depended the successful outcome of the enterprise, would be made through the good offices of the Commission would have removed all opposition, even on the part of the most radical Labourite in Australia. Each side had be sure in their minds that the type of settler was the best in every respect, destined to work exclusively in the agricultural sector and not be a threat to the labour markets, which was a perpetual nightmare for the Labour Party. No longer hindered by local opposition, the Western Australian government, without hesitation, would have been able to enlarge the scope of its apportionments to our people.

With the problem solved in this positive manner it remained to come to terms with the already favourably disposed Western Australian government through an exchange of ideas leading to an eventual agreement, which, in time, would enable the scheme to proceed. In passing, I must say that, within our relevant spheres, apart from the inevitable opposition one encounters in any undertaking, the scheme was warmly backed by the majority. Among expressions of support I would like to mention that of the illustrious Senator Bodio, president of the Emigration Council, who, quickly grasping the great advantages of a settlement in Australia, dedicated all his formidable talents of mind and energy towards getting the scheme established. His backing and, I would add, his enthusiasm particularly helped remove the many fears and prejudices which some had expressed with respect to the plan.

At that time the same Mr James who had been Premier became the Agent-General for Western Australia in London. He had been nominated for the post following the rise to power of the Labour Party in

1904 which, by the way, was replaced a few months later by the Liberals (with Rason as Premier, followed by Moore) who now in 1909 are still in power.[2]

The Emigration Commission felt it would be opportune for me to confer with this distinguished statesman who was a true friend of Italy and well disposed towards opening up his country to Italian immigration, while enjoying the full support of his government. We were to examine all aspects of the problem together and reach some preliminary agreement.

I arrived in London at the end of December. Mr James found Admiral Reynaudi's proposals excellent in that they effectively removed all obvious obstacles. James told me he was sure that the government, as well as public opinion in Western Australia, should be more than favourably disposed towards the scheme. However, he felt that, in the mutual interest of both nations, it would be useful if a delegation of prospective settlers could visit Western Australia to study the country and obtain a fundamental understanding of the situation before a final decision was reached. The impressions gained by the delegates would, no doubt, be excellent but it was important that the families who proposed to take the step learned from those of the same class as themselves exactly what they could expect so that they could make their decisions fully apprised of the facts. 'We do not want disgruntled persons,' he told me, 'but settlers who are satisfied with their new country and the conditions which apply.' So convinced was he of the necessity for a delegation that he immediately undertook to get the required funds for the trip from the government.

I had several further meetings with Mr James during which we went over the fundamentals of the settlement scheme while striving to ensure it was practical in essence. Agreement was quickly reached and in three days the preliminary negotiations were complete.

The Commission accepted the Agent-General's proposal with respect to the delegation which would number three persons. A special representative of the Commission itself, familiar with the place and able to speak English, should accompany the farmers. His presence would be needed not only to oversee the journey but also to liaise with the Western Australian government should the mission find it convenient to begin negotiations.

---

2 Each Australian government has its agent in London: his main task is to watch over the interests of the state he represents. Even the Federal government has its own agent.

The exchange of ideas between myself and Mr James in London was confined to laying down a base for future negotiations; many other issues of detail and principle remained to be resolved. The most irritating was always the question of guarantees on the part of the Commission. From my point of view it was better, in practical terms, to accept these guarantees as a matter of necessity in order to hurry things along so as not to risk the possibility that public opinion in Italy might turn against the scheme. After all, it would have been very difficult for the Western Australian government to do anything without such a clause, given the conditions prevailing in the country, the mood of the Labour Party and public opinion in general towards immigration, and the fact that our settlers would arrive with hardly any capital. Reconciling opposing interests and at the same time ensuring the well-being of our settlers was a problem which would require long and detailed negotiations which necessarily had to be undertaken on the spot.

The selection of the three delegates took some time. The Commission decided that the Emilia region would provide the best kinds of families. Thus, the prefects of that region were asked to nominate three reasonably educated persons, particularly versed in the practical aspects of agriculture, who would have the trust of their fellow farmers in the region. Those selected were: Ricci from Portomaggiore, Bottoni from Molinella and Ruozi from Reggio Emilia. Bottoni was no newcomer to such missions having already taken part in a similar expedition to Eritrea.

Initially, there was some uncertainty about who would accompany the delegates; but, when Admiral Reynaudi intimated that he wished me to undertake the mission (as had the Agent-General in London), I willingly accepted, pleased with the confidence he had placed in my abilities. It was May by then and we could have left immediately; however, I suggested that we wait until mid-August so as not to reach our destination during the rainy season which would have made our inspection of the country difficult.

In the meantime Mr James arrived in Rome and I took him to see Admiral Reynaudi and the Minister for Foreign Affairs, the Hon. Francesco Guicciardini. His visit produced some excellent results. Mr James received assurances of the good will of the Italian government; the Minister and the Commissioner-General remained convinced that the enterprise could not fail to achieve its aims, guaranteed as it was by the favourable climatic and soil conditions and by the active backing of the Western Australian government. The Commission, for its part, feared that the Immigration Restriction Act might cause some embarrassment to the three delegates, but the Agent-General was completely reassuring on this point. In fact, he predicted there would be the warmest reception on the part of both the authorities and the populace, and, in truth, events proved that he was an excellent prophet.

It was decided to embark at Genoa, the port nearest to the homes of the delegates, on one of the steamers belonging to the Norddeutscher Lloyd. This shipping company was preferred, both for the conditions enjoyed aboard its steamers and because the Western Australian government, which, as noted, was paying the fares, had a special arrangement with the Company regarding the transportation of emigrants.

I note in passing that Australia is linked to continental Europe by four main shipping lines: the Orient Line and the Peninsular and Oriental Line (known for short as the P&O) which are English, the Norddeutscher Lloyd (German), and Messagéries Maritimes (French). Italian ports are served only by the Norddeutscher Lloyd (Genoa and Naples) and the Orient Line (Naples). Marseilles is the closest port of call to Italy for the other two lines.

I have travelled in steamers belonging to all these companies but I must say that the Norddeutscher Lloyd, in every respect, provides the best service and facilities. It is unbeatable as far as third class is concerned. Sufficient to say that for an extra £2 (the entire passage from Genoa to Fremantle costs £13) the third-class passenger is entitled to a place in a two-berth cabin in which he is often the only occupant. Furthermore, when one considers that most of the voyage is through tropical regions, where the heat is often excessive, the advantages of having as much room as possible may be readily appreciated. Added to which the food is plentiful and varied. For this reason Italians have a marked preference for these vessels and rarely travel on the English or French lines.

We set sail on August 21 aboard the steamer *Gera* under the command of Captain Prosh. I had met the three delegates on the 20th at the Genoa offices of the Commission and had been most favourably impressed. They showed themselves to be enthusiastic and identified with the importance of the mission assigned them. At the office I received a telegram from Admiral Reynaudi who, while wishing us bon voyage, added his best wishes for the enterprise now under way and hoped that it might achieve a good result for the sake of the country. Both the delegates and myself were grateful to this distinguished man for his kind sentiments.

As soon as I boarded I went to see the cabin which had been allocated to the delegates. It was a four-berth one, entirely at their disposal. It had external portholes, which meant the cabin was light and airy. Moreover, it was equal to my own in terms of space. The delegates were very pleased, particularly Bottoni who was able to compare it with third class on our steamers, a comparison which, unfortunately, was not very flattering to our mercantile marine.

The voyage, which was excellent throughout, began in magnificent weather. We were in Naples on the 22nd; we then passed through the Straits of Messina enjoying the marvellous view of the Calabrian and Sicilian coastlines: Reggio to the left, and farther off, to the right, Messina, Etna and enchanting little white villages and brilliant green vegetation as far as Catania. Leaving such natural beauty behind is always hard on those obliged to depart from the motherland for lengthy periods. No wonder we Italians suffer from nostalgia. Where would one find a country more beautiful than ours? For Ruozi and Ricci, who had never been to sea before, everything appeared new and extraordinarily interesting.

Near Crete one of the usual melancholy events occurred. A waiter threw himself overboard and it was impossible to rescue him. On the 26th we hove in sight of Port Said. The lighthouse, equipped with a powerful beam, came into view first; gradually trees and houses took shape, then the wharf at the end of which towers the statue of De Lesseps. The Egyptian coast is low and sandy and the sea for many miles off-shore is a dirty yellow. The city of Port Said had little appeal so we were not unhappy to leave it. We passed through the canal with its bare sandy banks at snail's pace (if such an expression is permissible); overall, the landscape could not be more depressing. Then we reached Suez and before us were the blue waters of the Red Sea. August was the least favourable month for the crossing; the heat was suffocating and unbearable. We coped reasonably well for the first two days but the last few gave us a foretaste of the fires of hell. However, once past Bab-el-Mandeb and the island of Perim, a fresh breeze from the Indian Ocean brought relief.

On the 31st we entered the very large roadstead of Aden, surrounded by tall, dark and astonishingly bare mountains. The Hadramut coast, the most gloomy, wild and miserable of all Arabia where the mineral kingdom rules supreme, begins at Aden. We arrived very late at night. The vessel was surrounded by innumerable boats and rafts crammed with blacks who performed dances and other wild rites. For Ricci, it seemed as though he had been transported to another world and he was almost afraid of the quite diabolical appearance of the natives.

Another eight days sailing and there before us lay the enchanting sight of Colombo. I invited the delegates to visit the city with me. What most impresses the visitor to Ceylon is the extraordinary richness and enormous variety of its vegetation. The weather was extremely hot, but bearable and relatively healthy. We availed ourselves of the local means of transport, the rickshaw, a lightweight, two-wheeled little cart pulled by a native. It is amazing that a man can have such powers of endurance; one of these men-horses can trot along calmly for two hours or more without showing any sign of fatigue except for the sweat which drips profusely down his ebony skin. Surrounding the commercial district and the native quarter, which forms the centre of the town, innumerable bungalows—small, architecturally distinctive villas—set in large gardens, spread out to make the city seem much larger.

We travelled for hours and hours along endless avenues, never tiring of admiring the beauties of tropical nature. The dark green of the foliage, the strange gaudy-coloured flowers, the vast grassy glades, the avenues of bright red earth, the cloying perfume of aromatic spices wafted on warm breezes, the crowds of shapely, brown, half-naked Singhalese, all combine to give Colombo its special character and its irresistible appeal.

We went back on board to find that the deck had been taken over by peddlers trying to sell their wares at exorbitant prices. Every port in the orient has its speciality. In Aden the poor passenger is hounded until he buys an ostrich feather fan or loose feathers. For a fan they start off asking £3 or £4 but, after endless protest and whining, they will let it go for 10 shillings, even 5 shillings. I have been told that these fans, which are very roughly made, come from Germany. This does not surprise me greatly because I believe that very few of the so-called oriental articles are manufactured in the countries in which they are sold; almost all are made in Europe. Thus, the gold-embroidered silk fabrics which are a speciality of Tunis and Algiers are, for the most part, produced in Lyon. Colombo's speciality is precious stones. One might expect, given Ceylon's rich ruby, topaz and sapphire mines, and its extensive pearling beds, that real stones would be offered for sale. But, in fact, more often than not, the natives bring on board pieces of coloured glass. The seller begins by asking £4 or £5 each for a stone and, to prove they are genuine, cheekily resorts to methods that prey upon the ingenuous traveller. He puts one of the stones on the ground and places a copper coin on top: he then stamps his heel on it and then triumphantly shows how the stone has not shattered but has perforated the coin; therefore, it is genuine. Some people fall into the trap and buy. However, usually the honest merchant is lucky if, of his boasted rubies, emeralds and diamonds, he can sell half a dozen stones for sixpence.

Nevertheless, there are shops in town where one can buy precious stones at really moderate prices, about 20 per cent less than in Europe. Of course one needs to know something about the goods or else be introduced to the merchant by officers on board or by passengers who have been there previously.

Soon we were on our way once again and due to arrive at our destination in another ten days. The impatience which hits the poor old sailor towards the end of a voyage is strange; one literally counts the hours. As far as I was concerned the impatience could be readily understood given the unfortunate position of my cabin, right in the middle of the noisiest part of the ship. This was because the ship was full of so-called 'wool-buyers,' representatives of firms in London, Berlin, Brussels, Paris etc.—plainly none was Italian—who for ages have travelled to Australia to buy wool. They know months ahead which ship they will take and thus have the opportunity to appropriate the best cabins aboard for themselves; their being legion in number there is obviously little worthwhile accommodation left for the ordinary passenger who finds himself belittled and humiliated in front of individuals who, from the way they behave, might be thought to be princes incognito.

At one o'clock in the morning on September 19 we were in sight of the Fremantle lighthouse. At two, the pilot's launch came alongside carrying a representative of the government bidding me welcome to Australia. I had a heap of questions for him and he was keen also to hear about our mission. I then went to my cabin to snatch an hour or two of sleep but a wretched noise kept me awake until six o'clock. A Commonwealth official, charged with the task of checking the passengers disembarking at Fremantle, had installed himself right in front of the door to my cabin.

I have already mentioned the restrictions against immigration that exist in Australia. Some major points with respect to this matter might be apposite. Individual Australian states had already enacted very strict laws in this area prior to Federation. After Federation one law, covering all the Commonwealth, was enacted. Australia had two aims: 1) to prevent the influx of yellow peoples who, if left free to do so, would have flooded the country in a few short years. In fact, if one considers that Australia has an area of some three million square miles and a population of less than five million, one can understand that the fear of seeing the white element overtaken by the Asiatic is not without foundation. The White Australia policy, therefore, can be judged to have been useful, and even necessary. Sometimes, however, it can be carried to extremes as, for example, when it legislates to force ships that ply Australian ports to exclude non-Europeans from their crews unless they get proper wages. 2) The Australian government has a second aim in view, to which I have already referred: that is, to hamper foreign competition on the national labour markets. As a result the law provides the means to exclude not only the so-called coloured population, but also white immigrants who are subjected to a dictation test of fifty words in a European language. But, as the language to be used in the test is not clearly specified, the government has the power to exclude any individual it wants.

The law may be invoked not only against foreigners but also against the British. The clause which prohibits anyone coming into the country as a contract worker also applies to them. All England was up in arms when six English workers, specialists in the manufacture of hats, who had been engaged to develop or at least improve the industry, were prevented from disembarking in Melbourne. The case of the 'six hatters' has, in fact, become legendary.

In practice, it should be noted that there are very few such cases, although the means to implement the law are in place and continue, with some exceptions, to exclude black and yellow people. Naturally, whites, whether they be British, European or American, are allowed to disembark on the understanding that they are healthy, have the means to support themselves and at least appear as if they have not arrived under a work contract. However, that the full rigour of the law might be applied in particular circumstances cannot be completely ruled out.

As I have already noted, there has been a considerable change in public opinion over the years with respect to the immigration issue. Firstly, under pressure from the Labour Party, which detests any competition, the attitude of the public was generally unfavourable to whatever scheme was proposed. But the Russo-Japanese War opened many eyes. It was realized that an invasion of Australia by the Japanese, or even at some future date by the Chinese once they were organised, would be extremely easy. The British fleet was the only obstacle but, in the event of a general conflagration, it would, in the first instance, have to defend its own homeland. The achievement and daring of the Japanese fleet in the Russian campaign indicated that a landing on the coast of the uninhabited north, an attack on un-defended Fremantle and the occupation of the goldmines at Kalgoorlie would take only a few days. Western Australia would not be able to mount any semblance of resistance. How could a state with a population of only 250,000 persons in an area of one million square miles, without railway communication to the eastern states, possibly defend itself? While England is allied to Japan the threat does not exist; but who can predict the future? The hatred the Japanese have for Australians, whom they consider to be an inferior race, is almost equal to that which the empire of the Rising Sun harbours towards the United States.

The Russo-Japanese War, therefore, marked a change in the de-velopment of Australian public opinion towards immigration matters. As I have already said, it spurred on a change similar to that in Canada, which has developed amazingly in wealth and prosperity through its wise policy of encouraging people from all European countries.

However, it must be remembered that the only kind of immigration wanted, at this point, is of an agricultural nature and possessed of a certain amount of capital: capital which, as I have noted, is necessary because of the very special conditions applying to land that is covered by limitless forest, and also because, according to ideas which hold sway here, it confirms the upright intent of the immigrants. I shall discuss this last point in more detail later on.

Enough of my digression. Just as I was leaving my cabin I ran into my very dear friend Ramacciotti, one of the editors of the *Morning Herald* and temporary secretary to Mr Morgans, the acting Italian Consul and a wealthy mine owner. He brought greetings from his chief and, loyal to his profession, wasted no time in subjecting me to a probing interview. Ramacciotti was born in Italy, or more precisely in Livorno, but he has been resident in Australia since he was a child. He has won a highly respectable position in Perth and, to his merit, is well regarded everywhere. He it was who introduced me to Henry Ranford one of the high ranking officials from the Lands Department (the Lands Department is separate from that of Agriculture). Mr Moore, the Premier, had entrusted Ramacciotti and Ranford with the task of welcoming us and escorting us to Perth. As the narrative that follows will show, Mr Ranford would be our guide in our journeys through the state's agricultural districts.

Among the many individuals who came to meet us, I saw Mr Ratazzi, the representative of the Norddeutscher Lloyd Line and our consular agent in Fremantle. He had held the position of consular official in Western Australia before the post was occupied by career diplomats.

Chapter Three

Arrival in Perth—Democracy and Railways—
Hotels—Newspapers and Journalists—The Midland
Company.

Fremantle is linked to Perth by a double tracked railway about twelve miles long. It is an excellent service; trains depart every quarter of an hour and even more frequently on occasions. Delays (blessed country that this is) are completely unknown; moreover, there are many intermediate stations, at least on this line, and considerable traffic. What lessons this new country, civilized for barely twenty years, has given! Travelling on the Australian railways I frequently experience a sense of humiliation when I think of ours, particularly that along the coast of my Liguria, a single track throughout its course, whose interminable delays drive the traveller to distraction. Of course the Western Australian railways are not without their own problems. The spacious compartments have nothing of the elegance found in our first-class section. And the engineering of the lines themselves is somewhat rudimentary. Some, in hilly areas, resemble ours in Sardinia, where the train is forced to go slow on the uphill sections and at breakneck speeds on the descents. However, one must realize that, in a country of enormous distances and scanty population such as this one, where the railways through necessity must be widely developed (the Western Australian network is composed of almost 2000 miles of line), their mode of construction is governed by the finances available.

There is also a problem in that the division between the classes, which are only two in number, is not rigorously maintained. As a result, the company one finds is not always the most select; but here in Australia one must accustom oneself from the outset to the ultra democratic ways of the country which, while they may offend the more sensitive, also have their good side.

Australia is perhaps the most democratic country in the world. The stranger arriving here notices it immediately in the manner of dress. For example, all the women go out wearing hats; all are neatly, I would even say elegantly dressed, and it is impossible to distinguish between the wife of a worker and that of a rich man. The same neatness and elegance can be observed among men when they change out of their work clothes. It is a simple fact that poverty does not exist in this country and that every class, even the most humble, enjoys considerable affluence.

Not only is the lack of social division noticeable in external appearances, it is also firmly rooted in the soul and spirit of this people. While the English have the utmost respect, in fact I would say adoration, for their aristocracy, a lord or a duke would be treated here with the same familiarity and *sans gene* as any worker.

This, basically, is the reason for the deep dislike of Australians which exists among the English upper classes, a dislike that, at first, seems inexplicable to the foreigner and in Europe is largely unknown. It is a fact that the English nobility rarely choose Australia as a destination for one of their many peregrinations. Rather they can be found in Southern Europe, Egypt, the Indies and now in numbers even in China and Japan, all places where they are certain to be accorded due admiration and respect. These entrenched democratic attitudes may also be seen in the sphere of government. In Europe, ministers are like gods who are rarely exposed to the human eye. Here, instead, ministers love to be seen in public, they are accessible to everyone and are treated with the same familiarity as most ordinary people. Whether in cabinet or at public functions, they often dress with a simplicity which seems, at times, to be too much. But how often are intellect and cultivation masked by this modest appearance! What deep love they have for their country; what drive they possess to raise the glorious 'Commonwealth' to the prosperity and the power of the more advanced states in the world!

Australian democracy, which may appear excessive to some, has this tremendous advantage—it makes all citizens, from the Prime Minister to the most humble worker, aware of their rights and duties and that they are men beholden to nothing except the law of the land. There is no abject class here which, caught between hunger and want, harbour hatred in their hearts for the rich and for the government and see revolt and plunder as the only solution to their ills. Here everybody is a citizen in the true sense of the word.

Now I find myself drifting from the railway system to a discussion of socio-political questions! And I am afraid there will be several more such digressions in this work. Notwithstanding my admiration for Australian railways, particularly their punctuality, we decided to make the trip from Fremantle to Perth on the river. The Swan River in this section is navigable by small launches, barges and other craft of low draught. Perth actually is a port of some importance given the volume and weight of goods transported by water.

The vistas along the river are really charming; for two or three miles the river flows between rather high rocky cliffs before it widens out near Claremont (about the halfway point) and Melville, just before Perth, to form something like a lake. At Perth, too, the expanse of water is also quite extensive. The delegates, especially Ricci, were enchanted by the wonderfully picturesque scenery.

We arrived in Perth towards evening. I took my companions to a small Italian hotel owned by one of the Italian pioneers in Western Australia, a Mr Oldrini. Ricci would have preferred an Australian hotel where he could have practised English, which he was learning with ardour; but, in the end, as his studies were not very advanced and he would have needed to have an interpreter at all times, he gave in and accepted my decision.

Actually, Perth has little cause to praise itself over its hotels; naturally I am referring to their quality and not their quantity, which is very great. Only two, the Palace and the Esplanade, are tolerable. The former, without doubt, is the best. But the thing which all hotels lack in this country is comfortable rooms. They are microscopic in size and furnished with the bare minimum. For example, there is no such thing as a commode, and consequently, certain necessary items which one places in this piece of furniture are exposed to full view. There is never more than one chair. The mattress is paper-thin, through which the long-suffering guest can feel the cool touch of the metal base underneath.

On the other hand, the cuisine in the two aforementioned hotels is good (in so far as English or Australian food can ever seem good to the Italian palate). But no Continental European stomach could get used to the food served in second-class hotels in Perth, let alone in those of country towns. They would have to spend many years here before such a miraculous transformation occurred. The menu is almost always limited to roast beef, drowned in a black, evil-smelling sauce made separately; roast or boiled mutton, or corned beef. Sometimes they serve fish or poultry. Vegetables (usually cabbage and potatoes) are served with the meat, however they are always boiled and without salt. The helpings, if they are not drowned in the above-mentioned black sauce, are usually spread with an indefinable, whitish, viscous substance which resembles remarkably the paste used by bootmakers to stick the soles of shoes; I presume it has the same flavour. All this is washed down with tea or coffee (which means chicory). Don't even mention fruit. In second-rate hotels and boarding houses, meat is rarely served hot, with joints of meat weighing ten or twelve pounds being cooked in a piece and carved daily for meals until they run out.

The day after my arrival I went to call on the authorities, that is, the ministers, the under-secretaries (who here have no parliamentary position but correspond to our directors-general) and all those who had anything to do with the mission with which I had been entrusted. I received a kind, warm, and frequently enthusiastic welcome. The project was already known in the country and, save for the most rabid Labourites, it could be said that all were favourably disposed towards it.

The first thing to which anyone who is briefly popular or is classed as a celebrity must get used is the onslaught of reporters. The influence of newspapers here is incredible. The newspaper is read by all classes and reaches all homes, not only those in the towns but also in the smallest and most remote country centres. Even on isolated farms in the bush fifty or sixty miles from the post office one finds the inevitable *West Australian* or *Morning Herald*. The wide circulation enjoyed by these newspapers is due in large part to their advertisements. It could be said that all events, all transactions from those of commercial importance to the most mundane domestic sphere, are announced through the press. Also, everybody takes a great interest in politics and government, and illiteracy is completely unknown here. The politician, the scholarly expert, the reformer, the entrepreneur, in fact anyone who wants to make their ideas known, get publicity or exert influence, whether for some public or private reason, cannot hope to do so without the help of the press. It may be true that the same thing also happens sometimes in Europe; but, without doubt, the influence of the press is much greater in Australia. My arrival with the delegates had roused great curiosity and interest in the country. I had become the man of the hour and had my moment of glory. Therefore, I had to expect to be besieged by all the reporters in Western Australia. These indefatigable individuals would not leave their victim in peace, even at night. I remember being awakened at one in the morning, as I slept peacefully in my room, by a bold, not to say importunate, newshound who wanted the usual interview.

The most important and widely circulated newspaper in Perth is the *West Australian*, which also does very well financially. It is run by Dr Hackett, a member of parliament. It is followed by the *Morning Herald* and the *Daily News*; one of the directors of the *Morning Herald*, as I have already said, is our fellow countryman, Luigi Ramacciotti. There are also several weekly magazines, which belong to the ranks of the so-called popular press, to which I have already referred.

The success of the mission entrusted to me was due, in large part, to the excellent relations I enjoyed with the staff of several newspapers who welcomed and supported the immigration project. Such good relations were also useful from another point of view. As I have already explained I found public opinion to be steeped with the oddest prejudices against our nation, stemming mostly from a complete ignorance of the real state of affairs. The interviews, talks and publicity of all kinds that I had undertaken continuously during my four year residence had produced a result for which not even I had dared hoped, and the change in public opinion was quite amazing. But, without the goodwill accorded me by brave editors who desired only truth and justice, my efforts would not have been crowned with success.

One of the most outstanding personalities who earned the admiration of the public for his honesty and integrity, even though his *frangar non flectar* [to break, not bend] had aroused many enemies, was Mr Dreyer, the *West Australian*'s well-qualified agricultural correspondent. Through his insightful writings he had been able, in a relatively short time, to give a great fillip to agriculture in this country. Through our mutual concerns and ideals we became close friends. He rapidly declared himself to be a fervent supporter of the project, convinced of the enormous advantage that an influx of our peasant farmers would bring to the country. As far as he was concerned, the example of Argentina, where the Italian presence had enriched that vast territory, was conclusive.

The day of my arrival in Perth I had a visit from Mr Gardiner, formerly the Treasurer in the James' government and presently the agent for the English Midland Company which owns the railway line that runs from Perth to the outskirts of Geraldton (a distance of 277 miles), as well as vast tracts of magnificent land. The Midland Company had only recently begun to sell off some of its land and Mr Gardiner would have liked to reserve some of it for our settlers.

A brief account of the company, one of the strongest and most important in the state, may not be inopportune. It was founded around 1890 for the purpose of constructing the above mentioned line, destined to link the central and southern railway network with that of the northern goldfields (Geraldton–Nannine). The construction was undertaken and financed entirely by the company, but the government, in compensation, had granted it 12,000 acres for every mile of rail line, that is, a total of 3,324,000 acres. The agreement had been in place before the extraordinary development of Western Australia was foreseen and, too late, the government realized its mistake in granting such a large tract of Crown Land for a very dubious return. It tried several times to buy back the enterprise, that is, railway and land together (the railway is now the only private one in the state); but it was never able to make an appropriate deal. Some time ago (1905), under Daglish's ministry, the company had settled on the sum of £1,500,000, but parliament had not wanted to accept this figure, however much the government may have been in favour of the purchase. Thus, the company, under the direction of the wily Gardiner, abandoned any idea of negotiation and, with alacrity, began to realize its property through a partial sale by public auction. The land was divided into lots of 200 acres or more, with fifteen years to pay. Sales were extraordinarily successful as a result of astute advertising, although the best advertisement for the land was the fertility of the soil; the land brought up to 45 shillings an acre. This way the company will be able to recoup from the sale of the land alone all that it would have obtained from the government for both the land and the line, without taking into account the increase in traffic and profits implicit in the settlement of colonists along the way.

The government now bitterly regrets that it let such an excellent business opportunity slip by and that it has lost control of such a large section of Crown Land to an English company not based in the state and therefore considered to be barely more than foreign. It has been a hard lesson, and cannot but reaffirm the tendency, already so entrenched in Australia, to involve the government more and more with public works.

Mr Gardiner had immediately grasped the fact that our peasant farmers would be very useful in Western Australia and he was, therefore, most desirous that some of them be settled on company land. The appreciation in value of these lands and the subsequent establishment of populated centres would, without doubt, have given a boost to the sale of remaining lands and, at the same time, have increased prices. Moreover, Mr Gardiner offered very advantageous terms, principal among which was the establishment of settlements near to the railway line and the construction of a railway station for their exclusive use. Being close to the railway line, as might be imagined, was a tremendous advantage for settlers; their success in a new country depended almost entirely on the ease of communications. In Australia it is said that it is not practical for a farmer to establish himself beyond a twenty mile radius of the railway line. Naturally, I am referring specifically to farmers, that is, those individuals who are engaged in the cultivation of agricultural products and not squatters, that is, sheep and cattle breeders whose 'stations' may be situated further from the line. Cattle, for example, have less need to be transported because they can be made *to walk* to market.

Nevertheless, I felt it necessary to point out to Mr Gardiner the many pitfalls I foresaw in his scheme, the worst being that, as a private company whose immediate purpose was to make a profit, it could not enter into such generous agreements as could a government, whose sole aim was the general prosperity of the country. The Midland Company, as previously noted, had already put different sections of its property up for sale and had realized between 20 and 45 shillings per acre. The government, on the other hand, was prepared to allocate the best land for a single price of 10 shillings (without counting the 160 acres which would be free in any case). As well, it would make cash advances to enable our settlers to survive the initial period during which they would be unable to count on a harvest or a loan from the Agricultural Bank. Clearly, the conditions offered by the government left little to be desired. Was the company prepared, or better still was it in its interest, to do the same thing?

Mr Gardiner accepted that the idea I mooted earlier, that is, the establishment of a group of hard working people in the middle of their property, would result in an increase in the value of the surrounding land. With this in mind the Midland Company could certainly propose special terms and conditions which, in other circumstances, would never have been practicable. He told me, however, that the details could be discussed at a later date, if not in Perth then in London where the management of the company was located. Nevertheless he wanted me to promise that, as soon as I had visited the government land, I would, together with the delegates, inspect that under his jurisdiction. I happily agreed to this proposal.

Chapter Four

Australian Agriculture—Tours to the Harvey River and Kalamunda—The Arduino Farm—Fruit Cultivation.

The government had arranged an itinerary that would enable us to become acquainted with Western Australia's various agricultural districts. They wanted the delegates to have a complete picture of the state, its climate, products, agricultural practices, methods of clearing and so on, which were all so different from Europe. The settler coming here must really struggle hard to gain a firm understanding of the country. In the first place, he is used in the Old World to the very domesticated aspect (if you will excuse the expression) of the country-side. Everywhere the fields are under crops or fodder, and there are orchards and vineyards; the houses are close together, all of which give a vitality to the landscape. Here, instead, there is an immense boundless forest of eucalypts (or 'gums' as the many varieties of this family are known in Australia). Their uniformly greyish foliage and the coarse, thorny grasses which flourish beneath, lend the landscape a sad and melancholy aspect and the earth appears sterile. Not surprisingly the European arriving here for the first time is not very impressed. It is true, however, that, as soon as he has had a chance to study and observe in a little more detail, he changes his opinion and realizes what magnificent products a country, blessed with a climate unequalled in the world and with soil which in many parts is comparable to the most fertile in America or Europe, is able to produce. But this understanding cannot be gained in a day!

Let us suppose that the settler has overcome the initial feelings of dejection and bewilderment common to all new arrivals and has carefully selected his allotment. Many difficulties still remain to be overcome. First of all he will have to familiarise himself with the agricultural practices which, particularly in the early stages, are so different from ours. Meanwhile the land has to be cleared. It is not possible to utilize the timber given the enormous distances, the very high cost of labour and transport difficulties. Therefore it is burnt on the spot, the ashes being almost always an excellent fertilizer. In many cases it is impossible to knock down a still-green forest and then burn it; moreover, it would be a vast, time-consuming task if the trees were big. Therefore the trees are ringbarked, that is, a ring is cut through the bark around the tree; shortly thereafter the tree dries up and is burnt. The stumps are left, and wood and branches are heaped around and on top of them and set alight. The fire gradually consumes the roots until there is nothing left to burn. The smaller trees are knocked down while still green and their stumps and roots are pulled out with a jack. Sometimes the forest is not knocked down but entirely ringbarked. This usually happens when the land is designated for pasture. A strange phenomenon then occurs. The grass, formerly scant and thorny, becomes thick and luxuriant and provides succulent fodder for cattle; the reason for this change is that the eucalypts draw a huge amount of water from the soil. When the tree is dead all that moisture helps the growth of the grass.

In the southern region where the trees reach colossal proportions because of the excessive moisture only the smallest are knocked down; the biggest are left standing and later destroyed. The earth is immediately cultivated and the crops grow amid the dense bush. After the rains the countryside presents the strangest of scenes. In the warm and scented air flowers and rich green grass flourish beneath a serenely clear blue sky; they are in marked contrast to the trees which, like a mass of whitened skeletons, raise their denuded branches as if seeking revenge against the greed and cruelty of a mankind which, in killing them, has robbed them of their glorious mantle; it is the luxuriant spring of a semi-tropical country (and a great contrast to the severe northern European winter). However, the land reserved for cultivation is almost always completely cleared and then ploughed. This operation requires a certain amount of care; a plough with movable prongs which lift up when they encounter a root, then drop back when the obstacle has been passed, is used. In fact, it would be almost impossible, or at least it would take a considerable amount of time, to clear away all that is left after the forest has been knocked down. The bits of stumps, branches and roots are left to rot where they are. The ploughed earth is ready for seeding; but for the first two or three years it is, as they say in Australia, 'sour' and lacks the friability that soil acquires when it has been cultivated for some time. In this condition the soil is only fit for certain crops.

I could go on at length to describe the differences between European and Australian agriculture; one could discuss the way in which crops are rotated; the custom, held to be essential over there, of leaving the earth to lie fallow every two years; or the development of artificial fertilizers that have been adapted for agricultural and pastoral use. I shall refer to this matter at a later, more opportune, point. Nevertheless, from the foregoing, the reader will have realized that the European farmer will not immediately be able to get his bearings, to use an Australian expression. One should also add that the methods and manner of cultivation vary considerably according to district, not all being situated in the same latitude nor blessed with the same climate. It was, therefore, a wise decision on the part of the government to show us all of the state's agricultural areas. The delegates were intelligent observers who, with the assistance of technical personnel, would quickly gain a detailed picture of the country which would enable them to report back competently to their friends in Italy. Mr Ranford, who had been assigned by the government to accompany us, estimated that the tour would last for about five weeks, time enough to achieve the above mentioned aims.

Our series of tours began with brief excursions to areas close to Perth. As I noted earlier, the capital is situated on sandy soil which surrounds it for a ten mile radius. In the east, however, a very long chain of mountains, or better, hills (no peak is more than 1200 feet), known as the Darling Ranges rises. The base rock of these hills consists of iron nodules mixed with clay. In the valleys, or 'gullies' as they are called, the alluvial soil is very fertile and particularly well-suited to the cultivation of fruit which brings fabulous prices in Western Australia. The dark red clay soil of Guildford, an oasis situated a few miles from Perth, is extremely fertile. To the south, along the South West Railway line, between the Darling Ranges and the sea, there is an enormous area which includes some of the best land in the state. Travelling along this line one feels, in certain spots, as if one were in Italy on the plains of Emilia. The hand of man is everywhere; the forest has almost entirely disappeared giving way to cultivated fields of wheat, and meadows where thousands of sheep graze. The holdings are generally privately owned; the government, or as they say in Australia, the Crown, no longer owns any land in this area. One has to go thirty or forty miles away from the railway to find Crown Land and even then

Jarrah Forest
FROM: *Western Australia, Its Agricultural and Mining Interests, 1909.* Battye Library

there is only a limited amount. Further south, near Hamel (83 miles from Perth), there are enormous tracts of swampy land which the government is presently draining. The extraordinary fertility of the soil will certainly repay the considerable costs incurred in such operations. This area, together with another in the extreme south between Albany and Denmark, is one of the few marshy areas in the state. Both would be suitable for the cultivation of rice, although the high cost of labour rather suggests it may be better to use the land for raising cattle.

Near Hamel is an area known as Harvey River (98 miles from Perth), one of the most important agricultural areas in the state, particularly for the cultivation of oranges. Harvey River was the first of our excursions.

At this point, for the sake of clarity, my narrative will take the form of a diary.

September 22. The local agricultural show was held in Harvey today. Ranford, myself and the three delegates went there by train. Premier Moore had preceded us. On our arrival we found several vehicles waiting to take us to the Agricultural Hall that had been chosen as the site of the show. Even the smallest town or hamlet in Australia has its Town Hall if a municipality, or a Roads-board Hall, or Agricultural Hall, if a locality. These venues are the meeting places for the community. There they discuss matters of public interest, hold meetings, agricultural displays, dances, functions and banquets. These edifices fulfil the role of city hall, theatre and sometimes even church. They are the settlers' link with society, isolated as they are by great distances and the wildest solitude. We went into the exhibition hall where we were received with great courtesy and immediately several exhibitors offered to show us around and explain anything we wanted to know.

Harvey River, as I have said, is one of the most important centres with respect to the cultivation of oranges; not surprisingly, therefore, the golden fruit was one of the main exhibits. All the tables were covered with them, there were basketfuls everywhere and they were even hanging in bunches from the ceiling. I have never sampled oranges as delicious as those found in Western Australia anywhere else in the world. The area, which stretches for some 200 kilometres to the south and north of Perth, appears to be best suited for their cultivation. The variety known as 'navel' or Washington navel, imported from California, is the most delicious. These oranges were larger than the biggest oranges found in Palermo but the flavour of this local variety, which is faintly reminiscent of pineapple, is far more delicious. The navel has no seeds and a very thin skin; its flesh, reddish yellow in colour, is very friable and can splatter all over the place. It takes its name from the protuberance on the underside which resembles the human navel. This swelling sometimes appears like a rudimentary second fruit growing out of the skin of the original. Until recently the navel variety was impossible to find in Italy where the only sort cultivated was that which is known in Australia as the Mediterranean. However, several trees were recently introduced into Sicily.

The Premier made his opening speech and kindly extended a welcome to us, inviting the local farmers to supply us with any information we needed. Actually there was no need for such a suggestion as they could hardly have been more courteous towards us. Naturally I had to act as interpreter for the delegates who did not understand a word of English. In the course of his remarks Mr Moore made reference to some interesting statistics in respect to the district: I recall that, among other things, he mentioned that there are about five thousand acres planted with orange trees whose nett yield, at times, amounts to £60 per acre.

At present, the cultivation of this fruit is, without doubt, most remunerative. Oranges sell at between 2s [shillings] and 5s per dozen. I myself bought some a while ago for 7d each (a penny is worth a little more than 10 *centesimi*). They were, however, magnificent fruit and at the end of their season. But in any event the profit deriving to the farmer is quite considerable. On the way back to Perth I had occasion to discuss this subject with Dr Horrocks and Mr Howen, a lawyer, both of whom, while professional men, have found it profitable to invest part of their time and money in agriculture. They confirmed that orange groves were profitable and that, even if the price of the merchandise were to drop considerably, to say 3d a dozen, it would still be worth while. The 'even if' says it all.

However, the prices referred to above are not those received by the producer. They are retail prices and the difference between the two is considerable, even for the buyer. Unfortunately in Australia, this state of affairs holds true not only for oranges but for fruit in general, which is extremely expensive. This is the cause of much discontent among the populace. Australians, who in this semi-tropical country have retained the almost exclusively meat-based diet of their homeland, must, necessarily, consume a good deal of fruit if they are to offset the bad effects of an overly rich diet. Fruit, therefore, is an item of primary importance. Thus it follows that outrage over the middle men who have been accused of creating 'rings' or 'trusts' and other odious means of keeping the prices high, such as the mass destruction of con-signments of goods, is general. Radical changes to the system, such as the creation of municipal selling outlets, would be needed; but that runs against the spirit of total freedom which underpins British law. I do not know if any European countries would be so docile. In Italy, where sometimes the fruit is left to rot beneath the trees, some Australian prices may appear excessive if taken on a yearly average. As a matter of interest I can quote some of them: apples, between 4d and 10d per pound (a pound is about 450 grams); pears between 6d and 10d; plums 6d; peaches from 4d to 8d; walnuts 1s a pound; strawberries in punnets (25–30 per punnet) for between 1s and 1s 6d per punnet. The only fruit that actually starts off at a reasonable price is grapes which sell for between 2d and 4d per pound. We stayed in the exhibition hall for about two hours, as it was raining torrentially outside. We saw several varieties of vegetables and forage (particularly lucerne and rape which grow very well in the district).

In a nearby hall there was a poultry show. They are still very much behind the times in raising these useful birds for the table. The chickens and hens eaten here are usually too thin. Suffice to say that they know absolutely nothing about castrating these birds, with the result that the delicious capon never appears on Australian tables. On the contrary, all the experiments focus on obtaining a large number of eggs and in ensuring the fowl's high pedigree. Nobody here wants to keep animals of uncertain pedigree. (Australians, like all Britishers, have a passion for breeding domestic animals and strive to achieve the greatest degree of purity in every species. Almost every day in one city or another they hold exhibitions where the champions of every kind of animal, from the noblest to the lowest order, are shown for the admiration of the public. As one might suppose, the more profitable species receive more attention and special treatment.)

We admired some splendid white and black leghorns (*livornesi*)—I have been unable to learn why they are so named—not a particularly robust breed but excellent egg producers; some enormous orpingtons, somewhat similar to our *padovane*; and some brown and white spotted wyandottes. There were also some splendid examples of geese and turkeys.

Meanwhile, the rain had stopped momentarily and the Premier invited us to accompany him on a visit to some orange groves. From our carriage we could see a magnificent stretch of country covered with dark foliaged trees and golden fruit. Where there were no trees, we saw paddocks planted with forage (lucerne, clover and rape) stretching away into the distance; the grass everywhere was tall and vigorous. The soil, as they say here, was 'chocolate,' that is, more or less dark brown. In some places it was almost black and lightly mixed with sand which makes it extremely friable.

We visited the highly cultivated and well-tended orchard owned by Mr Smith. He welcomed us cordially and loaded us up with some exquisite oranges. I asked him how much land in the district was worth. He told me that, if the trees were already mature (six or seven years old) and therefore fully bearing, it would be impossible to buy land for less than £160 an acre, a not excessive price considering the return one would receive. We noticed some extraordinarily vigorous trees; it was as if the bark did not have the strength to hold back the sap. In some places the bark was swollen and sometimes cracked, the phenomenon being particularly noticeable in the case of apple trees. The fertility was also phenomenal. Mr Ranford cited a particular orange tree which in one season produced 3300 oranges.

It began to rain heavily again and we were forced to spend more than an hour under the verandah waiting for the weather to clear. By the time the sun reappeared it was too late to visit other properties; and so, sinking down to mid-calf in the mud, we set off across the paddocks to find the vehicles which took us to the railway station in a few minutes.

September 24. Mr Ranford and the delegates went to Kalamunda, a small agricultural centre situated in the Darling Ranges, about 300 metres above sea-level. It is linked to Perth by a railway which, allowing for its relative proportions, reminds me of the line in Peru that connects Lima and Oroya. Likewise, the engineers here, to avoid the costs which would have been entailed in constructing a circular line, opted for the easier zig-zag system. However, while such a system is explicable in the Andes where the heights to be conquered are in the range of 4800 metres, I fail to understand its application in this case, where elevations are no more than 350 metres. However, it is a trunk-line, constructed by a private company to facilitate wood cutting. The said company certainly did not have the comfort of passengers or speedy communications in mind. The line, which has been bought by the state, is about twenty miles in total length.

Because of their modest height, the Darling Ranges differ in their weather little from that in Perth. Nevertheless Kalamunda was quite crowded with visitors from the capital and Fremantle who delude themselves in thinking they go there for a change of air. There were two or three guest-houses and a hotel where, as usual, the board and lodging were dreadful.

Western Australia has the misfortune to possess no mountains in the true sense of the word. This configuration has had an unfavourable effect on the atmospheric and climatic conditions of part of the state. Moreover, the absence of these great condensers of moisture means there is also a lack of big rivers. Even though they appear as rivers on maps, most streams are, except in the rainy season, really just a series of ponds or else a dried-up bed. However, in the extreme south, under the influence of moisture-laden winds from the Southern Ocean, the rainfall is significant and the rivers, at least in their lower reaches, are reasonably full and permanent.

The highest hills in Western Australia are the Hamersley Ranges (north-west) whose peak, Mount Bruce, is less than 3800 feet. The Stirling Ranges (near Albany) follow, with Bluff Knoll reaching 3600 feet. There are some higher peaks in eastern Australia, with Mount Kosciusko at 7945 feet being the highest point on the Australian continent.

Having been to Kalamunda several times I did not accompany the delegates who, in any case, were in the capable hands of Mr Ranford, an excellent guide. Nor was there any shortage of interpreters as there were many Italian farmers living up there. Among them I would like to mention Mr Arduino and his two brothers, natives of Ormea in the Ligurian Appenines. Through their intelligent application to the task and their perseverance, they now find themselves in an enviable situation. One ought to see how they tend their orchard! Rows of trees stretch as far as the eye can see and the earth beneath the trees is ploughed to keep it free of weeds which spread everywhere here. The vineyard is immaculate; one could be in Monferrato, such are the modern and scientific methods used by the Arduinos. The delegates were amazed to learn that, in order to get rid of the insects which sometimes infect the trees, they use bacteria bred for the purpose.[1]

The battle against the forces of nature has not been easy. The trees were enormous and the soil was generally stony iron-stone; but the outcome was excellent. Mr Arduino told me that this year the profit

---

1 The government provides farmers with the eggs of these insects packaged in small tubes. It is thought that for every type of parasite there is a particular microbe. Intensive and continuous study in this field, undertaken by both government and private agencies, reflects the great importance placed on agriculture in this country where it is fundamental to national prosperity.

had been about £300. However, like all Italians, he suffers from home-sickness; he has no family and as he grows older he dreams of the mountains, the cool streams and the shady forest of chestnut and beech of his native Appenines. Australia is beautiful, he told me, but what can compare with Italy?

The bed-rock of the Darling Range, as I have said, is composed of iron-stone, that is, lumps of iron mixed with clay. Cultivation is only possible in the valleys and adjacent slopes where the soil is alluvial and the rock not so compacted. Iron-stone, however, once broken down makes an excellent soil for fruit trees but the cost and time needed for such a task are excessive.

The Darling Range area would not be a suitable area for Italian settlement in any significant number, given the lie of the land and the shortage of arable soil. Further south the mountains are flatter on top and there are stretches of marvellously fertile terrain. However, that section is reserved as the catchment area for the dam that feeds the 400 mile long Coolgardie pipeline supplying water to the arid goldfields. The acquisition of land in that area, therefore, would be impossible.

Furthermore, the Darling Ranges being, for a variety of reasons, only suited to the cultivation of fruit trees, means that Italians who might settle there would have to dedicate themselves completely to this activity. At present, in my opinion, the farmer in Western Australia must apply himself to present day agriculture with a wide range of products if he wants good results.

It is clear that the cultivation of fruit has been very profitable up to now, but I have major doubts that this can continue indefinitely. One must bear in mind that the amount of land assigned to this kind of farming was very limited until two or three years ago, while the consumption of fruit, as a result of the very rapid increase in the population, continued to grow. A large amount of fruit, therefore, has to be imported from outside, which is not easy, both because of the enormous distances which separate Western Australia from the other states of the Commonwealth and the difficulty of transporting such an unwieldy and perishable commodity. Local producers could thus count on a virtual monopoly. Now, however, the number of orchards is increasing steadily and the time is not far off when the Western Australian market will end up being saturated and they will have to seek outlets overseas or establish a preserving plant which can never provide the handsome returns which they received from the sale of fresh fruit to the local consumer. I foresee that Western Australia will end up like Victoria, Tasmania and New South Wales, where the price of fruit has fallen to such a low level as to leave little profit margin to the producer. Therefore, it would be a good thing if Italians who come here to settle bear this situation in mind.

Among Kalamunda's specialities are its most flavoursome strawberries; there are two varieties, medium-sized red, and the white whose fruit reach an enormous size. Because of the labour-intensive nature of their cultivation it is not possible to grow strawberries on a large scale, two or three acres being the maximum. Mr Urch, an expert in the field, told me that an acre of strawberries can realize a profit of £300.

Chapter Five

*The Main Inspection Tour Begins—Some
Geographical Notes about Western Australia—
Its Agricultural Areas—Settlers and Squatters—
Northam—Drinking Habits in Australia—
The Flora of Western Australia—Agricultural
Shows—Competitions.*

The excursions to Harvey River and Kalamunda were both one day trips: each time the group left Perth in the morning and returned the same evening. Now it was time to undertake the more extensive inspection tour that I mentioned earlier. The government had submitted an itinerary to me which I found most acceptable.

Firstly we would travel to the wheat belt along the goldfields line as far as Kellerberrin (almost on the easternmost edge of the regular rainfall zone and therefore at the limit of cultivation). We would then head northwards to Goomalling and follow the north–south route of the Great Southern Railway which runs through the best cultivated areas of the state. From Albany, the furthermost point of the Great Southern, we would return following the line to Katanning. From there, cutting through the bush as far as Bridgetown, a small hamlet situated on the Blackwood River in an area of dense bush, we proposed to turn still further south to the Warren River which flows through yet unexplored country. Then back to Bridgetown and, following the coastal (South Western) line, we would head back to Perth. From Perth, as guests of Mr Gardiner, we would travel as far as Geraldton, virtually the northern-most limit of the state's agricultural area, to inspect the Midland Company's land. As can be seen, it was a most interesting programme which allowed us to learn, in some depth, about those areas of the state most suitable for European agriculture.

At this juncture I think it would be useful, for the sake of clarity with respect to the narrative that follows, if I make a couple of general points about the geography of Western Australia and about its administrative structures from an agricultural perspective. Western Australia has a total area of 975,920 square miles, that is, about two and a half million square kilometres. Its maximum length from the extreme north to the extreme south (latitude 13° 30' to 35° 8' south) is 1400 miles and its maximum width (from longitude 112° 52' to 129° east) is about 1000 miles. It is easy to see that such a vast country has an extremely wide range of climatic conditions and products. The Land Act of 1898 divided the state into six huge divisions: Kimberley, North-West, Eastern, South-West, Western and Eucla.

Kimberley. Area 144,000 square miles. Contains majestic, permanent rivers and is favoured by abundant rainfall. It is particularly suited for the raising of cattle which thrive marvellously. The climate, even though hot, is considered to be healthy. The soil, which is alluvial in parts, is excellent and, when irrigated, lends itself to any kind of tropical agriculture.

The main rivers are the Fitzroy and Ord which are permanently flowing. The main towns and ports are Derby, Wyndham and Kimberley which are linked to Perth by telegraph and a monthly steamer service. The average temperature is 83° Fahrenheit (F). The average rainfall is 24 inches.

North-West. This area consists of a series of grassy plains intersected by rocky hills. Spinifex (*Triodia irritans*), a shrub which is almost the only kind of vegetation found in the central Australian desert, covers a great deal of terrain, such is the configuration of the region. It is said that it is ideal country for sheep rearing. Its most fertile areas can support an average of two sheep per acre. The climate is very healthy, but summer is very hot. Rich mines of gold, tin and copper have been recently discovered here.

It covers an area of 81,000 square miles. Its main rivers are the Ashburton, the Fortescue and the DeGrey. The main towns and ports are Onslow, Roebourne and Port Hedland (in the mainly pastoral sections the population centres are almost all situated on the coast). Inland is Marble Bar which is gaining considerable importance as a mining centre. The average temperature is 76° F and the average rainfall is 13 inches.

Western. It comprises an area of 133,000 square miles of virtually limitless plains. There is little water, except in the immediate vicinity of the main rivers (the Murchison and the Gascoyne). However, artesian water can be found at a shallow depth. The climate is good, although it is hot like the North-West.

The main town and port is Carnarvon. The average temperature is 72° F and the rainfall is 8 inches.

Eastern. This huge region, comprising some 491,920 square miles, encompasses the entire inland area of the state. Despite the fact that the soil is extremely fertile in some places, regular cultivation is impossible because of the shortage of water; however, there is some good pasture land. The mining industry flourishes in this area which includes the world-famous Kalgoorlie and Coolgardie goldfields (Western Australia is the third largest gold producer in the world). The main towns are Kalgoorlie, Coolgardie, Southern Cross, Leonora etc.

South-West. This region has an area of 77,850 square miles and includes the major part of the temperate zone that extends along the coast south of the Murchison River and, for some distance, along that of the Southern Ocean. The extreme south-west is covered by an immense thick forest. The soil is generally very fertile and suited to European-style agriculture. The light and friable soils are considered to be the best. Large expanses of sand are noticeable here and there but, if irrigated, they yield good crops.

The climate is very healthy and completely fever-free. The average temperature varies between 66° F in the north to 59° F in the south. The rainfall is very regular, ranging from 10 inches in some parts of the north-east to 53 inches in the south-west. The average is some 22 inches.

There are many rivers, however their courses are mostly short and they flow the year around only in the extreme south. The first European settlers in Western Australia arrived in this area in 1827. The state capital, Perth, is situated here, as well as such other important centres as Fremantle (port), Geraldton (port), York, Bunbury (port), Albany (port), Northam etc.

Not surprisingly it was this region that the delegates and I proposed to visit as soon as possible.

Eucla. The area comprises 48,150 square miles. With the exception of some parts where there are sheep stations the country is completely uninhabited. The section to the east of Cape Culver is utterly devoid of water, while that to the west, although it has sufficient supplies, is not very fertile. To the north of Eucla there is a high plateau with excellent pasture but it is also short of water. The average temperature is 61° F and the rainfall is 14 inches.

The above named divisions were in effect until recently. However, a new act of parliament has brought several changes. The Western Division has been joined to the North-West. The borders of the South-West, or agricultural zone, have been pushed further east as far as the rabbitproof fence (I will discuss this enormous enterprise presently). A third of the Eastern Division has been excised to form a separate division known as the Central Division and includes the rich goldfields, with Kalgoorlie as the main town.

The South-Western Division, as I have said, includes the land best suited to agriculture and, in particular, because of its temperate climate and regular rainfall, to the production of European crops. It is, in practical terms, almost exclusively set apart for the so-called settlers, that is, farmers who acquire title to the land and settle there per-manently.

The other divisions, by contrast, which, because of the climate or lack of rain, are better suited to grazing, are completely taken up by squatters, that is, cattle farmers who do not own the land but who rent it for long periods, with each 'leaseholder' or lessee having preferential rights with respect to the renewal of the lease.

The settlers in the agricultural areas (as noted, mostly in the south-western area) have a near monopoly because they always have the right to purchase any land even if it is leased at the time. The squatter can not oppose the sale and must immediately give up occupancy. Thus, for the squatters there is no advantage in settling in agricultural areas unless they buy the land themselves; but, then, in common with other settlers, they become subject to the special conditions concerning improvements to the land. Generally speaking, they only buy when they want to go in for intensive pasturing which, incidentally, is one of the more remunerative activities. Conversely, they could also incur enormous expenses without gaining much profit.

Despite the fact that the law clearly states that whosoever leases the land has no rights apart from the basic right to graze animals and that the state may sell, grant or dispose of it in any way it sees fit, in actual fact the squatters, in their turn, are effectively protected in their divisions. First of all, it would not be worth the settlers' while to take themselves to areas which are unsuitable for agriculture; and also they must bear in mind the law which states that whoever buys land for farming purposes can do so only in those zones and districts which have been expressly designated *open for agriculture*. At present that designation applies to almost all the land in the South-West Division; outside this area such a designation is rarely put into effect and, anyway, in the majority of cases the Kimberley, West and North-West Divisions are excluded from such an eventuality.

Given the diverse circumstances of climate and fertility, the Land Act, especially with respect to grazing, is applied differently in each division. So in the North-West and Western divisions the rent is 10s per 1000 acres. The minimum holding one can take up is 20,000 acres. In the Eucla Division the rent is 5s per 1000 acres with a minimum of 20,000 acres. In the Eastern Division no less than 20,000 acres at 2s 6d per 1000 acres for the first seven years and 5s thereafter. In the Kimberley the 'blocks' must be a minimum of 50,000 acres, or 20,000, depending on circumstances, and the price is 10s for every block. In the South-Western Division no less than 3000 acres can be taken up at £1 an acre, or 10s, depending on the situation. But, as I have said, few persons lease in this section unless in areas at some distance from lines of transport, in which, at least for the foreseeable future, settlers will not establish themselves.

There are general rules that apply to grazing all over the state. I shall discuss the regulations which govern agriculture and the acquisition of land separately. Such rules usually apply for all the sections declared open to agriculture in whatever part of the state they may be situated. The divisions, with the exception of some completely unexplored areas where whites have not penetrated, are sub-divided into districts with different names.

And now to return to my diary.

September 26. Today we began our main tour of inspection. We left Perth at ten a.m. and travelled directly to Northam. This little town, one of the oldest in the state, is also one of the most prosperous, being at the centre of the splendid agricultural district (the Avon district comprising 3,500,000 acres) particularly noted for cereal crops and sheep raising. Moreover, Northam is a commercial centre of primary importance in that it is at the junction of three railway lines branching off from the line from Perth: one, to the east, is the main line to the goldfields (Kalgoorlie–Laverton 520 miles), another heading south to Albany (826 miles) and the other, 115 miles, serving agricultural areas in the north as far as Goomalling.

Northam is 66 miles from Perth. We travelled the distance in about five and a half hours. The line crossed the Darling Range; however, there were very few bridges or other earth works of any importance because the highest point, Chidlow's Well, is less than 1000 feet. A few bridges across creeks and a tunnel, the only one in the state I think, represent the greatest obstacles the engineers had to overcome.

The land we passed through was generally barren and rocky. It was the customary iron-stone which forms the base of many hills in Western Australia. There was virtually no cultivation; only after the Chidlow's Well incline did we see large expanses planted with vines and fruit and, further on, brilliant green plains. We were on the edge of the cereal zone.

We arrived in Northam about three in the afternoon. I was already familiar with the town, having accompanied the Premier, Mr James, on an electoral tour two years earlier. The delegates were pleasantly surprised by the town's European aspect. Even though it has no more than 3000 citizens it is very spread out because, as in most Australian towns, the houses are single-storeyed and surrounded by huge gardens. Several of the larger structures, particularly public buildings and hotels, could well fit into any centre in the old world. A stranger arriving here quickly realizes that he is in a country where there is a general sense of well-being and no poverty.

We went to the Shamrock Hotel which, because of its fine cuisine, was highly esteemed by Mr Ranford. The name was enough to suggest that the owners were of Irish origin. The foreign visitor finds the proliferation of hotels in Australia astounding. Every little hamlet of 50 to 100 inhabitants has one, sometimes two or three, and they are always the best buildings in town, built without regard to cost and often truly luxurious. Northam for its part has about ten of them. If there was the same ratio of hotels to population numbers in Europe nine out of the ten would have gone bankrupt in a week. Although it is difficult for us Europeans to understand why there are so many hotels, it is explicable when one considers the enormous amount of alcohol consumed in Australia, and particularly in Western Australia, where the adult population is proportionately higher than elsewhere in the Commonwealth. One must also add the fact that the law here does not permit liquor to be sold in liquor stores or bars, unless they form part of a hotel.

The passion for alcohol in Australia, in particular for whisky and beer (wine consumption is very low) is indescribable. Esau sold his inheritance for a bowl of lentils; here, if not their inheritance, Australians sell their health, well-being and family happiness. The bar is a den of iniquity where countless numbers leave their wages down to the last penny only to emerge totally brutalized and unable to face up to life's struggles. Unfortunately this vice is not limited to men; even women drink, and how! They do not frequent the public bars but either get drunk at home or in one of the private rooms provided in the hotels where they cannot be observed. It is a disgusting sight, particularly in small country hotels, to see workers completely drunk for weeks on end. They have worked hard for a few months, clearing or shearing sheep on the stations; they have saved up £10 or so and they go and spend the last penny of their hard-earned money on the awful concoctions which publicans foist on them; like opium smokers they find supreme happiness in disgusting, revolting drunkenness. However, as soon as the publican sees that they have no more money he ejects them without compunction, despite their snivelling and pleas to have another longed for drink.

Drinking has become so commonplace and has entered into the customs and ways of this populace to such an extent that the greatest sign of friendship and courtesy that one can extend to another is to say 'have a drink.' The worst thing is that one generally has to reciprocate the invitation, so that among a circle of friends the drinks never stop and everyone gets intoxicated.

All thinking Australians realize that drunkenness is the greatest scourge of their country and one of the more serious impediments to its progress. As in the case of all such extreme evils, cures, far more drastic than the complaint, have been devised which we may find exaggerated. Nevertheless, a number of people are 'teetotallers,' that is, abstainers who would not for the world have a glass of alcoholic liquor. Thus, one goes from one excess to another. However, the law strictly forbids the sale of alcohol on Sundays to anyone who is not a 'bona fide traveller,' that is, a complete stranger. In New Zealand it has reached the point where several towns have banned the sale of wine, beer and spirits altogether (Sundays or weekdays, no exception). However, the legislative measures and the unceasing efforts of private individuals do not appear to have produced any very reassuring results up to now.

Before lunch we paid a visit to the Lands Office. The Minister for Agriculture, or more precisely, for Land, there being two separate departments, has an agent stationed in the main town of the more important agricultural districts. This official is assigned to deal with all matters pertaining to the sale of Crown Land; for example, he receives the offers to buy (the bill of sale, however, is handled by Head Office), transfers titles of ownership, presides over auctions, collects annual

77

taxes etc., etc. As well, he must also provide intending settlers wishing to purchase land with all the relevant information, and accompany them, or arrange to have them accompanied, to inspect the property. Each office has guides, horses and carriages at its disposal for this purpose. This assistance is free to the settler, as well as a ticket on the state railway. Obviously these concessions are made only in cases in which the agent is satisfied with the genuineness of the prospective settler; otherwise it would mean encouraging tourism at government expense with little return to the taxpayer.

The agent provided us with a deal of useful information and, before anything else, showed us examples of the district's products. We were particularly impressed with some wheat plants which, including their heads, were about two metres high. The land around Northam is almost all in private hands, a fact which is easily explained in that the area was one of the first settlements.

Some years ago, before the law concerning the acquisition of land was in force, there were many individuals in the state who, urged on by greed alone, bought tens of thousands of acres of land for next to nothing. They were, for the most part, persons who had little money and who would not have been able to make use of the vast expanses, even had they so wished. Thus, the land remained uncultivated, hindering the development of the country. For a while the government instituted a system of buying back these holdings. Based on market value, the land was sub-divided into small lots which were sold at public auction with the same obligation to improve which the law now generally requires of purchasers of Crown Land that has come up for sale. There are still many of these vast estates in existence, but a goodly number are disappearing in the manner already mentioned, or being divided up as a result of inheritance provision, and they are also being gradually developed by their owners both for farming and intensive pasturing. Near Northam the largest single block comprises some 37,000 acres.

To avoid the revival of large-scale estates, the law has now instituted very strict regulations concerning Crown Land which is gradually being allotted. Thus no one can acquire more than 2000 acres in his own name. Within ten years they must have made improvements to the value of the purchase price (usually 10 shillings a year). Every two years they must spend a fifth of that amount, so that the farmer does not, through negligence, put off improvements until the last moment, making it impossible, as a result, to meet the prescribed conditions. In such an event his land would be confiscated.

It must be said, however, that the regulation limiting the maximum allotment of land to 2000 acres per person is circumvented by an infinite number of ruses. One of the most common means employed is to buy it in the name of another person, from whom it is then transferred. Thus, despite the severity of the law, one actually sees the formation of new estates. The problem, however, is not as bad as it was in the past. In fact, in certain circumstances, the accumulation of property represents an advantage for the national economy in that the land is often held by capable people who have capital and have bought the property to improve its value.

The land under wheat in the Northam area yields an average of 11 bushels an acre (a bushel of grain is about 28 kilograms). In many parts of the district it reaches 20, 25, even 30 bushels, though this last figure is exceptional. Clearly this is nothing like the 40 bushels which, according to Ricci, who had converted decimal measurement to those used in British countries, could be had from the recently reclaimed land around Ferrara. But it must be remembered that here we are dealing with virgin soil, not well suited initially to production and where cultivation is entirely large scale.

I believe that the following table which compares wheat production in Western Australia with that in other states of the Commonwealth will be of interest.

Annual averages 1903–1904 (bushels per acre)

Western Australia	13.60
Queensland	17.75
South Australia	7.72
Victoria	14.49
New South Wales	17.51

(The acre has an area of about 4000 square metres. The bushel, as I said, is a measurement of wheat by volume and is equal to some 28–30 kilograms.)

The land in this area, if not far from town, costs about £2 per acre whether still virgin or whether it has been improved to the extent of ringbarking. If it is completely cleared and ready to sow it can cost up to £10 per acre. It should be understood that, in the case of virgin land, I am referring to private property because, as I have already noted, the state now holds very little land in this district.

In the evening we visited a flower and homecraft show: the entry fee went towards the new Anglican church. Therefore the Irish, all fervent Catholics, were conspicuous by their absence. The opening address was given by Bishop Riley, the Anglican Bishop of Perth, with whom I had travelled in the train to Northam.

His Lordship (the title is equivalent to our Monsignor) is an extremely intelligent and educated person and an excellent speaker. He knows Latin very well, even though the liturgy of his church uses English. We had spent two hours of the journey engaged in a long etymological discussion which, in Italy, I might have found rather boring but which, here, I found most pleasurable, reminding me as it did of the tongue of my far-off homeland.

We found the local show crowded mostly with farmers and their families. Mr Ranford was our guide and I, as usual, acted as interpreter for the delegates. We saw quite a lot of European flowers, particularly carnations, stocks and roses; nothing exceptional, save for the last-named, several of which were very beautiful. However, there was a large collection of splendid native flowers.

The flora of Western Australia is extremely rich. In September and October especially, the magnificence of their colours is most evident. According to Baron Von Mueller, a specialist in the field and author of a very fine work on the botany of Western Australia, there are about 9050 kinds of plants in the state, 2460 of which are not found elsewhere in Australasia or the world. The plants vary greatly according to different areas. The green kingdom is incomparably rich in the south-west region where the rainfall is abundant. Rain is scarcer in the north, particularly in the central sector where salt-bush (of the *Chenopodiaceae* family) is predominant; with five or six varieties it makes excellent pasture. In the more barren areas, spinifex occupies an enormous area.

With the exception of the desert region, Australia is almost entirely covered with eucalyptus forest (54 varieties, some of which produce flowers in many shades of red with surprising effect). However there are many other species mixed with the eucalypt. Some shrubs, particularly those belonging to the *Myrtaceae* and *Protaceae* families, are covered with brilliantly coloured flowers. These flowers grow particularly well in the most arid desert regions. Being a country without high mountains, the state lacks alpine flora entirely.

The flora of Western Australia is set apart from that elsewhere in the world, a distinctiveness which is probably due to the great geological age of the continent and the fact that it does not appear ever to have suffered any major cataclysms. The more ancient species have been preserved and, perforce, have adapted themselves to their environment. This transformation and adaptation process is particularly noticeable in the hot dry central region, where the plants have had to cope with an almost complete lack of water and intolerable heat.

As I have noted, native wildflowers were in abundance at the show. The kangaroo paw (*Anigozanthus*), with its unusual formation, was one of the most beautiful. There are four varieties: the most common is the red and green, another is green, another black and another orange. They are all covered with light hairs which gives them the appearance of fine velvet. Another unusual flower is the Sturt desert pea (*Olianthus dampieri*) which is bright red in colour and elongated in shape with a black protuberance in its centre. The flowers hang in bunches.

We admired some boronia (*megistima*, of the *Rutaceae* family) with small brownish yellow flowers and sweetly scented. This family has sixty varieties. The climber, kennedya, with its bunches of blue flowers is very common here and is used, in particular, to beautify the facades of houses. When in flower it forms a solid mass of dark blue. There is also a red variety (*Kennedyae prostrata*). There are many cream coloured clematis (*Ranunculaceae*); some very beautiful, delicate, exquisitely formed orchids (at least seventy-five varieties in Western Australia). The flowers of the bright yellow Western Australian wattle (*Acacia cyanophilla*) are outstanding, and similar in shape and perfume to the European mimosa. With the exception of the wattle, the boronia and two or three other plants, few Western Australian wildflowers are perfumed.

From the flower display we moved on to the less poetic but more practical homecraft section. There was a large display of pastries (puddings, scones etc.) and pats of butter of all shapes and sizes.

While we were touring the exhibition halls Mr Ranford pointed out to me that this show was fairly small and limited to certain items, but that other shows I would see in the future would give me a better idea of Western Australia and its products. This month and next they would be inaugurating five or six shows devoted to displaying agricultural produce and homecrafts. I could not but help think that, in this lucky country, these shows spring up like mushrooms. Every small town and hamlet wants to have its own and is not content with one a year. Almost always a member of the government is at the opening. Even in Australia, it should be noted, political life is not without its drawbacks.

In one way, shows such as these, in a country which is just beginning to develop, are useful in that they offer an opportunity to learn something about the state's potential and its production methods and, of most concern to all, the results which are gradually being obtained. However, the frequency of such shows can, I believe, be harmful. It is difficult for very small townships with few resources to do anything worth while; they might be better advised to conserve their energies. A show in a larger centre, which brings together the products of a wider area, would also allow a greater opportunity of comparing products and methods of different districts and the diffusion of technical expertise.

The shows are also the occasion for games, or competitions as they are called here. The inventiveness of Australians in this area is amazing, they have competitions for all kinds of things from the most useful and practical to the most frivolous. Some are directly related to the shows themselves: one of the most common is the egg laying competition, that is, a race for egg production. By the way, this produces some splendid results, some hens laying as many as 280 or so eggs a year. Other competitions are more in the nature of hobbies, such as log chopping, that is, who can chop a log the fastest.

My trusty delegates were amazed to see a number of young women line up in the lounge of the hotel where we were staying and start hammering nails into the tabletop with all the force their delicate arms could muster. What could this display possibly mean? It was simply a nail hammering competition. The first girl to hammer a certain number of nails into the wood was acclaimed by all and received an appropriate prize. Actually, I don't think this kind of thing is completely unknown to us, at least in a metaphorical sense.

We Europeans find it hard to understand the appeal of some pastimes; but one must not forget that this is a land almost totally lacking in social life and where the more refined entertainments, as we know them, are so few that one can forgive a populace that chops wood or hammers nails. At least no one will deny it is the most innocent of pastimes; the worst thing that can happen is that one will crush a finger or cut a foot, a mere bagatelle which would not preoccupy these country people for a moment.

Chapter Six

Goomalling—The Battle against Rabbits—
The Rabbitproof Fence—Agricultural Machinery—
Intensive Pasturing and its Profits—Cereal
Cultivation.

September 27. We left in the morning for Goomalling, a fairly important place and centre of one of the state's best grain growing areas. Goomalling is thirty-three miles from Northam and linked with it by rail. It has a population of 300, scattered widely throughout the district. There are a few houses in the town, a couple of little shops and the usual hotel, which is, as always, the most conspicuous building. One of the inspectors of the rabbitproof fence travelled with us and furnished some interesting information about this enormous undertaking. I must say at this juncture that rabbits are a real scourge in Australia. These animals, which are not indigenous but descended from stock brought from Europe, have multiplied in extraordinary numbers, finding in the local conditions an unexpectedly favourable environment. Their first incursion was in the eastern part of Australia, where they were introduced by early settlers, and they gradually spread through much of the continent. The damage these little creatures do is indescribable. They destroy and completely devour crops which are not protected by fences, and they also threaten pastures because they deprive the sheep of an enormous amount of grass.

Some interesting, seemingly incredible, facts have emerged concerning the voracity of rabbits; a pair of them, released on a small wooded and grassy island in the Southern Ocean, in a short time grew to be a horde. However, their numbers soon outstripped the amount of food the soil could provide; they ate not only the grass and the roots but also the bark of the trees. The island became sterile and bare, the plants dried up and soon the land, which had earlier been like a garden, became a desert strewn with corpses.

All means of eradicating these animals have been investigated and the government has offered rewards to those who submit the best schemes, but until now the results have been strictly limited. Recently, it was proposed to inject a number of rabbits with infectious diseases which would then be passed to other rabbits by natural means. The experiments proved to be satisfactory; germ cultures were scattered about a large area and it was estimated that 95 per cent of the rabbits in the prescribed area died. However, there was a danger that the disease could spread to other animals, particularly sheep; thus the cure could be much worse than the complaint. On the other hand, one must acknowledge that rabbits are important both in terms of local consumption and export for their meat, which is excellent and moderately priced (6d or 1s each in the shops; a large amount is exported frozen to England) and for their fur (used in the production of felt): their destruction would seriously damage the livelihood of many sections of the public. However, I do not believe that such a consideration alone would be enough to halt the elimination of the 'pest' (as the scourge of rabbits is called here), because the damage to grazing and agriculture is incalculable.

Until now, Western Australia has been almost immune to the invasion (which as I said has travelled from east to west) because of the wide band of desert which covers a third of the continent and almost completely isolates Western Australia from the eastern states. However, it has not proved a completely insurmountable barrier as the number of the beasts which have managed to overcome it demonstrates.

To protect the agricultural zone and part of the grazing lands the Western Australian government has conceived the idea of a system of fences composed of metal mesh and wire. The construction of this enormous project, which is now nearing completion, has taken less than three years and has already cost £328,636 (8,215,000 lire). There are three main lines; the first (No. 1) and the most important crosses the state from one ocean to another (south-north) for a distance of 1135 miles and is the closest fence to the eastern border of the state. The second (No. 2), which is much shorter, also begins at the Southern Ocean, 75 miles from the first. They run parallel for some distance, then veer away to form a large semicircle before coming together again at a halfway point. Its total length is 724 miles. The second fence is meant to protect the so-called agricultural zone after rabbits were detected in what is now the area between fence No. 1 and fence No. 2. The last line (No. 3), some 160 miles long and running due east from the west coast and converging with line No. 2, completed the defence of the agricultural zone. The area is thus protected by a triple barrier, in iron if not in bronze, as Horace declared.

Two thirds of the state, or more precisely the Eastern, Central, Kimberley and Eucla divisions, lie outside the protected area. However, with the exception of the Kimberley Division and a small section of the Eucla, all this area can be said to be completely barren, with the result that the damage caused by rabbits is not severe.

The technological detail employed in constructing the fences was most ingenious and apposite for the purpose they were to serve. The fences are formed by posts about 2 metres high placed about 4 to 6 metres apart. The posts, which are sunk to a depth of 60 centimetres, have four lines of wire strung equally apart. The top wire bristles with spikes (barbed wire). A metal mesh, with openings of 10 centimetres width, is nailed to the posts. To prevent rabbits getting underneath by digging tunnels, 15 centimetres of the mesh is buried, a depth thought to be sufficient. The height of the mesh is about a metre off the ground and its lower part is covered with a thin layer of tar to prevent possible damage by moisture. And special traps have been laid every five miles.

When animals encounter an obstacle in their path, their instinct is not to turn back but to run alongside it until they find an opening which enables them to continue in their original direction. I have often had the opportunity here in Australia, where even the largest property is fenced, of noting this phenomenon, particularly with respect to kangaroos. Rabbits conform to this general rule; when they collide with the fence they run alongside it until they fall into traps that have been laid for such an eventuality. For the convenience of cattle and travellers, there are four-metre wide gates at every intersection with the road; by law there must be a gate provided at least every ten miles. The maintenance of the fences, the wages of the employees and associated expenditure costs the government a considerable amount.

I have rambled on somewhat on this matter because, in terms of farming and grazing, it is of major importance to the country. An invasion of Western Australia by rabbits would immeasurably damage the state, if not bring complete ruin. However, the big question is whether a undertaking of this magnitude, which has cost so much, is really an efficient defence against the dreaded peril. First of all, it has not been shown that the rabbits definitely cannot dig warrens under the fence; nor can the possibility be excluded that some ill-disposed individuals, whose only pleasure is to cause damage, will not throw live rabbits across the fence; in fact it seems certain that this has happened. For some degenerates, wrong doing, just for the pleasure of it, has a special attraction; let us imagine a situation in which, with the minimum of effort, it is possible to frustrate such an enormous and extremely expensive undertaking. A small number of rabbits have been found in the agricultural zone; but, as I said, surveillance is extensive and they were quickly destroyed. In any event, the work undertaken has secured the desired result. If nothing else it will delay a general invasion of rabbits for some time which will be of considerable advantage to the country.

It is pleasing to the traveller to observe that almost all the land along the way between Northam and Goomalling is cultivated; whereas, on the section between Perth and Northam, because of the sandy and rocky nature of the soil, there is little to see besides the monotonous bushland. Instead, in this area, the work of man has completely transformed the landscape. Vast fields of wheat, oats and rye extend as far as the eye can see. It was the beginning of spring, the glorious Australian spring, unfolding in the widest variety of colours. In the cultivated paddocks millions of a kind of dandelion were growing, a yellow daisy which gave the landscape a greenish gold hue; some of the nearby hills, whose slopes were covered with masses of everlastings, appeared fiery red, others as white as snow and still others pale pink. Along the railway line there were clumps of different kinds of shrubs, literally smothered with flowers to the extent that no leaves can be seen. The blue of the *Leschenaultia bilboa* and the pure white of the smoke-bush predominate.

Mr Ranford pointed out a small tree which is important in a practical sense; it is known as the 'lucerne tree' and makes excellent fodder, especially for horses. It grows to a height of three or four metres; its leaves resemble those of lucerne but are rather lighter in colour; it has bunches of white flowers like those of the wattle family to which it belongs.

Our travelling companion, the expert on the rabbitproof fence, was also well versed in aspects of practical farming and gave us interesting information on working the land in this district. The soil is ploughed to a depth of 8 centimetres the first year and 10 the second. My men were very surprised by this. Ricci told me that in the Ferrara countryside they plough to a depth of 30 centimetres. The topsoil here varies in depth from 3 to 10 feet. It is a dark reddish colour caused by the large amount of iron oxide which is mixed with the clay. In some paddocks we noticed that particular stands of wheat were a darker green and more lush; these were the spots where the tree trunks had been burned and their ashes had fertilized the soil. The earth in this area is very productive. Between 18 and 25 bushels per acre are harvested. However, a certain amount of artificial fertilizer is used. The rainfall in the area varies from 17 to 19 inches which is the ideal for the cultivation of cereal crops.

Throughout Western Australia, and particularly in the wheat belt, as I have noted, the land is left fallow every alternate year. I was assured that, failing such a measure, the productivity of the land would be much diminished, if not rapidly exhausted. However, I believe that, with a more intensive use of fertilizers and rotation of crops, the system, which leaves large tracts of land unused every year, could be done away with.

During the trip we had the opportunity of seeing the system of ploughing used in the district. My peasant farmers were amazed to see horses labouring instead of oxen. Usually the plough is drawn by two animals, sometimes four. The ploughman steers by walking alongside the plough or perched on top of a high and narrow seat fixed to the plough itself. The number of ploughshares varies between two and four.

Western Australia imports almost all its agricultural machinery from outside the state. It comes from the eastern states of Australia, the United States and Canada (Toronto). Italy might, perhaps, be able to compete in this kind of trade; however, it is worth remembering that this country is quite advanced in terms of agriculture and very modern machinery is used. Therefore we would need to offer the best equipment in order to be competitive.

At Northam we saw some examples of local manufacturing. These were the initial efforts of a new nation trying to free itself from foreign trade. Until now such efforts have been confined, almost exclusively, to ploughs made of iron and steel; they have three shares and weigh about a third of a ton. They sell for £25.

My farmers were glued to the train window so as not to miss a thing about the country through which we were passing and which seemed to be well-cultivated and very fertile. Large flocks of sheep, one of the most important sources of wealth in the district, came into view. It was not sheep breeding on a large scale like that practised in the Northern and Central regions, with their endless expanses and where one proprietor can own a million acres and hundreds of thousands of sheep. We were in an agricultural zone where animal husbandry is carried on in a smaller but more intensive manner.

To this end, the first step, as I have said, is ringbarking, which entails making a circular cut in the bark of trees which then rapidly (in about two or three months) dry up. I have already explained the wonderful effect this process has on previously barren scrubby land, clothing it with thick soft grass, excellent for fattening sheep. Moreover, it is not only the grass that grows, but often springs bubble up to form small bodies of water 'soaks' where previously there was no trace of water. In areas where running water is scarce one can see how useful, if not indispensable, ringbarking can be. However, not all trees are killed off; a certain number are left green to protect the stock from the sun's rays.

Killing off the trees is but the first stage of preparing the soil for intensive pasturing. Many farmers go no further, happy with the relative increase in the nutritive value of the pasture provided by this process. And it is not insignificant. In the Northam district, for example, one can observe that 1000 acre lots, prepared in this way, can run 600 to 700 sheep where previously less than 300 could have been raised. The cost of cincturing the bark is between 1s and 3s per acre.

After ringbarking, the more enterprising farmers, with greater means at their disposal, clear the bush completely, plough and seed the paddock. A blend of grass seed is used to create a permanent pasture that will not require further attention for a number of years. This system is suitable only for those districts where there is abundant rainfall and the grass remains green for a relatively long time. The results are excellent and large profits are made. Near Tenterden (see Chapter Eleven) we visited a property where, they assured me, they could raise ten sheep to the acre on cultivated pasture, a figure considered to be a record in Western Australia. However, not all cleared land is turned into pasture; some is set aside for growing such forage as rape, lucerne, Italian rye grass, English grass and sometimes turnips and beetroot, in rotation.

In the arid districts of the north, where the rainfall is much lighter and the summers are extremely long, the grass stays green only for a few months. It is, therefore, preferable to sow wheat in the cleared areas. The crop is then cut high with the remaining stalks and mixed with some of the heads of wheat fallen from the harvester, providing an excellent fodder on which the sheep thrive admirably. Nevertheless, experiments in the cultivation of both native and foreign heat-resistant grasses are being undertaken in the north on a continuing basis. The best plant appears to be the *Paspalum dilatatum*, an evergreen, long-leaved grass that at times reaches a height of one or two metres.

Raising sheep is evidently a good business in Western Australia. The state has tremendous advantages over the central and eastern states in that drought is almost unknown in its agricultural areas, even in the far north. There are areas where it has not rained for twenty months, but the drought has never lasted for two or three years as it has in Queensland and New South Wales, where it has destroyed more than half the flocks.

In the less favoured areas, there are numerous rivers in which, even in summer, one can find water, if not flowing at least in ponds. In the flat areas away from the rivers, wells are now dug and water is raised to the surface by means of wind-mills. One of these wells can provide water for herds in a radius of ten miles. Periodic water shortages, albeit brief and rare as noted, are overcome by this method.

Western Australia, in contrast to the rest of the country, is almost free of rabbits, and it shares, with the eastern states, the advantage of having few infectious animal diseases.

A few salient points suggest the benefits to be had from sheep farming; a flock doubles in size in little more than two years, even with selling off the male lambs (with the exception of those retained for breeding purposes). To be more exact, one hundred ewes give birth every year to 85 to 90 lambs, of which almost half are female. Fat lambs sell for between 7s and 14s each and sometimes the price is even higher. Every adult animal gives wool worth between 4s and 6s. Sheep can be bought for 15s each but in general the price may be set at £1. Anyone starting up a stud always buys far fewer sheep than the property can run. They are then left to multiply until they reach the maximum number; then the flock, including the lambs, is sold off, a certain number being retained to replace the older animals or those that have died. The breeds of sheep raised in Australia are very select and care is continually taken to improve them; the wool is long and plentiful and the meat most flavoursome; they are sometimes extremely heavy. Our Italian sheep, in contrast, cut a poor figure. The favoured strain is the Shropshire, renowned for its meat and its crossing with the Merino and the Lincoln; no less the Leicestershire which has excellent wool.

We arrived at Goomalling at three o'clock in the afternoon. We went immediately to the hotel where lunch awaited us, although, perhaps because it was past the sacred lunch hour, it had been prepared in a very offhand manner. Never mind, we were, after all, used to the menus in small towns in Western Australia and we could put up with almost anything!

We went for a quick stroll about the place and observed the sur- rounding countryside. The possibility of settling Italian families in the area was discussed with Mr Ranford. I was opposed to the idea and Mr

Ranford shared my opinion. The annual rainfall, which is between 12 and 14 inches, is enough to grow wheat (this is even possible with a rainfall of 9 inches) but not sufficient for mixed farming. It is a mistake for a settler, particularly one without funds, to rely on a single crop alone. If it fails for one reason or another he is ruined completely.

The price of wheat is very low at present. While production was insufficient to meet local needs the price remained very high; I recall that, in 1903, the year I first arrived in Australia, they were talking about 6 shillings a bushel. When production outstripped local requirements they were forced to consider exporting the surplus and the price fell to less than 3 shillings.

It is true that the farmer in this district is not confined just to wheat growing because that enterprise is usually accompanied by raising sheep and sometimes pigs, both of which give a good return but require capital; therefore, such an undertaking would be impossible for Italians, at least at present. To find empty land here one has to go more than twenty miles out of town. The government had created a reserve of fifty square miles nearby which included the best land. I have noticed that large tracts of land are sometimes reserved in areas that have already been opened up for farming, where an individual could freely select some blocks for those who immigrate in groups and want to stay together. Without such foresight it would be impossible for an immigrant group to obtain a sufficiently large and compact area when needed.

Chapter Seven

Return to Northam—The Robustelli Farm—
The Spencer Farm—Chaff—The Chinese in
Australia—The Extreme South of Western
Australia—The Minister for Agriculture—
Mr Throssel—Catholics and Protestants—Car Trips—
Mount Dick.

We returned to Northam in the evening. The mayor of the town, Mr Bernard, was waiting at the Shamrock Hotel to tell us that the local club had made Mr Ranford and me honorary members. We much appreciated the courtesy extended towards us. We spent the evening at the club where, as usual, drinks flowed. I had a most interesting conversation with Mr Bernard who appeared keen to learn about events in Italy. I realized that, as always, our country was completely *terra incognita*. He found the information I gave him about our commercial and industrial progress amazing. I am more than ever of the opinion that it is impossible to think of increasing, or in this case creating, commercial links with Australia without careful preparatory work which would enable us to know and respect one another. It would be like trying to establish friendly or business relations between two people when one ignores, or, worse, scorns, the other.

September 28. The local office of the Lands Department sent us an open buggy drawn by two lively horses. We travelled along a pleasant road between fields of green, budding wheat and hedges whose flowers smelled sweetly like honey. I regret that I have forgotten the name of this plant.

Half an hour later we reached the farm belonging to Mr Robustelli, a fellow Italian. I feel I must say something about this hardworking absolute model of honesty and industriousness. He is a native of Grossotto in the province of Sondrio and came here about twenty years ago. Like many of his fellow countrymen he began working in

91

the goldmines; then, following his natural bent as a farmer, he acquired 300 acres near Northam. He was virtually without funds, having no more than £20 to his name, but he made up for it by hard work and rectitude. Within a few years he paid off the debt he had taken on to buy the property which he has turned into a veritable garden. As he told me yesterday, he made about 20,000 lire per year. He owns 100 sheep and a good deal of machinery (all very modern) worth 8000 lire. The property is valued at more than 75,000 lire. Robustelli is universally admired and respected for his scrupulous honesty, farming know-how and his friendly, open and jovial character. I am not exaggerating when I say that, if Italian farmers in this country are well respected and if the Western Australian government decides to go ahead with Italian immigration, much of the credit must go to him.

In fact I remember some three years ago when I accompanied Mr James, then premier, on a tour of the Northam district, we visited the Robustelli farm. He was enthusiastic and from that time began to formulate a scheme to attract our agricultural workers to Western Australia, having seen for himself the enormous advantages it would bring to the state. Recently Robustelli gained second prize in a nationwide model farm competition. Some time ago, in a letter from the president of the Milan Exposition, he learned that there, also, he had been awarded a silver medal for the products he had exhibited.

I have referred more than once to instances of persons who, when they came to Australia, were able to create an enviable position for themselves in the field of agriculture. At first glance this statement seems to be at odds with the principles I set down, namely that the peasant farmer who wishes to settle in this country needs to have a certain amount of capital. This apparent contradiction is explicable, however, when one realises that some farmers who came here, even genuine ones, like Robustelli took up other jobs, particularly in the mines, and were able to save up the required money before they turned to agriculture. Others, with relatively little capital, having managed to obtain land near the township, worked in their spare time for their neighbours who needed labourers. However, few have been able to avail themselves of these exceptionally favourable conditions. Anyhow, these are isolated instances and could never be cited as the norm with respect to large scale immigration.

Robustelli wanted us to stay for lunch and his good wife served us a delicious meal, prepared strictly in accordance with Italian culinary tradition which, sadly, we had almost forgotten. After lunch he took us to visit the property. Passing through the orchard we were amazed to see that all the trees, particularly the pears, had a large stone placed in the first fork of the tree. Robustelli assured me that fruit production was increased by this method; the stone, positioned at the time during which the sap is flowing at its maximum, hampers the growth of superfluous foliage in a way beneficial to the fruiting. Doubtless, years of experience have proved the worth of this rather unconventional, though fundamentally sensible, method. By three o'clock we were on the move again. Robustelli revved up his Ponej and off we went at a great pace to Mr Spencer's farm about five miles distant.

With the man of the house away, we were met by his wife who, in honour of the occasion, had invited several of her women friends from nearby. We went into the dining room where we were pleasantly surprised by the sight of a large table laden with all kinds of food, especially desserts and fruit. We drank the indispensable tea and needed little prompting to do justice to the delicacies offered us. The long drive had sharpened our appetites, and anyway the European adapts without noticing it to the Australian custom of having six meals a day.

Mrs Spencer, a typically frank and open Australian, wanted to explain everything to me in minute detail; she stationed herself at my side and made sure I missed nothing. The farm comprised some 1500 acres almost entirely under cultivation. Few Western Australian farms, as I have already noted, are completely cultivated. It was, therefore, an achievement of which the Spencers were justly proud. As elsewhere in this excellent grain producing district the wheat was growing extremely well. They run 500 sheep which have a nett worth of about 12 shillings a head. With six cows they produce an average of 60 pounds of butter a week, a high yield that I believe is due mainly to the Jersey breed which gives excellent milk, but also to the quality of the pasture and forage.

I must mention that here in Australia chaff is used as forage for both horses and cattle. It is made by chopping up wheat, barley and oat plants while they are still green but have formed the ear. Everything is used, stalk, leaf and ear, to make a most nutritious blend which cattle relish. In the goldfields area it is easier to turn the crop into chaff than to utilize it in the normal manner. As I said, the price of cereals is down, while the local demand for forage in the central region (where none is produced but where there are countless numbers of horses employed in the mines) is always very high. Because of the warm climate, which gives them an early crop, the northern districts, including Northam, have come to have something of a monopoly over the supply of forage.

I was struck by the complete absence of cherry trees in all the orchards we visited, Mr Spencer's being no exception. I was told that attempts to acclimatise them had been in vain. A vegetable garden was flourishing in a plot of land reserved for the purpose. We saw onions, potatoes, lettuce, beetroot and a large amount of peas which are eaten here by man and beast alike. The gardener was a Chinese. In Australia vegetables are grown exclusively by orientals, with excellent results. The Chinese farm worker does not like to work by the day for a boss, especially if that boss is a European. If possible he prefers to work for himself and, really, he is right because a more conscientious, sober worker would be hard to find.

An Australian would never dream of working all day, and often into the night, without a break. He thinks he has done more than his duty after a couple of hours of not too hard work. As a result many light industries in Australia have fallen into Asian hands. The local worker sees this and fumes with hatred against the yellow race whom, first the state and then the federal government have contrived to keep out through the application of strict entry requirements.

Of course the Australian populace is not entirely wrong in supporting their 'White Australia Policy.' The influx of Asians, from an economic point of view, might lower the wages of the local worker to such an extent that he would no longer be able to support himself. From an ethnological aspect, it could signal the deterioration of the present race and the formation of a half-caste element which, in every nation, has shown itself to be inferior to the pure race in both moral and physical terms. From a political standpoint, a vast, scarcely populated continent which leaves itself open to the swarming hordes of Chinese and Japanese will certainly be transformed into an Asian nation in a decade or so.

However much one might want to repulse coloured immigration, it is essential that the doors be widely opened to that from Europe. The idea of Australia for the Australians, entailing extending the ban even to the white races, has had its day.

Now, back again to Mrs Spencer's garden. The Chinese who tended it was paid by the day, or rather by the week (30 shillings plus board). The owner's share of the profit was considerable. Last year it was £30 from a plot of land measuring not more than a third of an acre. The Spencers, like the Robustellis, exemplify the prosperity to which those who work hard in Australia can look forward. Fifteen years ago they were poor; now they have a nett income of more than £1000, plus the worth of the property.

29 September. The Minister of Agriculture, Mr Mitchell, arrived from Perth early in the morning and most courteously called upon me at the hotel immediately. We met for some two hours and talked about the proposed settlement and its likely location.

He was of the opinion that the best area was in the south-west corner of the state where there is an abundant rainfall and where the very fertile land is criss-crossed by a number of permanent rivers. He gave me many good reasons for his choice. In the more northerly areas the main crop, actually the only crop possible at least initially, is wheat. As I noted earlier, Western Australia at present produces more wheat than is needed for local consumption; some of it, therefore, must be exported and the price must be competitive on world markets. But, while the country is more than well-provided with grain, it must still import more than £1,500,000 worth of so-called 'dairy products' (ham, butter, milk, eggs etc.) which is an enormous sum for a country with a population of only 260,000. These goods bring very high prices. Therefore, it is useful, not only in the interests of the state but those of the settlers themselves, that they be sent to a region where these products can be more easily produced.

I concurred, for the most part, with the Minister's ideas. Moreover, the climate in that area would be most suited to our farmers. Down there they would be able to harvest a variety of crops, everything needed for their own sustenance and more. With the exception of a small area, vines will grow very well. The olive bears abundantly and the mulberry thrives. Plantations of mulberry trees would open up new horizons for local industry given that silk-worm keeping is completely unknown in Australia.

From our point of view that region would be the most preferred. That far corner of the state has been sparsely populated till now as immigration has been directed towards the capital and the gold-bearing inland areas. Our fellow countrymen would be able to settle there peacefully and increase without fear of resentment and confrontation. They would have the advantage of having ports near at hand enabling them to trade with the rest of the continent and Europe. The Great Southern Railway is very close and the new settlements could be very easily linked to it by short secondary lines.

The fertility of the soil down there is much better than that in the north in terms of the nature of the land and, particularly, with respect to the rainfall and the amount of running water. In the north a settler needs at least a thousand acres, whereas in the far south, where intensive cultivation is possible, nay extremely easy, one or two hundred acres are sufficient.

However, one serious problem exists; in some places the forest is gigantic and clearing is consequently very slow and costly. Of course that does not mean to say that one has to select land where the forest is so thick. In fact such areas are, by law, reserved for the timber industry and excluded from settlement. On the other hand, there are areas in the south where the bush is relatively light; in fact there are large sections covered with grass and shrubs. In any event a decision will not be taken until we have visited all the various districts of the state.

The long conversation I had with Mr Mitchell left me in no doubt that the widespread respect he enjoys is well justified. With his impressive turn of mind and distinguished character he is, without doubt, one of the most outstanding personalities in Western Australia. Well versed in the agricultural field, he is really most suited to his portfolio (something which rarely happens in states governed by parliamentary process). Moreover, as a long-time farmer and still the owner of large estates which bring in a considerable income, he possesses both theoretical as well as practical expertise; thus it is possible for him vigorously to promote and direct agriculture in his country. To his rare intelligence is added great modesty and an exceptionally courteous manner, gifts that have afforded him widespread popularity.

Mr Mitchell exemplifies a style, common to politicians in this quite fundamentally democratic nation, in being accessible to all and retaining a simple way of life and an affability with the general public. He is enthusiastic about his country, in which he has total and unlimited faith, and to which he dedicates all of his considerable energies. I often think how satisfying it must be for a man to find himself in charge of such an enormous, young and resource-rich state which is presently going through the most important phase from infancy to that of a strong and forceful youth. It seems to me that a minister in a country like this would be the envy of his counterparts in the Old World where everything has already been done and settled for centuries and where everything moves at the slowest pace possible. He holds in some ways God-like powers. He can shape at will the rough clay placed in his hands and leave upon it his own creative imprint.

I explained my own feelings to Mr Mitchell. He smiled and approved, while in his eyes there was a flash of pride and satisfaction.

I had the Minister to lunch with me. I must say that from the time we set off on our tour Mr Ranford, the delegates, and I have dined at the same table. Ruozi and Bottoni were somewhat uncomfortable at first but, within a short time, they were at ease. It would be hard to imagine a happier, more companionable group of people. Mr Mitchell wanted no exceptions made for him and we all dined together. He tried to start up a conversation with Ricci who was beginning to stammer the odd word in English, but the attempt was rather futile.

After lunch Ranford and I went to visit Mr Throssell at his magnificent home situated on a hill outside Northam. This man, a real country gentleman, belongs to a distinguished English family which settled in Northam about fifty years ago when the district was all bush. Through utter integrity and hard work they have accumulated considerable property. He was the Minister for Agriculture and later Premier but has now left politics and lives in retirement on his farms. He is still hale and hearty despite his seventy-five years and leads an amazingly active life.

I stayed at his place for more than an hour and he was at pains to let me know of his great liking for Italians and his admiration for the fine qualities of our farmers. He spoke from experience, having had frequent occasion to employ our fellow countrymen whom he found to be honest, sober and hardworking. He asked a lot of questions about the state of agriculture in Italy and, for his part, gave me some useful and practical advice regarding the successful outcome of our immigration project.

He insisted on putting his automobile (a four-seater, 18 horse-power De Dion) at my disposal to inspect the surrounding areas and most courteously offered to accompany me. It was amazing to see him leap from his seat like a young man as soon as he saw a gate, of which there are many here, blocking our way. I tried to stop him but his son-in-law told me it was his custom, in fact one of his ways of showing courtesy to guests; also I thought perhaps it was a way of letting strangers know what a good climate Northam has and how its citizens stay full of vigour into their later years.

We went for a long drive through delightful country, all beautifully cultivated and undulating as far as the eye could see. It reminded me of some parts of the Umbrian countryside. On the way back we stopped for some time at the home of Mr Dempster, one of the oldest settlers in the district. As always, we were greeted with open arms and offered a lavish selection of wines, liquors and sweets. The conversation centred on items of local interest: the price of land, the chances of a good

Motoring Party: The Throssell family, Northam
Battye Library 23714P

harvest that year, horses that would be raced in forthcoming events etc., etc. Mr Throssell, even in such mundane conversation, demonstrated, as always, his great spirit and wit. Mrs Dempster discussed a complex genealogical matter at length with Mr Ranford which, as I was an outsider, did not interest me greatly.

Back in town, our friend Throssell wanted to meet the delegates. The first thing he looked at was their hands. He judged the future success of a colonist by the existence or not of callouses on the hands. And he is not mistaken: here, as elsewhere, hard work and no nonsense are what is needed. He was very pleased with Ruozi whose Herculean frame impressed him, reasonably happy with Bottoni, and little, in fact not at all, with Ricci, who was somewhat put out. However, I hastened to explain to him that, in the delegation, the first two were direct representatives of actual farmers whereas Ricci was involved in the more theoretical aspects.

I saw Mr Mitchell again in town. He told me that a meeting of farmers had officially passed a motion of welcome to the Italian mission. As one can see the farming sector is entirely favourable to us.

In order to stretch my legs, I accepted the Minister's invitation to go to the club for a game of billiards. We were both fairly good players and our game threatened to go on for ever. Luckily we were alone in the saloon. By the way, I must note that here in Australia, as in all British countries, billiards, including the manner in which it is played, is very different from both ours and the French version. The tables are very big, about twice the size of ours. Like ours they have six pockets but players do not use ninepins. The most common game is a mixture of billiards and snooker. Bridge followed billiards, and good luck favoured me and I won all evening which, as a guest, disturbed me somewhat.

September 30. It is Sunday, one of those silent, dark and dismal English Sundays. I went to the Catholic church in the morning. In Australia all Catholics and Protestants are most assiduous in their religious observance. It is most surprising to us Italians to see the composure of the faithful in church. No one is allowed to say a word, a jest or to make any movement. The Catholics, almost all Irish in origin, make up about a third of the Australian populace; in terms of wealth and status they are a significant force which the government must bear in mind.

In the afternoon the mayor came in his carriage to take me for a drive. I was very sorry to have to decline but I had already been invited by Mr Throssell to go for a spin in his automobile at three o'clock. At the appointed hour Mr Ranford and I went to the old gentleman's home. We found him surrounded by about twenty people including his children and grandchildren. He told me that his family numbered some fifty persons, a real patriarchal tribe! Last Christmas they all dined together. We partook of the customary tea and cakes, then off we went in the automobile.

My host realized that friend Ranford, who had been in an automobile for the first time only yesterday, was terrified that the vehicle would roll over. His little eyes gleamed mischievously as he planned to play a mean trick on poor Ranford. He motioned to his chauffeur and off we went at break-neck speed. The road, a country track which twisted through half-cleared bush, was anything but good; deep ruts formed by the wheels of carts, potholes full of water, creeks that cut across the path without any sign of a bridge, unexpected twists and turns at right angles, and dips that gave one the shudders, all combined to make our progress more than a little dangerous. The automobile bounced, twisted, collided with fallen branches and scraped against enormous tree trunks. Poor Ranford did not know which saint to invoke and only just managed to have the presence of mind to hang on like grim death to the back of the seat in front of him. Even those more accustomed than he to mad sprints at forty miles an hour found little pleasure on such roads. At one point we avoided disaster by a miracle; at a sudden turn we missed an enormous tree by millimetres. Luckily we got out of it with only a fright.

All at once the sky clouded over and torrential rain began to fall. I offered Mr Throssell my raincoat. He waved it away and it was charming to see this hale and hearty old man challenge the wrath of the elements unflinchingly. At last, as the fates decreed, it stopped raining and the automobile came to a halt. Well-pleased with himself Mr Throssell turned laughingly towards Ranford who vowed he would never get into that invention of the devil again as long as he lived.

We arrived at Mount Dick, an old property belonging to our host. Years ago he had sub-divided the land into lots which he had given to poor families. They have cleared their land and planted fruit trees and cereals. They all live now in great comfort. Mt Throssell's generosity in this instance has few peers. He advanced them everything including land, money and tools and was content to be repaid when the families were able to do so. They paid punctually and the little settlement is now prospering. He put the same system to work in other areas with good results. I was not surprised that this charming old man enjoyed the love and respect of all. Everyone doffs their hat as he goes by and speaks of him in reverent tones. He is the true father of the district.

At the hotel I made the acquaintance of Dr O'Connor, a former member of parliament and one of the richest landowners in Western Australia. He had been to Italy, which he loved and respected, but, like all the Irish, he had no time for either Garibaldi or Mazzini. However, he admired Cavour.

In the evening there was a large gathering of the elite in the hotel lounge. There was the usual game of bridge that went on until two o'clock in the morning.

Chapter Eight

*Trip to Kellerberrin—Artesian Wells—The Water
Pipeline to Coolgardie—The Leake Farm—Granite
Outcrops—Aborigines—The Mitchell Farm—
The Wheat Belt—The Harvest—Wool and Sheep
Shearing.*

October 1. I think that last night's game was the reason that I got up with
a violent headache this morning which prevented me from enjoying the
countryside along the railway between Northam and Kellerberrin,
which last is a small agricultural centre on the goldfields line going
towards Kalgoorlie which Mr Ranford felt would be useful to have us
visit.

Twenty-five miles out of Northam the railway cuts across the first of
the rabbitproof fences. The weather was splendid; the sky was a
pristine blue like it is in Italy in July. Here it is already high summer,
the long summer customary in this part of Australia where for eight
months there is not a drop of rain nor a cloud to dim the sun's
implacable rays. The countryside was very monotonous; endless
undulations interspersed with sandy plains. When the train reached
the top of one of these rises one could see what appeared to be an
immense, greyish-green sea, relieved here and there by small
yellowish oases. It was the endless virgin bush that the settlers had
already claimed; in some places the land had been cleared and the crop
that had been planted was beginning to turn golden.

The line ran in an easterly direction; the further we went the more
arid the area became and the lower the rainfall. In Kellerberrin they
still get twelve inches of rain a year but, thirty or forty miles further
on, the rainfall is so sketchy as to preclude any kind of cultivation. By
that I mean regular cultivation, because there are regions inland
where, with falls of only seven or eight inches, one can harvest a crop
on an average of every three years. It is a pity that the climatic

conditions are not better! A huge stretch of land, perhaps a third of Western Australia, is composed of very fertile soil, a mixture of clay, silica and ferrous oxide which, if irrigated, would be able to produce any kind of crop. Attempts have been made to obtain the water needed for agricultural purposes through artesian wells but they have only produced salty water laden with mineral substances that burn and make the soil sterile.

However, artesian wells have proved successful in the coastal regions where they are often used to provide drinking water to settled areas like Eucla where the land is most suited to grazing cattle but where the rainfall is lacking. Much of the land that comprises the Australian continent is artesian by nature, and, as one knows, this particular geological configuration has been put to good use elsewhere. Eastern Queensland owes its agricultural and pastoral prosperity to an excellent and inexhaustible supply of underground water. In Western Australia there are forty-four artesian and sub-artesian wells whose depth varies from 400 to 3000 feet. The cost of excavation is estimated at £2 per foot.

When speaking of Australia, one often hears mention made of the central desert and other desert areas. The term desert does not, perhaps, convey the real meaning. Here there are none of those endless barren stretches, devoid of vegetation, one encounters in the Sahara, Arabia and the Chilean coast. Of course there are some very barren, sandy and rocky sections but generally, in the so-called Australian desert, various types of shrubs, mainly spinifex, have taken root and in winter the earth is almost completely covered with grass, which in some places grows feet high, although it withers and dries up in a few weeks. Nor are trees entirely absent.

The particular thing about the Australian desert is the complete lack of fresh surface water, be it in rivers, creeks or lakes (exceptions being a very rare spring or rainwater trapped in rocky caves called rock holes). The so-called lakes, many of which appear on maps, are no more than extremely shallow, salty ponds which are completely dried up for ten months of the year. They are really only extensions of the salty land which becomes swampy during the rainy season. Lakes, in the true sense of the word, are very rare in Australia.

The water pipeline to Coolgardie, or the 'goldfields pipeline' as it is now called, runs beside the railway line. This colossal undertaking, which demonstrates the tenacity, the spirit of initiative and faith in the future of the small population of Western Australia, was built to provide water to the arid mineral area of the centre. The discovery of gold some twenty or so years ago produced the usual rush of miners, but it was almost impossible to extract the gold because of a lack of water. Rainwater was caught in special receptacles known as tanks but the amount was barely enough for personal use and there was none whatsoever for industrial purposes. Such was the shortage that it was said that bar tenders were meaner with the water than the liquor.

Therefore the state decided to construct the pipeline which turned out to be a truly colossal undertaking. It begins in the Darling Ranges near Perth where a dam, with a capacity of 4,600,000,000 gallons (a gallon is equivalent to 4.54 litres), has been built. The main pipe, which has a diameter of 30 inches, runs for a length of 350 miles with numerous branches. It has a potential to pump 5,000,000 gallons a day. Its construction, begun at the end of 1896, was finished in 1903 at a total cost of £3,078,500. Because there is no slope the water does not flow naturally and has to be pumped by means of powerful turbines situated at eight pumping stations along the line. Not only the mineral regions benefit from the pipeline but also other centres along the line. Besides its use in mining and for domestic purposes, it also provides a small amount for pasture and agriculture (mainly irrigating gardens and orchards).

Kellerberrin is about sixty-five miles from Northam and we covered the distance in just over three hours. As soon as we arrived we went to lunch. The hotel, which was recently built, was very nice. It is said to have cost £3000. I cannot understand the point of spending so much money in an area with no more than a hundred inhabitants. However, it reveals a good deal about the future development of the place which is the centre of a very promising grain growing area. And it must not be forgotten that Australians drink a lot! The prices in Kellerberrin were already on a par with those in the goldfields, that is, a shilling a glass. An unpleasant surprise, like the one we encountered at Goomalling, greeted us at the hotel; they knew nothing whatsoever about our coming and so we had to make do with a dreadful meal consisting mainly of salted tongue which did not stop the proprietor charging us top price. The land agent in Northam, Mr Euston, accompanied us on the trip. He knew every inch of this part of the state which was why Mr Ranford had asked him to be our guide.

Two carriages were waiting outside the hotel to take us through the bush to the Leake farm which was situated in the middle of a very picturesque area. The house was built at the foot of a huge, solitary, dome-shaped granite outcrop which reared up in the middle of the countryside. One encounters a good many of these granite domes, clearly of volcanic origin, throughout Western Australia and particularly in the area through which we were passing. One advantage of these outcrops is that there is never a shortage of water as it is caught on the rock and the run-off flows to the surrounding area. We climbed up its steep slippery slopes to the top where we enjoyed a view of the property; like a wide green belt, standing against the grey of the bush, it spread out around us.

The family, aware of our presence, came out to greet us. We quickly descended from our vantage point and were treated to the usual Australian hospitality. They invited us to have tea which was served outdoors. A number of neighbours had joined the family on this occasion. Among them I noticed several elegantly dressed, aristocratic looking young women. One did not feel that one was in the Australian bush but rather taking one's ease in a European city. I would never have believed refined persons, particularly women, could possibly pass almost all their lives so far from civilization and in a place where, it must be said, there is a complete dearth of comforts and diversions.

They assured me, however, that they were very happy and that country life had many attractive features. Continual visits with neighbours, sports of every kind such as riding, tennis, hunting etc., to say nothing of their domestic chores, did not leave them much time to be bored. It must be remembered, however, that many of these country landowners are very well-off and spend the summer either in Perth or Melbourne or, sometimes, in Europe.

We watched a wild horse, recently captured in the bush, being broken in. These animals, called brumbies in Australia, are descendants of horses of earlier times which got lost in the bush or escaped from the paddocks. One encounters great bands of them, among them there being some magnificent animals. On the stations, situated at the edge of the bush or on the plains, hunting wild horses is one of the favourite pastimes of the squatters, a pastime that is often not without fine profits, as a yet unbroken brumby sells for about £5.

To catch them, a palisade, shaped like an elongated 'V', is erected around the springs and ponds where they come to drink. As soon as the animals enter the area the entrance to the palisade is blocked off and the prisoners are tied up. The methods used to break in the animals are not very humane, although the horses are soon resigned to their destiny and often prove excellent as work and saddle animals.

In discussion with Mr Leake he provided me with a deal of information about his farm of 5000 acres, of which 1000 acres are under wheat, 50 acres under vines and about 10 acres of orchard; there are 3000 sheep and many horses and pigs. With all this God-given bounty the family lives very well.

We set off on the homeward journey after sunset. A strange and picturesque landscape unfolded before us. On the horizon was a strip of violet and orange sky and lower down, the black of the forest was relieved by the bright red glow of hundreds of fires. The settlers were burning the dried-out trees in the bush and, next year, where these had stood, there would be ripening crops.

We went close by an encampment of partly civilized Aborigines. They were dressed in a grotesque semi-European manner. The men were involved in shearing sheep on nearby properties. They are paid 5 shillings for every 'score,' that is, every twenty animals. Some more adept individuals can shear up to sixty sheep per day. It is a good wage; but it should be noted that the shearing season is very short and lasts no more than a month. We continued to meet groups of blacks along the way. Our driver greeted them with the usual, 'Good-bye, Billy.' They replied by waving their hats.

A number of geography and travel books contain many inaccuracies concerning Australian blacks. It is commonplace to say that they occupy the lowest rung on the human scale. But, if that means that they are bereft of any kind of culture, then the statement is far from the truth. They rarely adapt easily to hard work but one must not forget that their muscular force is much inferior to that of the European and to certain African peoples.

This is how Australian Aborigines and their customs have been described by Mr Malcolm Fraser who is most knowledgeable in the field:

> The Australian aborigines are slightly shorter than the European, but they are often more corpulent, even though their limbs are very thin; a particular characteristic is the almost complete absence of calves on their legs. The skull is long and narrow, the cheek bones prominent and the lower part of their forehead protrudes. The nose, thin at the top, is large and flattened below. The mouth is large, the teeth usually healthy and white, the chin small, the hair which is very black and sometimes curly is not woolly but very shiny when clean. Their skin is dark brown in colour and at times close to ebony. Their life expectancy rarely exceeds fifty years.
>
> These aborigines are unsurpassed as 'trackers' (those who follow the tracks of both criminals and persons lost in the bush and stolen cattle); they frequently make excellent messengers, divers, shepherds, horsebreakers, drovers, hunters etc., in general any kind of activity that does not require heavy muscular work. The names of many aborigines who accompanied the

early explorers in their dangerous journeys across the Australian continent, and whose worth and loyalty proved indispensable to the success of these enterprises, have become famous.

Scientists like Dampier, who declared the natives of Western Australia to be the most wretched people on the face of the earth, forget the ability and the knowledge they have displayed in the making of items for domestic use, in building habitations and weaving the fur of possums (a small native quadruped) with human hair. It is true that the methods they use to record the passing of time and to calculate are quite crude and, in this respect, they are inferior to other primitive peoples.

Contact with Europeans, instead of educating and civilizing, has, as a rule, served only to make them more brutish. The abuse of alcohol has had a disastrous effect on their already frail bodies and has accelerated the ultimate extinction of their race. Venereal disease will account for the rest. The early settlers spoke of the natives who lived in the northern part of the state as being a relatively strong and well-formed race and there was no shortage of women who were attractive even to European eyes. Now, however, with the exception of those in the inaccessible interior, the race is in complete decline. Both men and women are covered in ulcers and sores, they have runny eyes and are old and worn out at twenty.

Parliament, on a number of occasions, has voted on laws for the protection of the natives. It is absolutely forbidden for whites to sell them liquor. All blacks are supplied with blankets and food (tea, flour and meat) on request and are provided with medicines if they are ill; orphans are cared for in special establishments. To cover the costs incurred a sum of £11,500 per annum is allocated. However, it is not enough. The position of Protector of Aborigines was established and its incumbent charged with the task of overseeing the strict application of the regulations made for their benefit. In particular he tried to prevent cunning whites from exploiting them with respect to work contracts, which often happened in the past and still occurs.

Unfortunately, despite the best of intentions, the condition of the ancient owners of Australia is not a happy one. The expansion of agriculture, particularly grazing which requires a large amount of land, has robbed them of their main means of sustenance, that is, hunting. The food provided by the government does not make up the difference because only those who live near towns can take advantage of it.

Driven by hunger they often steal a sheep or kill a couple of head of cattle. Then the squatters treat them like wild animals and on occasions slaughter them without mercy. The police also frequently treat them cruelly. While the original Aborigine was very moral and had strict laws governing marriage, marital fidelity and the purity of young girls, contact with whites has completely debased them.

In the more remote areas, miscegenation among whites and young black women is common, often not based on persuasion alone. Thus the head of a family may readily accede to the desires of the white who hands over some tobacco, whisky or a bit of bread.

It must be said, however, that the government has shown some good intentions. Some time ago it ordered Dr Roe to conduct an inquiry which, without fear or favour, exposed to full view the evils and shame of the situation. Remedies were taken which are still in effect; but the population is sparse, the area immense, management is lacking and, especially, the shortage of funds hinder any satisfactory outcome.

There are also several religious missions whose brief is the material and moral welfare of Aborigines. Generally they have produced excellent results. Noted among them is the Benedictine establishment at New Norcia, founded in 1846 by Father (later Bishop) Salvado. In 1904 there were 163 Aborigines and half-castes being cared for at this mission.

The origins of the Australian Aborigines have been the subject of considerable debate, but up to now no firm conclusions have been reached. They have nothing whatsoever in common with such peoples of nearby countries as Papuans, Malays or Polynesians. It is generally supposed that they are descended from a very old race, in existence before those mentioned above, which in its place of first origin had been wiped out by more recent arrivals.

The only people with whom the Aborigines have something in common are the inhabitants of the mountainous regions of central India. From both a physical and linguistic point of view one could presuppose some common ancestry. One cannot overlook those that like to think of the Aborigines as descendants of the inhabitants of the ancient continent of Lemuria which, according to some scholars, linked Australia and Africa in prehistoric times. However, these speculations have no scientific basis. The recent discovery in Egyptian tombs of weapons similar to those used by Australian Aborigines (particularly boomerangs) may cast some light on the matter.

With few exceptions, Australian Aboriginal tribes are essentially nomadic, having no fixed place of abode or shelter. They roam about continuously, although they do not go beyond their tribal limits as delineated by ancient custom. Their sustenance comes from hunting, fishing or digging for roots. They shelter in huts made of branches, open at each end and shaped like a semi-circular hedge, leaning slightly at the top and serving mainly as a protection from the blustery winds. In the northern areas they live completely in the open around big campfires. Their clothing is very primitive: a belt and a cloak fashioned from the skins of the kangaroo or possum. Their main weapons are the spear, which they throw with great strength and accuracy, and the boomerang, a piece of curved wood which is used to kill birds and small animals. Their skill in throwing it is amazing; sometimes its flight is in a straight line, sometimes a curved trajectory, or else they make it come back to where it was thrown with marvellous precision. Rarely is a white able to emulate their skill.

In the northern part of the state many paintings depicting human figures, reptiles, quadrupeds etc., have been discovered on sandstone rocks. The colours used are generally ferrous oxide, white clay and coal. These paintings and the fact that one encounters among the northern tribes individuals with regular features and paler skin, suggests that in ancient times a race more civilized than the present one may have existed there.

I beg the reader's indulgence for my long digression occasioned by our meeting with the black shearers. It was already dark when we arrived back in Kellerberrin and, as there were no theatres or clubs, I decided to follow the example of my companions and went to bed immediately after supper.

October 2. During the day we visited two farms; in the morning we toured that owned by Mr Mitchell (the same surname as that of the Minister of Agriculture), situated seven miles out of Kellerberrin. He had previously lived on the goldfields where he had a lumber business providing wood for the mines. He then decided it would be easier to go into farming and he bought a thousand acres from the government and, a bit at a time, he is planting his land with wheat. In the middle of the property rises one of the common granite outcrops; we struggled to the top to find a mound of cyclopean rocks balanced one on top of another. The weathering of the outcrop has produced this effect. The rocks have been transformed into fantastic shapes; some were like huge elephants, others gigantic towers, still others were perfectly spherical and seemed as if they had been placed there with mathematical precision. One had the feeling that a puff of wind could send them hurtling into the chasm below. In fact, we suddenly heard a loud rumble and a deafening crashing sound. Whatever had happened, we asked ourselves. It was simply Ruozi, the Hercules of the group, who, having climbed to one of the higher points of the outcrop, was amusing himself testing his strength by rolling down an enormous rock, fragments of which fell quite close to where we were. Luckily we were in a cavern formed in the outcrop, and so were safe. Our good friend had looked down and, seeing no one, thought we had gone to the opposite side of the hill. We begged him to come down and stop his dangerous game. I tried to dig in the earth inside the cave to see whether I could find a fossil. There was nothing except two tiny skulls, one of a lizard and the other of a rodent.

We crossed a field of green wheat which in some parts was already beginning to turn golden. The crops here were the best I had ever seen in Western Australia. Even I, in spite of my height, disappeared from view in the middle of the crop. The ears of wheat are very big, full and heavy, several reaching 13 centimetres in length. It is unlikely that wheat with such resilient stalks would be flattened even by the most boisterous wind; at its base the stalk was as thick as a boy's little finger. Without doubt, this strength derives from the chemicals found in the soil. All the shrubs in this part of Australia have very hard, almost woody, leaves and stalks; the grass is also very strong.

Mr Mitchell attributed his abundant harvests firstly to the position of his farm, situated as it is at the base of the granite outcrop which, as I have said, acts as a collector and distributor of water to the surrounding area, and secondly, to the tilling of the soil two or three times a year before the grain has germinated. Such a practice preserves a considerable amount of moisture in the soil. Tilling, in fact, breaks up all the fissures and cracks formed by the rapid heating and drying of the topsoil, through which the moisture normally evaporates.

On the way back we passed through country which showed the harsh and melancholy aspects of the Australian bush. Nevertheless, we saw some beautiful flowers and, in some places, some wild peaches, reddish in colour and acidic to the taste, which the blacks eat avidly and whites use to make jam. This peach is one of the few native fruits found in the Australian bush, where often in a thousand acres there is hardly anything that can feed a man. In this area the timber is sparse and scrubby. Thus clearing costs only about 15 shillings per acre.

I asked Mr Euston for particulars concerning the cultivation of grain in the area. These details are relevant to the situation where an owner has employees to work the land. If he works it himself the expenses, as one might imagine, are much less. The costs per acre are as follows: ploughing and seeding 12s 6d an acre; seed (per bushel) 3s; artificial fertilizer with superphosphate at the rate of 50 pounds to the acre, 2s 6d; reaping and binding, chopping up for chaff or threshing the actual wheat, and transportation to silo 6s; total 24s 6d or 25s. Bearing in mind that the average production in the district is 15 bushels to the acre, the cost is low and, given that wheat sells for about 3s a bushel, it is clear there is a nett profit of £1 per acre. The initial costs occur only once, that is, the purchase of the land (normally sold by the government for 10s an acre payable in twenty years without interest), the clearing (15s per acre in this area), and fencing (£25 a mile). Machinery can be paid for in a very short time. (On smallholdings the machinery is usually hired, but on larger properties it is more convenient to buy it.)

It is a fairly rosy picture. It must be admitted that, as I have said, the price of grain, has tended downward but, with prices having already reached close to those offering on the world market, it is difficult to believe that they will go much lower.[1]

After visiting the Mitchell property I changed my opinion about the area completely having previously believed it to be totally unsuited for our settlers. Mr Euston told me that about twenty miles south-west of the railway, that is, in the area where the rainfall tends to be greater, there were some 15,000 acres of excellent land most suited to cereal crops. The lie of the land is the same as here, gently undulating plains with frequent granite outcrops. Obviously it would be impossible for every settler to be allotted land of the sort mentioned above, that is, with granite outcrops. However, one must not forget that, even if one is not in the immediate vicinity of such a natural feature, the soil for several miles around is still very good for cereal crops and other products.

The advantages of the area are as follows: the bush is lightly timbered and could be ringbarked and burnt in two or three months; it is the area closest to the goldfields where much fodder is required; the climate is very hot which means the harvest is two or three weeks ahead of the south-western districts; as a result the prices are higher and the crop is easier to sell. In this area the land allotted to each family ought not be less than 1000 acres minimum. Otherwise they could run the risk of having to struggle in straitened circumstances without any hope of increasing their holding because all the available nearby land had been taken up by new settlers.

---

1   Unfortunately at present (March 1907) the price has dropped to little more than two shillings a bushel but I believe this is a passing slump.

Keeping the above-mentioned particulars in mind, it would be possible for a family, comprised of husband and wife and two or three robust sons, to bring all their land under cultivation in a relatively short period (say ten years). In any event, five or six months after they established themselves, assuming this occurred at the right season of the year, it would be possible for them to harvest up to at least a hundred acres of wheat. The cultivation of cereals does not require a great deal of man-power if one has enough machines. Mr Mitchell, who has a property of 200 acres, does all the work with three horses and two men.

We went back later to visit Mr Leake who yesterday had promised to let us see wheat being harvested and sheep shorn. The harvesting was done with a special machine called a 'reaper and binder.' Drawn by three horses with a man perched up on a high seat steering, the machine travelled across the broad expanses cutting the waving wheat in great longitudinal swathes. The wheat was cut close to the earth with horizontal blades and the stalks, by means of a canvas cylinder, were gathered into sheaves in a kind of a sack where, one at a time, a special gadget bound and tied them with string. The same gadget knotted and cut the cord; the sheaves were then dropped on to a horizontal wooden platform. When six sheaves had been accumulated the boards were retracted and the sheaves were dumped in heaps on the ground. This machine represents an improvement in the types of harvesters used previously which dropped the sheaves one at a time, causing a great waste of time and energy. Mr Leake told me that, in one day, one machine can reap and bind ten acres of crop. To do the same manually would require at least twenty people, whereas it needs only one person to drive the machine.

We then went to watch the shearing, which took place in a sort of open-sided shed with the floor raised about two metres above the ground. We clambered up on the platform where about fifty animals were held in five or six wooden pens. The shearer, stationed at the gate of each pen, grabbed a sheep, sat it down on its hind legs and, holding it firmly between his knees, proceeded to shear the long fleece with large shears or a little machine like that used by hairdressers. The sheep were very quiet and Mr Ranford reminded me of the bible saying, 'meek as a shorn lamb.' The whole operation was quite speedy, but sometimes a sheep is nicked here and there. In that event the wound is plastered with liquid tar and heals rapidly.

Sheep are mostly shorn once a year, sometimes twice. Mr Leake's flock had been shorn six months earlier. Each sheep produces an average of five to seven pounds of wool a year, but it is not unusual to find pedigree sheep which produce up to 18 pounds. As soon as it is cut the wool is picked over to remove any dirty or matted locks (however, these are also sold and absolutely nothing is wasted). It is then compressed into bales and sent to the market. The actual price varies from 12d to 14d a pound. In the eastern states the main markets are Geelong near Melbourne, and Sydney in New South Wales. In Western Australia the product is sent directly to the London market, but no doubt, with the increase in the local production, a market must also be established in Perth.

Thousands of wool-buyers, representing English, German, French and Belgian firms, go to Australia every year to buy wool. They constitute the aristocracy of commercial travellers and are, in fact, extremely well paid, receiving, besides their fixed salary, a percentage of the sales effected which can sometimes reach enormous amounts. I have always found the complete absence of representatives from Italian firms to be totally inexplicable. I shall refer later on to this point and to the wider phenomenon of inertia with respect to trade with Australia (see Appendix).

We partook of tea at the foot of an enormous granite hill. Skins and blankets were spread out and we all sat on the ground. The charming Mrs Leake carried out her duties as hostess with faultless grace. We were enchanted by her attractive and pleasant manner in conversation. Her three brothers were with her, all country gentlemen who, rich as they may have been, were not above maintaining a busy working schedule. One should see them, dressed like the lowliest peasant, taking on the heaviest tasks. It is a 'sport' as much as anything else! You would most certainly not connect the elegant gentleman, perfumed, spruced-up and dressed in the latest fashion, frequenting the clubs of Perth and Melbourne, with the man who, only a few days earlier, clad in workman's clothes, had driven the plough and baled the wool on his farm hidden away in the middle of the endless bush. They belong to an admirable race which will have a glorious future.

Towards evening we returned to Kellerberrin. Before taking the train to Northam Mr Euston showed me the town's future planning scheme which, according to him, was destined to proceed with all haste. However, until then, it comprised only a hotel and four or five houses; but who can forecast what the development of this new state will be in the next ten or twenty years?

Every six to twelve months, even in the smallest centres, the government puts blocks of Crown Land up for sale. When the country is not well known, the prices, as one might imagine, are very low; but some small agricultural or mineral centres which only a few years ago had barely thirty or forty inhabitants now are important cities and those who bought then did a good deal for themselves. For those who may be interested, half-acre building blocks in Kellerberrin sell for between £10 and £15 each. It is worth noting that, here in Australia, building blocks are not sold in terms of area but on the length of the frontage; the price is calculated at so much per linear foot.

Chapter Nine

The Northam Agricultural Show—Banquet and Speeches—Beverley—Sandy Soils—Narrogin—The Official Reception—Mr Brown and his Opinions—The Clayton Farm—The State Experimental Farm.

October 3. Today was a field day. The annual agricultural show began in Northam. It was a large gathering said to number not less than five thousand people among exhibitors and visitors, who had come from all parts of the district and elsewhere, particularly Perth and Fremantle. That number would not be remarkable in Europe, but it must be remembered that we are in an immense country with a sparse population.

The district show in Northam is second in importance only to that held at Claremont near Perth. The space allocated to the Northam show was 15 acres compared to 40 acres in Claremont. It had been organised by the local agricultural society. Mr Spencer kindly sent us tickets which also entitled us to attend the official luncheon. As a special honour we had been declared honorary members of the committee.

We were the recipients of all sorts of honours and kindnesses. At the entrance we were met by the Minister for Agriculture who, after conducting us on a short tour of the most important sections of the show, accompanied us to the banqueting hall. This was a large pavilion, completely open on the side, which looked out on to the showground. It was divided into two sections; on one side the officials were seated and on the other were the ordinary guests, in all some hundred persons.

The delegates and I were placed in seats of honour near the ministers; Bottoni and Ruozi sat opposite me. The latter was in a cold sweat; as he told me later he had never been so embarrassed in his life.

Close by me I saw the Minister for Agriculture; the former Minister Throssell; one of his sons (a member of parliament); Mr Dempster, also a member; the Mayor of Northam, Mr Bernard; and Mr Bennet, the London manager of Millars, an important company involved in the exportation of Australian timber; as well as other notables from Perth and Northam.

At the beginning of the lunch I was handed a list giving the speakers' names. Eloquence is one of the greatest attributes of the Australian who indeed can be a good talker and easy ad-libber. As Archbishop Riley, himself an excellent orator, told me, there are few Australians who cannot, at any given time, give a speech in which elegance of form is linked to the depth and substance of the topic.

I saw to my horror that my name was on the list. I do not really have the oratorical gift of the Australians—quite the opposite! To improvise in a language other than one's own in front of a hundred or so guests and a few thousand others crowded around to hear was easier said than done. But there was no way I could avoid it!

It began with the ritual call, 'Gentlemen, charge your glasses.' Bottoni, seeing his glass brimming over with champagne, drank the lot in a gulp. Everyone smiled at his naiveté and the ever patient Ranford poured him another. The first toast to the King is never omitted from any kind of an English banquet; not even socialists forget it. According to English custom, the various toasts (to the government, the parliament, judges, guests etc., etc.) are proposed by a designated speaker; the person representing the group to whom the toast is proposed then responds with a speech.

All the speakers referred to us in most flattering terms; especially well received were the frank, warm-hearted words of the Minister for Agriculture. The venerable Mr Throssell proposed the toast to the guests with a speech marked by expressions of admiration for our country and its people. My turn came and I really did not think I could cope. But one must put on a brave face. I began by expressing the deep admiration we felt for so prosperous a country which had made so much progress in such a short time. I spoke of the scope of our mission and of the advantages which the realization of the immigration project might bring to both nations. I mentioned the advantage of initiating reciprocal trade relations and I did not forget to thank the government for the many courtesies extended towards us. I concluded by saying, such was my enthusiasm for their country, that had I not been born Italian (of which I am immensely proud) I would have liked to have been a Western Australian. I thought the room would cave in under the thunderous applause which seemed to go on forever. The delegates told me that my speech had been the best of all; but really they were not the most acute judges seeing as they did not understand a single word of English! Perhaps they judged it from the applause which, by dint of good manners, was more generous towards me than to the other speakers. In any event, my last remark did the rounds of all the newspapers and was commented upon most favourably.

With the luncheon over we made closer inspection of the exhibits we had glimpsed earlier. We admired some splendid breeds of sheep: Shropshire, Lincoln and Merinos, these last named being particularly noted for their wool. I was told that, among the meat producing breeds, some animals become so fat that they are not suitable for butchering. We saw sheep which weighed more than 200 pounds live weight (the pound is equal to 450 grams). I was particularly struck by a splendid breed of draught horse. They were the famous Clydesdales whose fetlocks are covered with long hair. I also saw some excellent race horses. Lastly we saw the homecraft section, machinery, vegetables etc., etc.

We had to depart that evening for Beverley, a town situated on the Great Southern Railway. I very much regretted having to leave Northam, such a pretty little town where we had been greeted with much warmth, affection and enthusiasm. Even the delegates were down-hearted. When we made known our plans there was a general outcry. Quite plainly, for a variety of reasons, no one wanted us to leave. There was to be a ball that evening at which all the prettiest young girls in the district would be present and they would be offended if we did not attend; the next day there would be horse racing, what ever would they say if we did not go? It would be scandalous. Everybody was insistent and I, for my part, would have given in quite happily, but Mr Ranford reminded me that he had already telegraphed ahead to Beverley. Time was pressing and there were many other places to visit, so we had to say farewell to charming Northam and its hospitable citizens. Who knew when we might see them again?

Mr Throssell made me promise that I would go and spend a week at his place as soon as I have the time and I accepted his invitation with alacrity. Everybody was keen to ensure that we would return: we were truly touched by such friendliness.

Before leaving I had another long discussion with Mr Mitchell. He again stressed the opportuneness of settling our farmers and their families in the southern districts where, while there were some problems, there were also many advantages. Those districts, as I have already said, are particularly suited to the production of dairy products which still account for £1,500,000 of foreign debt in Western Australia.

He gave me a list of imports in this category for 1905. These were the main items (in £ sterling):

Butter	313,000
Fresh food and vegetables	185,000
Meat (fresh, salted and canned)	139,000
Ham and lard	116,000
Milk and cream	100,000
Potatoes	91,000
Eggs	70,000
Wine	34,000
Beef cattle (especially dairy cows)	36,000
Horses	64,000

At the show I had met Mr Teesdale-Smith, the technical manager of Millars Company in Australia. He told me that his company owns about 30,000 acres of excellent land in the far south which it had purchased many years ago to make use of the enormous amount of timber in the area. Felling being now completed, the company had no further interest in keeping the land, which they would be prepared to dispose of on advantageous terms. Mr Smith wanted us to go and see the area. From Albany, where we were heading in any case, he would put a special train at our disposal which would take us along the company's railway line as far as Denmark which is situated in the middle of the land referred to earlier.

I realized, however, that Mr Mitchell preferred that we negotiate with the government which, he told us, was disposed to offer us every assistance. It was clear that in this matter he did not view private proposals altogether favourably. And perhaps he was right because a company, intentionally or otherwise, always has profit in mind, whereas this is not an issue in dealings with the government. Furthermore, the calibre of the Minister ensured a successful outcome for any undertaking under his direction. Nevertheless, I did not think it was a bad thing to listen to any proposals the company might offer.

October 4. We arrived at Beverley late yesterday evening. This morning we went firstly to see Mr Walker, the land agent. He was a well-established farmer and therefore a most practical person. He lined us up in front of a map of the district. 'Have you enough land to allocate to about a hundred families?' I asked him.

'In the outskirts almost all blocks have been taken up,' he replied, 'but 20 to 25 miles away there are about two million acres still available. The land has not been taken up before this as it appears to be not very fertile. It is mostly clay with a strata, five to six inches deep, of fine sand on top. Trees do not grow in this soil, only shrubs native to the sandy plains.'

'Do you think it suitable for the cultivation of cereal crops?'

'Better than many other so-called first grade soil. With ploughing the clay gets mixed with the sand to form a light soil that retains moisture very well. A little while ago some important experiments were made. About 40 acres were planted with wheat which yielded an average of 20 bushels each.'

'You don't think those 40 acres represented a particularly good patch?'

'Certainly not; all this area is uniformly fertile, at least judging from the composition of the soil which is the same everywhere. I have convinced my sons who have acquired enormous holdings and I am confident of their ultimate success.'

However, Mr Ranford was very sceptical about the idea. Why select doubtful land when there was excellent land in abundance? Moreover the soil might easily become depleted and require vast amounts of chemical fertilizer or long periods of lying fallow. Mr Johnson, the land agent at Narrogin whom we met that day, was of the same opinion as Mr Ranford.

Nevertheless, with the little bit of local knowledge I had acquired, I begged to differ from these two gentlemen. How many of this country's misconceptions might be reversed as a result! How many soils have been judged unsuitable for particular crops and then have yielded magnificent results! My opinion was confirmed by maize plants I saw in the Narrogin office. They were more than two and a half metres high with enormous cobs and came from the above areas. But while I would advise anyone with capital to experiment, positive as I am that it would afford excellent results, I would not risk suggesting to the government that they send our farmers there. As far as they are concerned there must not be the faintest shadow of a doubt about the quality of the land they would take up. But, I repeat, if it was up to me I would not hesitate. Moreover this land has the advantage that there are virtually no clearing costs, the only difficulty being in transporting wood for the fencing.

Mr Walker gave me a sample of already ploughed soil. It was a white clay mixed with silica sand. I want to have it analysed as soon as I get back to Italy. He also gave me a sample of the so-called chocolate soil which is clay mixed with a good deal of ferrous oxide.

We stayed in Beverley for only a few hours. It is a vast district and would need several days to visit it all completely. But because of the shortage of land suitable for large scale cultivation Mr Ranford felt that the brief notes Mr Walker had given us were sufficient. Beverley has 318 inhabitants and, notwithstanding its small population, boasts three hotels. It is one of the oldest agricultural centres in the state; that explains why the land for many miles around is in private hands. It is the main town of the district which is particularly suited to sheep and wheat farming. The rainfall varies between 7 and 24 inches a year. Clearing (mainly York gum and 'jam') costs between £1 and £3 per acre. The main rivers are the Avon and the Dale; and excellent water is to be found everywhere at a shallow depth. In 1903 there were 28,592 acres under cultivation. Average production was as follows; 17.4 bushels per acre of wheat, 21.7 of oats and 2 tons of potatoes.

A three hour train trip took us to Narrogin (108 miles from Northam). It is only a few years old but destined for the greatest prosperity because of its position and the fertility of the surrounding land. It is situated 1100 feet above sea-level at the highest point of the Perth–Albany railway. The climate was completely different from that of areas visited thus far. The fresh, sparkling air made me feel as if I was in the hills of my native Liguria. Even the appearance of the vegetation was different; the grass grew thicker and greener because of the greater humidity in the soil. In the paddocks the wheat was barely a hand's breadth high whereas in Kellerberrin it had been already harvested.

As soon as we arrived we found all the notables of the district assembled at the station to bid us welcome; the mayor, with the councillors, all the town officials and even the Anglican minister. It was the customary, cordial welcome from this open-hearted people. They took us to the Town Hall where a sumptuous repast awaited. As per usual there was no lack of speeches. Everyone expressed great admiration for Italians and for our government which was such a friend of Australia. Even I had to speak, unfortunately off the cuff, without even the hour's notice I had in Northam! However it is all a matter of habit and I realized that I was becoming a first-rate speaker.

It was pleasing to note that our mission always roused a deal of interest and enthusiasm among the populace. This tour was a great advertisement for our country and its moral benefits are considerable.

How different now to when I arrived in Australia for the first time four years ago! Then Italians were not well thought of. As I have already said they were placed somewhere between the blacks and the Chinese. Instead, now we are the country of the moment; everyone wants to know about us, about our trade and industry and about our progress. One starts to realize that the resentment there was against Italy was, in large part, the product of ignorance. I felt very pleased, the more so because it seemed to me that this change in public opinion was linked to my work of promoting Italy which had occupied me continuously for three years.

We went to the town's main hotel kept by a Mr Brown, a full-blooded Irishman. The room assigned us was spacious and elegantly furnished; it would have stood comparison with any first-rate hotel in Europe. We were treated with every courtesy and respect; during lunch and dinner the owner sat at the table with us, this being a signal honour in Australia.

Mr Brown told us his history, a common one among peasants and workers who arrived penniless from Europe and were able, by dint of hard work and perseverance, to succeed. He left his native Ireland about forty years ago and settled in Australia without a penny. Now he is wealthy, owning more than 30,000 acres, 3000 sheep and 500 head of cattle. Hearing an enumeration of the riches of Australia was like going back to biblical times. Luckily, all this God-given bounty nowadays is linked with some modern conveniences such as the railway, electric light and telephone, making it hard to imagine how the patriarchs did without.

After lunch I had a most interesting discussion with our amiable host. He advised me against the land in the far south because of the tremendous amount of work needed to clear the bush, and because there is too much moisture in the soil and too many difficulties transporting produce. He might have been right in one way but essentially he viewed the matter in a pessimistic light. He was a dedicated proponent of cereal cultivation which obviously flourishes in the northern and central districts. His estimate of the costs and profits was about the same as those already quoted to me for the land around Kellerberrin. Given that the bush was still green, clearing would have to start in March and ploughing in June so that seeding could then begin.

Two years ago he and a not so young nor able-bodied worker began to clear twenty acres of land; in ten weeks the work had been completed. A family who began to clear the bush in February or March could have a harvest in the wheat shed by October or November. He estimated that the cost of clearing, ploughing, seeding, harvesting, seed, chemical fertilizer etc., etc.—obviously using machinery—would amount to no more than a total £2 per acre. The nett profit, in all cases, would be more than £1 per acre. A family of three or four persons could, in the space of a year, clear and work a hundred or so acres and earn a nett return of similar amount. In the years which followed they would be able to bring the rest of their allotment under cultivation. It would provide a ready-made and immediate source of well-being. Nor can it be said that only one crop can be cultivated in the cereal growing districts. The area is also suited to sheep, beef and pig farming. Thus a farmer could count on grazing and other allied products. Our conversation lasted for more than two hours. Mr Brown concluded by promising me a special report on the matter.

A long buggy ride took us to a farm on the outskirts of town where they have harvested as many as 37 bushels of wheat to the acre, an enormous amount considering no chemical fertilizers had been used. However, it should be noted that, apart from being blessed with an extremely fertile soil, this region is also most favoured in terms of rainfall. The annual average is 18 inches which is an ideal amount for cereal crops. It is not just the amount of rain that benefits the crop but also the period during which it falls.

On the way back we lost sight of Ricci who had shifted, with two other farmers, to a different carriage. We waited dinner for him in vain, for he did not arrive until almost eleven o'clock. We were very worried because it is the simplest thing in the world for an inexperienced person to get lost in the bush. We knew only too well how, when engrossed in his botanical and entomological pursuits, our friend can easily wander away from his companions to seek out an unusual flower or rare insect.

In fact, there had been no flowers, no insects. Rather, one of his friends wanted to have him to dinner at his place which was halfway along the road between the farm we visited and Narrogin. Ricci reported that he had spent a very pleasant evening; good wine, good food and unlimited cordiality. The only problem was they had to make each other understood by sign language.

With Ricci back safely, I resumed my discussion with Mr Brown and our chat went on until two o'clock in the morning. He hoped that some Italians might settle on his land. The Western Australian government could buy his properties (as I have already said, the government here often buys property from private landowners which it then sub-divides and sells) and in turn allot them to our families. He would be prepared to relinquish it for £1 per acre; he himself would take charge of the clearing etc. I neither approved nor disapproved. I advised him to deal directly with the government on the proposal. It was clear, in terms of what he told me, that several of his properties were first rate but why pay him £1 per acre when they could be had for 10 shillings? Furthermore, most were situated more than 25 miles away from the railway line which was rather a long way.

October 5. This morning we had to visit another property. Mr Ranford had been made responsible for waking us up. He was confused, however, and instead of summoning us at six o'clock, as we had arranged, he called us at four o'clock which did not please me greatly as I had gone to bed at two a.m. But one could never take umbrage with the man, who is truly as good as gold.

We took advantage of this unscheduled free time to discuss technical matters with Mr Ranford and Mr Brown, focusing particularly upon agricultural legislation in Western Australia. To prevent the accumulation of vast estates, which for the most part remain uncultivated, parliament, as I have noted, has for a number of years put in place laws which prevent anyone from purchasing more than 2000 acres of Crown Land. I believe this restriction tends to deter well-intentioned capitalists from acquiring land.

In fact it is very difficult for a capitalist or a European consortium to invest money in agricultural enterprises here and be subject to all the rules, regulations, costs and feasibility studies, only to be limited to a trifling 2000 acres. Why not allow them to purchase 20, 50, or even 100 thousand acres with the strict proviso that the land be placed under cultivation within a certain period of time? The advantages for agriculture are evident. It would allow capital to be used on large scale development with a minimum squandering of materials and with a much more scientific approach than that presently in use.

Mr Brown and Mr Ranford shared my opinions; but it is futile to hope for any change in the law given the semi-socialist spirit which influences all legislation in Australia. On the other hand, it would be unfair not to recognise the considerable advantages the current agricultural legislation has brought to the country. In fact, one could say that the small settler is practically assured of success given the organization and function of the Agricultural Bank which is more than laudable.

In biting cold and frequent showers of rain we went to visit Mr Clayton's farm. A sumptuous spread, to which we did full justice, was laid on for us. The temperature outside was very low and the fire that burned brightly in the dining room was much appreciated. The entire farm comprised 10,000 acres, about a thousand of which was under cultivation. Mr Clayton, a former miner, began his farm with £1000 which considerably eased his task. A man of rare energy and big ideas, he proposes to have all his land under the plough in a year or so. He would then own the largest tract of cultivated land in the state.

We first inspected a ten acre field which had been divided into rectangular strips. Part was destined to be a vegetable garden and part an experimental plot for forage plants. There was a considerable amount of beetroot, turnips, carrots, parsley etc., but few potatoes because it is believed they suffer from the cold and frost. We admired several examples of a gigantic cabbage with a stalk about two metres tall; they make excellent fodder for the cattle, especially for the milking cows. The orchard was beautiful also, some twenty acres planted with every sort of fruit tree. In one paddock a hundred or so pigs grazed happily. Mr Clayton has established an artificial pasture in this paddock, composed of different grasses, which, as I have said, is a system destined for big things.

From the pigs we moved on to the stables where Ruozi, who is a specialist on horses, was most taken with a magnificent Clydesdale stallion worth £120. His services at stud cost between £3 and £5. Lastly we saw the ultimate in farm machinery. Mr Clayton's farm was the best of those we had thus far visited in every respect. It was on a par with Robustelli's in terms of method and attention to detail but it was much larger in area.

It was already midday and Mr Ranford suggested we cut short our visit because we had yet to go to the state experimental farm which was close by. There are two such properties in Western Australia; one is near Geraldton in the northernmost part of the agricultural zone and the other is here in Narrogin. However, it seems that the former has been a failure and there is talk of shifting the school and its pupils to Narrogin.

The experimental farms were designed to give the necessary training and practical experience to young people who want to devote themselves to agriculture. However, in terms of teaching, I doubt if these schools are on the same level as similar institutions in Europe. The fees one pays here are minimal, only £2 per year. This sum provides for accommodation and plenty of healthy food. But the students must do the same amount of manual work as labourers.

The government farm was ten miles away from Mr Clayton's property. Land in the less fertile areas of the district was deliberately chosen to demonstrate what the soil can produce when it is cultivated by scientific methods. Plants of wheat and other cereals were exceptionally good. The breeds of pigs (Berkshires and Yorkshires) had been selected and the poultry stock selection was almost complete. Mr Baird, the farm's very courteous manager, after having guided us on our inspection tour, then took on a role which was really appreciated by our much sharpened appetites: he presided over a heavily laden table. We felt that, if the students' meals were as luscious as ours, they would certainly have little cause for complaint.

On the way back I was joined by the land agent Mr Johnson. We chatted about a number of things and I found him to be very knowledgeable and intelligent. Among other things, I asked him if he thought it feasible to settle some of our farmers in the district. In his opinion it would not be easy given that here, as elsewhere, the land closest to the railway had already been taken up. While it was true that there were still some blocks of Crown Land there would not be sufficient for more than eight to ten families. Enough land could be found for the whole company if they were split up into smaller groups and settled some distance from each other, a proposition that I consider inadvisable.

There was, however, a project to build a railway between Narrogin and Kellerberrin which would open up vast tracts of excellent land unsurpassed for cereal crops. A rail line between Narrogin and Williams (40 miles), running west towards a higher rainfall district, has been recently opened but, unluckily for us, almost all the land has already been allocated. When this line is extended further west towards Collie (the coal mining centre of Western Australia) it will open up more fertile land, blessed with a high rainfall of some 30 inches. However, one must wait until this project becomes a reality and that will not be for some time.

In the afternoon we left for Wagin, situated on the Great Southern Railway about fifty miles south of Narrogin. The local dignitaries who had met us at the station on our arrival were there to farewell us; we were most appreciative of their graciousness. About three o'clock we arrived at our destination.

Chapter Ten

*Wagin—Minister Piesse—His Properties—
Information on Sheep Farming—A New
Cincinnatus—Katanning—Piesse the Member of
Parliament—Vines and Fruit Trees—Wine Production*

I was settled in my room a bare five minutes when a visit from Mr Piesse, the Minister without Portfolio in the present government, was announced. He expressed his pleasure in being able to welcome our delegation and in learning that Italian farmers, whom he admired for their dedication and love of hard work, were preparing to settle in Australia. We talked together for half an hour, then with Mr Ranford I went to see the agent, Mr Wallace. It was the same old story here; nearby land had been almost all taken, one had to go quite a distance to find any that was unoccupied. It is true that the trunk-line railway under construction towards the east at Lake Dumbleyung will open up an excellent area with room for many families, but it would need swift action on the part of the local government to set aside the land by decree lest the offers to buy on the part of private individuals split up the area.

October 6. An excursion, in the now customary buggies, to Mr Piesse's home, an elegant little house situated two miles out of town.

This distinguished gentleman greeted us like old friends and insisted we partake of refreshments; then he took us on an inspection tour of his property. Chatting with him I had the opportunity of learning something of his history; he was the typical Australian 'self-made man.' About fifteen years ago he was working as an ordinary labourer making 3 shillings a day on a farm in Northam. Today he possesses an enormous fortune. Most of his land is under wheat or forage and a small amount is under vines which are most profitable here.

Along the way we met his son, a handsome young fellow who I recalled had been introduced to me the previous evening by Mr Wallace. We found him concentrating on steering a plough pulled by two pair of horses. I did not recognise him at first. Of course in Europe one is not used to seeing ministers' sons doing manual work, dressed like ordinary labourers. Our customs are quite different!

The sight of this new Cincinnatus filled us at first with wonder and later with admiration; I could not help congratulating Mr Piesse who had been able to raise his family in a love of work and of simple things. Obviously with men of this stamp the country has a brilliant future before it. It cannot fail because its foundations are solid. I do not know what some of our dandies, for whom idleness is synonymous with nobility and any kind of work is a dishonour, would say!

We crossed a magnificent high and undulating plain where cultivated land stretched as far as the eye could see. The weather was very brisk and the air sparkled; the recent rains had given the atmosphere an amazing clarity. We were at an altitude of 800 feet, 300 feet less than Narrogin, but there was no sign of the temperature moderating. Mr Piesse pointed out to me that the rainfall in the vicinity of Wagin is obviously too high for wheat to prosper as it does in the more northern and easterly districts. However, other cereal crops, especially oats and barley, grow extremely well. Raising sheep is also very successful. For this reason Mr Piesse and his brother (a resident of Katanning to whom I shall refer later), began intensive sheep breeding in Western Australia.

I have spoken about this system earlier. At risk of repeating myself I shall mention some statistics provided by my host which show the profits and costs of this enterprise which, while relevant to the Wagin district, are, save for the costs of clearing, applicable to the entire agricultural zone.

Mr Piesse's estimates related to the development of a property on virgin land: 1s for ringbarking, 20s to 30s for clearing, 20s for plough-ing, price of seeds and seeding etc. Of course it is obvious that he did not take into account such initial costs as that of the land, fencing, buildings etc., which are common to any agricultural enterprise whatever its nature. There are also a number of annual expenses, although they are relatively slight: 1) the cost of shepherds, 25s a week besides keep. But when one considers that for his 5000 sheep Mr Piesse does not usually employ more than two people it is clear that costs in this area are not very heavy; 2) cost of shearing (3d per sheep), baling and shipping the wool. The profits from the industry are, nevertheless, significant. One ewe in the Wagin district will yield more than 12s profit a year between lambing and wool. The amount says it all and there is no need for further comment.

For some years the Wagin district has witnessed a considerable increase in land prices as a result of almost daily sales. The region is perhaps the best suited of all to intensive pasturing and the squatters from the far north, seeing the fabulous profits accruing from the new system, are rushing to establish themselves in this part of the state. The gradual increase in land prices in the district and elsewhere in the agricultural zone is also, in its turn, quite an incentive to squatters. As I have already mentioned, outside the agricultural areas they are but leaseholders and, as such, cannot ever hope to profit from any future increase in the price of the land, while the opposite is the case when they become owners of a farm.

The carriages took us for another hour across paddocks, cultivated fields and bush. There were swamps here and there in which the horses sank up to their bellies. The ability and courage with which the Australian can handle a rig in areas which seemed impassable to us was considerable. He travels far and wide through the bush in his trap or buggy (two and four wheeled vehicles respectively) with the utmost disregard for the hazards. It may be agreed that the timber is sparse, but it is also true that the land is covered with fallen branches and tree trunks or thorny shrubs which sometimes reach a height of two or three metres. However, it must also be said that the country's horses are very sweet tempered and intelligent and often know the way better than their owner.

Nevertheless, there is no shortage of incidents (better still, accidents) and unfortunately the vehicle in which Ricci and Ruozi were travelling became a victim that day. The rig, travelling at full speed, failed to take a sudden bend in the track and smashed against the trunk of a tree right in the middle of the path. One of the horses was badly injured in the chest. Maddened with pain it no longer responded to the driver's commands and began to go backwards, pushing the buggy towards a nearby precipice. It was only the cool behaviour of the two Italians, who leapt out and brought the terrified horses to a standstill, that averted a tragedy. The driver was full of praise for their courage and quick thinking. He said that had English immigrants been involved (and he knows something about them, being the district guide), they would have been glassy-eyed and paralysed with fear, not daring to lift a finger. Ruozi, a mounted artilleryman of old, was experienced in such matters and could not understand why they were all praising him for doing something which was quite natural.

By the grace of God we returned safely to the hotel. There we took our leave of Mr Piesse who promised to visit us in Katanning, our next stop, where his brother, a wealthy vigneron and orchardist, lived. Before we left I had a visit from the editor of the Wagin newspaper who subjected me to a lengthy and probing interview. Like many others, he thought our project an excellent one, and without precedent. These interviews, although somewhat tiresome because I had to repeat myself *ad nauseum*, were very useful for our cause. As I have already mentioned, everybody here reads the paper so, if our nation gets a favourable press, it helps create a cordial atmosphere. I noted with great satisfaction that it was not only a liking for us that was stirring, but genuine enthusiasm. By evening we were aboard the train which took us further south. However, it was quite a short journey and we reached Katanning in two hours.

We were able to observe the surrounding countryside from the train. For many miles there were those strange granite, dome-shaped outcrops common to these districts. The land was gently undulating as always, however, gradually the undulations became definite hills. Along the railway line there was a narrow strip of cultivated land, beyond which a band of dead bush could be seen, while in the distance it appeared untouched. We would go around a bend and then suddenly everything changed; there were no more dead trees, no more bush. As far as the eye could see were fields of green wheat, meadows gilded by innumerable dandelions, and vineyards and orchards. And there, far off on the slope of a hill, was a grey spot which we guessed was the town. Gradually we could discern the larger buildings, the churches, the hotels and then the sprawl of houses. The train came to a halt abruptly and there we were on Katanning station. We were most impressed by the little town. It was extremely clean, had large streets and attractive buildings. For the first time since Northam we saw electric light.

Almost immediately we had a visit from Mr Piesse's son (the Piesse resident in Katanning, was a member of parliament and owner of the biggest vineyard in Western Australia). Seconds later Mr Cullen, the editor of the local newspaper, the *Great Southern Herald*, arrived and, like others of his ilk, put me through the customary interview.

One thing I do not have to account for is our non-existent leisure time. In the morning I had to get up before first light and, throughout the day, I was continually on the move talking with all kinds of people and being bombarded with a wide range of information. Back at the hotel there were visits to make, interviews, speeches and interpreting for the delegates. In the evening, when I was completely exhausted and longed to go to bed, I wrote up my diary until the early hours. Even so, I was exceedingly pleased with the way things were going and I felt the work would prove to be most advantageous to our country, which, while one loves it always, one loves the more when one is far away.

October 7. Today was Sunday, the usual miserable and boring Sunday common to these parts. After lunch I went for a long walk with Mr Cullen. His knowledge of all the Australian states was considerable, particularly New South Wales and its capital Sydney where he had managed a newspaper. He furnished me with a lot of vital information about agriculture and the agricultural legislation of eastern Australia. He was also of the opinion that the west offered more in terms of agricultural and pastoral undertakings. Our walk took us close to Mr Piesse's property. We admired his vast immaculately kept vineyards and orchards but waited until the morrow to examine them more closely.

We took a path through the bush on our way back. What an amazing sight! The earth was covered with countless varieties of flowers of every shape and colour. Many of them were completely unknown to me. However, I recognised some orchids; one most beautiful variety had delicate thread-like petals. I also saw some quite strange yellow and black jonquils and a kind of violet growing on a shrub whose leaves were invisible under the mass of flowers. Where the grass was greener and thicker the earth was covered with beautiful, if odd, fiery-red flowers shaped like a butterfly. Neither I nor Mr Cullen, who knows more about this than I, are aware of the name of this plant.

The animal kingdom was represented by numbers of parrots busily flying from tree to tree, filling the bush with their cries. Some were green and blue with a very long tail, other smaller ones were ash grey in colour, while others still were red and yellow, their feathers standing out in vivid contrast to the greenish-grey bush.

October 8. Just before lunch we made a quick trip around the outskirts of Katanning. Mr Ranford took the reins himself but, in his enthusiasm to point out the sights, did not notice a huge tree trunk and we nearly rolled over. We saw two farms, one of which was owned by a German.

There are quite a few in Western Australia and they have been very successful. There are more of them in South Australia, constituting a large colony in which, as in Brazil, they have been able to retain their own language and customs.

I asked the German for information about the wheat harvest in the district. He told me it was not that abundant; or, more precisely, that it was adequate at times but on occasions quite sparse because of the lack of regular rainfall. This year, for example, it had rained a lot and the earth, which was already moist by nature, had turned into a swamp and most of the crops were lost. It would be advisable to concentrate on barley and oats which do very well in the district.

Later young Piesse came with his buggies to fetch us. He apologised for his father who had had to go to Melbourne on urgent business a few days earlier. However, we would see him on our return to Perth. He took us immediately to his place, a magnificent home set on the side of a hill facing town. From up there one had a delightful view of Mr Piesse's extensive property stretching before us as far as the eye could see.

The vineyards occupied an area of 140 acres and yielded about 11,000 gallons (a gallon is equivalent to 4.54 litres); forty more acres were to be planted this year. There was a huge cellar that could hold more than 30,000 gallons, its lower floor being dug mainly out of the rock. They were working on enlarging it at the time. A German expert from the Rhine valley, who had been the head of the renowned Penfold winery in South Australia, was in charge of operations.

They had us sample a considerable amount of wine: three kinds of a red table wine (claret), one, two and three years old respectively. Even though it was rather alcoholic for a table wine, its aroma and flavour were unparalleled. As it ages the wine takes on that reddish gold colour of a ruby which the English call 'pigeon's blood.' The two varieties of chablis were excellent, particularly the dry one. The Piesse winery, after considerable effort, had been able to eliminate the sweetish flavour which lingers in local wines even after fermentation, and develop perfect dry types.

Of the bottled wines, the sweet muscat had reached true perfection. We sampled three different kinds: that known as Tokay, which was a golden amber colour, was on a par with, if not better than, any other Tokay irrespective of its provenance. Its clarity was perfect, its aroma the sweetest and its texture unsurpassed. I advised Mr Piesse to send samples to the European and North American markets where they would be very successful. In my opinion he would be able to export all the varieties of wine that he produces, with the exception of the claret which could not compete with similar Italian or French wines because of their very low price. However, he would, without doubt, be successful with the dessert wines (muscat, sherry, port etc.).

Mr Piesse and the winemaker were pleased to find someone who knew something about wine (my opinions were printed in local papers no less). Unfortunately, the ignorance which reigns in this field is indescribable. They are very well versed about beer and whisky but understand absolutely nothing about wines. Mr Piesse told me that, at some local shows, his wines had been beaten by badly made, inferior, worse still, acidic wines. He had been so disgusted at such treatment that he had declined to compete in any show for some years.

Having closely examined the cellar with its two long rows of barrels with a capacity of 1000 gallons each, as well as the gadget for picking grapes, we moved on to the orchard. A splendid sight greeted the eye; the trees were planted in even rows 27 feet from each other. It was most pleasing to see the way in which the plants were cared for. It was the end of winter and the leaves had yet to appear so we were able to view quite easily the careful pruning which gave each tree its chalice-like shape.

The trees which do best here are the apple, the almond, the peach and the apricot, followed by the pear, the plum and, to a certain extent, the cherry, which does not grow in the northern districts. Oranges and lemons hardly ever bear, even though they grow vigorously. While he expanded his orchard every year, Mr Piesse was careful not to neglect the other areas of his operation which would stand him in good stead should the price of fresh fruit drop. His trade in dried fruit, preserves, jams and similar products was already considerable and he looked to further increases in the future. By the way, I must say that the jams made in Australia, particularly in Victoria and Tasmania, are absolutely delicious. Enormous quantities are con-sumed all over the British empire because of the place jam occupies in the many meals the English partake of every day. Ours by comparison is much inferior!

Having made a close inspection of the orchard which, by reason of its size, we had to do in the buggy, we crossed into the artificial pasture. We saw some really beautiful lucerne. Mr Piesse believes lucerne, together with *Paspalum dilatatum*, to be the best forage for the type of soil in the district.

I have spoken of the great faith which exists in Western Australia about intensive pasturing. Although the results obtained thus far appear to be very encouraging, the system has yet to be perfected. But they keep on trying and trying again. The country is limitless, the range of soil and climate vast and they have only a few seasons experience. The most difficult problem always is trying to find a grass that stays fresh the longest and gives the greatest return. However, the same variety does not suit all areas nor is one variety enough. The problems, therefore, are neither simple nor few; but there is no lack of enthusiasm or perseverance here in Western Australia.

Obviously this state has not progressed, in terms of general agriculture, to the extent of other so-called new countries. But one must not forget that it was colonised quite late and has a very sparse population, particularly in terms of the rural class. When one considers that, even fifteen or twenty years ago, it was, with a few minor exceptions, nothing but endless virgin bush, the work done by a handful of men gives one hope for its future. The progress achieved owes much to the hardy pioneers of the likes of Throssell, Robustelli, Clayton, Piesse and many others, who have devoted their lives to the development of the country. Much yet remains to be done, and many clever, hardworking individuals will still find the country offers a superb outlet for their energies. Italians be advised!

It was late and we had to think about getting back as it had been decided that we should leave for Tenterden. However, the train was not due to leave for another half an hour so we took advantage of the time available to have a quick glance at the mill, situated quite close to the station, and owned by our host. Powered by steam, all the mill's machinery had been imported from England. It grinds about 100,000 sacks (110 kilos per sack) of cereals per year.

At the station I had the pleasure of greeting my fine friend Mr Cullen once more; I also saw the government engineer, Mr Bridley, who had just come back from a trip to virtually unknown areas in the far south. He told me that the land there, in terms of climate and fertility, was excellent. And so we found ourselves en route for Tenterden, which we reached at eight o'clock in the evening.

Chapter Eleven

Tenterden—Country Hotels—The Climie Farm—
More about Intensive Pasturing—Unexpected
Farmers—Mount Barker—The Sounness Orchard
and Apple Production.

We arrived in total darkness, so black that we could not see the station or any other buildings; nor, for reasons I was unable to fathom, were there any lights. Mr Ranford explained to me that we were not actually in Tenterden but at the stop before which was closest to a particular hotel, noted for its cuisine, where a delicious supper awaited us. The hotel was only half a mile away and he had telegraphed ahead to ensure they would despatch some vehicles and be ready to receive us decently. We were somewhat cheered by this news. However there was no sign of life, no buggies, not even the traditional lamp flickered in the distance. We had waited a good half hour when, thank goodness, a boy, sent to pick up some stores for the hotel, appeared.

He it was who gave us the disturbing news that the lady of the house had wired us that very morning to tell us that her husband had left the previous day for an unknown destination and had taken all the available buggies. The hotel was full and she advised us against going to their establishment. Our hearts literally fell to our boots; going to bed without supper was less than comforting but worse still when there was no bed either! The only consolation was the thought that an inefficient telegraph service was not just the province of European countries!

In the meantime we had to decide what to do; the only other hotel was seven miles away and impossible to reach. We decided to drop in at the decidedly inhospitable hostelry and, if necessary, sleep on the floor. And so off we set, each heaving his own luggage on his shoulders! As I said, it was completely dark and there were a few spills.

The half mile, as I feared, turned into a mile, then two, then three, but, finally, and with considerable difficulty, we reached our destination. Our troubles were not yet over. The owner, like the wily commandant of a fortress, had carefully prepared her defences. We got caught up in a maze of barbed wire entanglements: some were low down and caught at our legs, others, at head height, knocked off our hats and struck us in the face. Extricating ourselves from the wire was not easy and, when we did manage to overcome the barricade, we had to avoid being bitten by several savage dogs who hurled themselves against us. Thank God we finally made it to the door of the enchanted castle. We were then confronted by a strange edifice which Mr Ranford said dated from the early colonial period. It was shaped like a bungalow with a steeply pitched roof which protruded at least two metres beyond the walls to form a large verandah on all sides. The doors were so low that I had to bend in half to enter. Everything was virtually in ruins.

The attitude of the owner when she met us at the door, terrified by our arrival, was no more pleasant than the surroundings in which she lived. The news she gave us was depressing. All the rooms, with the possible exception of one, were occupied. Nor was there any supper available; she would see if there was a piece of mutton she could cook. And to think it was already ten o'clock and the freezing cold air had made us as hungry as wolves! We tried to make the best of it, chatting together in front of a roaring fire, but it is strange how the brain seizes up and conversation languishes when the stomach is empty.

Finally the long awaited mutton appeared and it was really delicious; bread, cheese, butter and plenty of beer completed our Lucullan feast. But what were we going to do about our sleeping arrangements? There was only one room free; the owner admitted that there could have been a double room available, but that was already occupied by one person who was dead drunk and could not be roused to change places. In Australia, for those of you who do not know, the drunkard enjoys universal attention and respect, something akin to that of the insane in Moslem countries. This being the case we had to make the best of it. Ricci settled himself on a sofa, the other two lying down on mattresses on the floor. Mr Ranford and I occupied two little beds in the famous empty room. But alas! I discovered too late that the good Mr Ranford had yet another quality of which I knew nothing. He snored so dreadfully that he kept me awake all night.

October 9. Up before sunrise. A surprise awaited us at breakfast. The day before they had killed a kangaroo and the owner served up steaks cut from the poor marsupial. My Italian companions were pleased because they could say that they had tasted a meat which, even in Australia, at least as far as the larger centres were concerned, was becoming rare. We found it to be very good, but with a somewhat unpleasant soft and rubbery texture.

Then, as was customary, off we went to visit nearby places. Tenterden was more a name than a place. There was no actual town centre and the houses were scattered about at a considerable distance from each other. We went firstly to a property owned by an old English colonel, whose wife had all the looks of a real English aristocrat. They were most gracious and answered all my questions. What were the clearing costs in the district? Between 30s and £2 an acre. Did they have good soil? Excellent in some places, less good in others, the soil changed its appearance and quality every few hundred metres. Sometimes it was a dark red, almost black; sometimes a greyish black and, as always, there was some white sand. What was the extent of cereal production? Wheat 10, sometimes 12 or 15 bushels to the acre; oats 25 to 30, sometimes 40. The price of oats on the local market was only slightly less than that of grain and, as a result, cultivation of the latter was somewhat neglected. Did they have any potatoes? Very few because the cold and the frost affects them badly. What were their labour costs? Between 25s and 30s a week plus board and lodging. Which crops did they consider most suited to the district? Oats, fruit and intensive pasturing.

Thanking my gracious informant we moved off once more and in half an hour were at the home of Mr Climie, a Scottish gentleman of the old school, a real country squire from the 'old country.' The family greeted us effusively and it took me only a couple of minutes to realize that they belonged to the higher echelon. The meeting turned out to be a very pleasant surprise for me, as rarely in these isolated places does one come into contact with real gentlemen.

Mr Climie was one of those intelligent farmers who run their properties along scientific lines. He owned about 2000 acres of land, most of which had been gradually cleared and cultivated. He also was of the opinion that the future of the country lay in intensive pasturing. The land in this district, in its natural state, would not support more than one sheep per five acres. If the trees are ringbarked, one sheep every one and a half acres would be possible. With a system of intensive pasturing in effect, the number of sheep increases markedly.

He prepared his land according to the system described earlier (in Chapter Six). He divided his land into two approximately equal parts.

Having ploughed one part he seeded it with about twenty different kinds of grass. These grasses are all perennial so a paddock seeded in this way lasts indefinitely and needs no further work. The second half was divided into several sections. One was planted with oats, another with Italian rye grass (*Festuca ovina*, the weed common to our fields), another with lucerne, another with rape etc. For the most part these special plantings are rotated annually so that the same seed is not sown for more than two years in the same plot. However, lucerne and Italian rye grass are left for many years. Using such a system, which no doubt is an excellent one, Mr Climie gets some magnificent results. One acre can feed ten sheep, although six would be the average number that could be fed with certainty.

To keep the sheep healthy and ensure a good reproduction rate for lambs as well as fine wool (bearing in mind that parasites are almost unknown here), he gives the sheep a pound of chaff every morning for six months of the year. Chaff, as we have seen, is made from chopping up the stalks and heads of half-green cereal crops. The costs run out at about 3 shillings per year per sheep. But the results obtained largely bear out the cost.

Mr Climie added that, as far as pastures were concerned, while he is an avid supporter of intensive pasturing, nevertheless he believes that the prudent farmer acquiring land should never limit himself to just the area which he intends to put under artificial pasture in the short term. Given the enormous amount of land available in Western Australia and its almost laughable cost, it would be better for the farmer, or the breeder, to secure a large tract in its natural state, part of which could just be ringbarked, where his flocks and his cattle could every so often be put to graze.

In conclusion, for those who come here hoping to raise animals the following points should be observed.

1. Part of the cleared and ploughed land should be put under permanent pasture.
2. Part of the cleared and ploughed land should be subdivided into sections and forage plants cultivated by the rotation system.
3. Part of the standing bush should be ringbarked.
4. The largest part should be left in its natural state.

Let us suppose that Mr X bought 5000 acres of land with a view to raising animals; 500 acres would fall into the first category; 500 into the second, sub-divided into five sections; 1000 in the third and 3000 in the fourth.

These figures can vary according to circumstance. If the farmer is well provided with capital he should increase the area under intensive pasture, the ideal being to have all his property fall into the first two categories. But, given the very low cost of land in Western Australia and the fact that most of those undertaking such enterprises are not generally overburdened with funds, I do not hesitate to maintain that the ratios referred to are, more or less, the best ones to follow.

Mr Climie also had fifty or so pedigreed milking cows (Ayrshires and Jerseys). The Jerseys in particular produce extraordinary amounts, from 10 to 20 pounds of butter a week; however, the record of 28 pounds is held in South Australia. One of Mr Climie's jerseys has won first prize in all the local shows. He estimates its value at more than £200. The Ayrshires are particularly valued for their reproductive ability. In one almost incredible case in point a single cow produced ten calves in four years. In Western Australia it is estimated that cattle numbers double every two and a half years; the same situation applies, I believe, in all other animal husbandry centres.

We were most impressed by our visit to Mr Climie's property. Mr Ranford told me that, proportionately, our host's farm produced about twice as much as other farms in the vicinity. That went to show, if proof were needed, that agriculture and pasturing are real sciences which need not only empirical knowledge but also technical understanding, study and constant practical application.

It seems that there are few in Western Australia prepared to dedicate themselves to such undertakings. As I have already had cause to note, more than a few of these so-called farmers were cobblers, blacksmiths, sailors, office workers etc., a short while ago. They think that a few days in the field, or even just having the best of intentions, is sufficient to transform them into experienced farmers. Luckily, thanks to the unsurpassable climatic and soil conditions bestowed by Mother Nature on this land, failures in the true sense of the word are rare. Also, the government does its best, through the press and through experts installed on site, to disseminate agriculturally oriented scientific information. There is no denying that there were some poor results during the early years of settlement in the colony; however, almost always, failure stemmed from fundamental ignorance.

I will cite a typical example of that ignorance and inexperience which one so often sees among those who, I suggest, are not fully cognisant of such matters. Many farmers in the district believed that cultivation of potatoes (which, by the way, is of considerable value to Western Australia, bringing from 10s to 15s per 50 kilos and yielding up to 10 tonnes per acre) was virtually impossible because frosts in the area damage the plants. When I pointed this out to Mr Climie he smiled and said to me, 'Winter in Western Australia begins in May and ends in September. Instead of planting potatoes in May or June, why not plant them somewhat later? That way the frosts are over before the leaves appear.'

We stayed at our host's home until almost evening. The time flew by quickly, conversing, as I was, on a topic which interested me greatly. Naturally we spoke about agriculture and animal husbandry, about the relevant legislation, and about how much land was still available. Mr Climie told me of the existence of enormous tracts of land in the far south, as yet virtually unknown. This seldom seen land was beautiful and extremely fertile. Perhaps the air of mystery which still surrounds the area enhances its beauty and fertility. In any event it made me want to visit the region as soon as I had the time and to have the joy of discovering treasures not to be found in the richest of gold mines. I asked our host the usual question about the availability of sufficient land for our settlement in the district. I received the customary reply that twenty miles west there was an abundance; the soil, however, was very 'patchy.'

We reluctantly took our leave of this lovely family, promising them that we would return. Mrs Climie most charmingly presented us with samples of the magnificent orchids which grew in the district. The bee orchid, whose pistils were shaped exactly like the insect, was very strange yet beautiful; the petals are joined in the centre of the flower by a fine filament which made it appear as if a bee were about to alight on the flower.

We returned to the hotel rather late, just in time to have a bite to eat and meet the local school teacher who, poor thing, had confided her troubles to us earlier in the day. What a ghastly life, alone in that little hotel, without family or relatives and far from any social intercourse.

We took the same road as the previous evening and arrived safely at the would-be station where we picked up the train which would take us to Mount Barker.

October 10. Beginning at Mount Barker is an area which is given over to fruit production, apples in particular. In Western Australia, as I have already indicated, fruit commands fabulous prices and is one product which actually makes a profit. Doubtless an increase in the number of orchards would lead to a drop in prices, but there is no immediate danger of this, nor in the long term as there will always be some margin of profit for the orchardist.

We visited the property belonging to Mr Sounness situated about three miles out of town. The orchard occupied an area of some 140 acres almost entirely given over to apples, except for ten acres that had been planted with other kinds of fruit. The profit from this undertaking, without exaggeration, was enormous. Every acre had fifty trees planted 30 feet apart. A ten year old tree bears an average of almost eight cases of fruit, each weighing about 18 pounds and selling for between 8s and 20s, even 28s a case (official wholesale prices). Even supposing a minimum price of 8s a case on only a half of the projected 400 cases, there would be a profit of £80 per acre. With older trees the yield, up to a certain point, is much greater. The cost of cultivation is minimal, bearing in mind the initial cost of clearing the land and planting the fruit trees. Mr Sounness was lucky to have a large family comprised of some eleven children, who did all the work on the property. Obviously not all farmers can hope to be similarly blessed!

But even assuming that all the work would be done by paid employees, a property as large as that of Mr Sounness would not require more than six men, the cost of whose board and wages would amount to £12 a week, in other words, £5 per acre annually. Even taking a third off the profit margin for packing costs, the construction of cases, cost of transport to the Perth and Kalgoorlie markets, commission, interest on mortgage for land, clearing, purchase of plants etc., there would still be the respectable sum of more than £50 per acre. And, it should be noted, my calculations are rather conservative.

Apricots are very profitable and produce excellent fruit. A mature tree can produce ninety cases of fruit which sell at 12s a case. However, growers mainly prefer pears and apples, especially the latter, because they keep longer.

We then inspected Mr Smith's orchard, comprised of some 120 acres, planted with apples, pears, plums, apricots and almonds. However, Mr Sounness' orchard was more impressive in terms of the manner in which the trees were pruned. Mr Smith allowed the branches to grow unchecked and the extra wood, without doubt, adversely affected the fruiting.

The last orchard we visited, comprising some 40 acres planted with different kinds of fruit, belonged to Mr Mitchell. Mr Mitchell was one of the very few proprietors who made use of the timber on his property by means of a sawmill furnished with a petrol-driven power saw. On both the Smith and Mitchell properties we saw several good artificial pastures.

Chapter Twelve

Albany—The Millars Company—Denmark—
A Ghost Town—The Impenetrable Forest—
Good Fishing—Denmark's Resources—
Millars' Intentions.

October 11. We arrived in Albany last night and I found the town to be much improved from when I had left it three years earlier. The main hotel, the Freemasons, had been completely transformed and would grace any first class town. I could find no trace of a certain little suite, the only one in the hotel, which I had occupied during my time in Albany and which I always remember as being completely devoid of any comfort. The bedroom, in particular, was virtually uninhabitable. In the middle of the room, for reasons unknown, there was a sort of wooden tower or column which, linked as it was to the bar below, carried the voices or rather the shouts of the drunken sailors into my room with extraordinary clarity. The bed was so ancient it could have come from Elizabethan times; the upholstery on the sofa and chairs was so worn that the stuffing was bursting out all over the place. Now, however, all is changed, with everything refurbished and very elegant; there are electric lights everywhere and excellent service. However, the prices, as we later learned, had gone up proportionately.

Albany and its surrounding district numbers no more than 2000 inhabitants and it is the most important town on the south coast of the state. Its magnificent and immense natural harbour is one of the best and safest in the world with few peers anywhere. A few years ago, when the international shipping lines stopped at Albany, the town was much more important. However, most liners now berth at Fremantle, and Albany, despite its ten hotels, is in a commercial decline and supports itself as a seaside resort. In fact during the summer months the weather is gorgeous and hordes of people, particularly from the goldfields, gather there. For the rest of the year the weather is dreadful, continual rain and wind. Without doubt Albany will regain its former prosperity as soon as the agricultural areas, for which it is the natural port, are under cultivation; then its traffic will be more important than ever.

Mr Ranford's itinerary had from the outset included a visit to Albany but, because time was pressing, we might have omitted it from our schedule had not an invitation from Mr Teesdale-Smith to inspect the Denmark district persuaded us to prolong our stay. I think I have already mentioned that he is the managing director of Millars, which, with a capital of some £40 million is the largest exporter of timber in Australia. The areas to which the company has felling rights are vast and extend over the whole state. The cutting of timber in any particular area lasts only a few years and then moves elsewhere, although there are always five or six sawmills working at the same time in different places. The company rarely, in fact hardly ever, owns the land, but rents it from the government for an annual fee. The Denmark land was the exception. It had been bought but now that the timber had been taken out Mr Teesdale-Smith had decided to sell it off.

Denmark is thirty-eight miles from Albany and is linked to it by means of a railway. The line has been maintained in good condition, even though no trains have run since 1902 when the populace of the hamlet moved on as the work ran out. The company put a special train at our disposal for our journey to the townsite.

We left early in the morning accompanied by Mr Tompson, the company agent in Albany, who had come to meet us at Mount Barker. He brought us the unwelcome news that Mr Teesdale-Smith had been detained at the last minute and was unable to come. However, we found Mr Tompson to be a very courteous and well-informed person, well able to substitute for his superior. We were joined by the land agent in Albany and by Mr Gerdes, the old chief clerk in my office when it was situated in Albany. Another ten or so persons, who had taken the opportunity to visit the area, were in a separate coach.

The railway follows the coast. The soil around Albany is generally sandy and barren (white sand) but, after a few miles, it gives way to a very black and extremely fertile humus. We noted many swampy tracts which at relatively little cost could be drained and transformed into rich pastures suitable for raising dairy cattle.

Halfway along the track the train stopped to enable us to visit a ten hectare potato plot. We also noted the black humus there. The fertility of the soil is reflected in the harvest which amounts to ten tons per acre. When one considers that this crop is sold for £10 or more per ton it is clear that the profits obtained are not insignificant. Potatoes, like onions, are consumed in vast quantities in Western Australia. Local production, however, is very sparse because of the prolonged summer drought and, in the case of potatoes, because of frosts (although, as I have mentioned, a delay in seeding can overcome the problem), and is not enough to satisfy, even partially, the demands of the market. In the region we were crossing, where damp soils abound because of the moderating influence of the nearby ocean, neither frosts nor dews occur, and so the terrain would be very suitable for the production of the crops in question. In summer particularly, when all the other districts are in the grip of drought, one would have a sort of monopoly here. About twenty-five miles from Albany the quality of the soil changes completely. The black humus, of which traces remain along the coast, gives way to a very deep, light, reddish, friable clay which is also very fertile.

The first of the giants of the forest now began to appear. I had never seen trees of such size. There were some which reached 300 feet in height with a circumference of thirty feet or more. Several of these giants have been ringbarked but they have not actually been vanquished, although the sharp eye of a woodsman would notice signs of internal decay. Others are still green. However, generally the virgin forest has disappeared and in its place one sees stumps and a dense, vigorously growing scrub. After having crossed two important rivers, the Hay and the Denmark, the latter which gives its name to the region, we finally arrived at our destination.

There, an unexpected and surprising sight greeted us. On the slopes of a gently rolling hill, at whose base the deep and dark waters of the Denmark River flow, was a completely abandoned hamlet, or rather a town. There were some two hundred houses lined up in five or six deserted and silent streets, where the grass grew tall and rank. The doors were tightly closed and the windows boarded up. It seemed as if the entire population had been destroyed by some plague and that the whiff of death had plunged the town, which had previously been animated and full of life, into silence. One could say it was a new Pompeii, except that here the houses are not built of brick or stone but of wood, not tumbled down into ruins but new and standing; instead of lava and lapillus, there was a reddish soil covered by a thick brush.

We walked through deserted streets bathed in splendid spring sunlight. The luxuriant vegetation which grew in the gardens covered fences and walls. Creepers climbed up to roofs and, where they found no support, sprawled across the ground. The native plants were mixed with and entwined among our European varieties; here an enormous stand of red geraniums flowered amid the shiny leaves of a gum sapling, the offspring of an ancient giant; further off a clump of pansies was smothered by Australian clover more than a metre high. Lemon trees and vine shoots were covered with bunches of blue kennedya and the yellow of wild acacia. It is the sight of such luxuriant growth which most strikes visitors after their initial sense of amazement and, I would add, of dismay, evoked by the prospect of the abandoned town.

We came to the workshops, vast buildings in which more than 500 employees had worked. Some of the machinery was in place and mounds of sawdust were heaped up to the roofs. It seemed as if, any moment, we would hear the shriek of the siren and the deep throb of the steam saw. Farther off there was another big building, once used as a library, and several churches. Here and there were shops and eating places and, naturally, numerous bars. There was even a club. Mr Tompson, the only caretaker assigned by the company to look after the ghost town, showed me about. He confessed to me that he felt badly about such desolate sights and was scarcely able to accompany me around the deserted townsite, for fear it would remind him of the times when the place bustled with life and work.

Mr Tompson pointed out to me that all the buildings, particularly the houses, were in an excellent state of preservation and could be restored to first class order with little work or financial outlay. In the event that any of our families acquired land in the area it would be useful to have accommodation already available.

We then went to inspect the land together. Mr Tompson had an expert bushman accompany us because the bush is so dense it is easy to lose oneself. We walked along a fairly wide path still covered with sleepers. Apart from the railway which connected Denmark and Albany, the company had built forty-five miles of tramways to transport the logs. The rails had been removed but the way was still there and could be very useful in the event that the district was settled.

Even though the giants of the forest had been almost entirely cut down, the return of the bush, as I have already noted, had been vigorous and incredibly rapid. The path was covered by the growth of branches and creepers which formed a solid and impenetrable mass of vegetation which made it almost impossible to proceed. One had to walk bent over, sometimes literally slithering on the ground, in order to keep going. The path ascended all the while and in about an hour and a half we had got to the top of the chain of hills which flanked the sea.

144

The mild and equable climate of Denmark owes much to this higher elevation which is so much better than that of Albany and its surrounds. Down there, unhindered, the biting south wind hurls itself continually against the benighted town, whereas in Denmark a delightful calm reigns. The rains, although more abundant here (Albany has 34 inches, Denmark 40 inches), fall at regular intervals, often interspersed with splendid, or as they say in Australia, glorious days.

On the summit the vegetation was somewhat thinner, although the soil was still excellent. We dug some holes and saw that the layer of loam was very deep. This was quite strange because in every hilly situation, not only in Western Australia, but elsewhere in the world, rocky outcrops appear on the slopes.

We had now left the old tramway and had taken a steep rocky track. Mr Tompson assured me that this path had been used to transport logs weighing up to 20 tons and 80 feet in length. Plainly the undertaking had not been one of the easiest. In fact we saw several trees left by the way; some were lying across the path and blocked our way. It proved a great opportunity for Ruozi to prove his agility and gymnastic prowess.

We returned to town about two o'clock, dead tired and starving. Luckily, an excellent lunch, to which we did full justice, awaited us. At first no one felt like talking; however, the conversation, after a few roast chickens, bottles of beer and innumerable whisky and sodas, brightened up considerably. Somewhat rested, we began walking once more, flanking the river, which, about a mile or so away, flowed into a big inlet of the sea, rather like a lake which is joined to the ocean by a narrow canal. What rich soil and vegetation was evident everywhere! What a riot of life and colour! Little by little our trek became easier and finally we came out onto a narrow plain from which there was a wonderful view of a vast lake and distant hills which enclosed it. We sat down on the ground and contemplated the landscape.

Before us was the calm expanse of the sea, to our left was the river with its black waters winding lazily between banks enamelled, it seemed, with many varieties of flowers. A lone, gently sloping hill clothed with gigantic trees was close by. What a wonderful spot for a country home!

There was life and movement everywhere. Little kangaroos bounded at high speed through the bush; innumerable parrots screamed and chattered in the branches of the trees; in the distance, flocks of wild ducks flew slowly over the waters of the lake. We literally could not get enough of the place and we plotted ways to come back and see it again and, if possible, take up residence. Unfortunately, our dreams will be difficult to realize.

The only inhabitant of the district, besides the caretaker of the ghost town, was Tom, an old fisherman whose shack was built near the river. He came to meet us and bid us welcome. He would be pleased if some hundred of our immigrants settled in the district. The good fellow had been a sailor or, as he said, had obeyed a master, for some fifteen years. For two years he had known no master but himself and was content with his solitude because at last he was completely free. Now he is employed fishing (this job, it seems, does not compromise his independence) on behalf of Mr Gerdes, our travelling companion, who sends the catch, packed in ice, to the goldfields. The lake is extraordinarily rich in fish (snapper, mullet, whiting) as is the river, which for many months of the year is salty for up to two or three miles from its mouth. Tom told me, and his assertion was corroborated by Mr Gerdes, that in just a few hours working on his own, he had been able to net more than four tons of fish. What a thrill for a newcomer and what a profit to be made for anyone willing to undertake large scale involvement in the industry.

Our ex-sailor wanted us to make our way back via the river and offered us the use of a large yacht. However, there was not a breath of wind and he had to man the oars in order to move the boat forward. Ricci, an old sergeant in the bridge building brigade, came to his assistance, although his prowess left something to be desired. In half an hour we reached a jetty beneath the railway bridge. The train was waiting and ready to leave. Exhausted once more, we hurled ourselves into the carriage and, by eight o'clock, we were on our way back to Albany. Poor Mr Ranford, who went to bed straight away, told me he had never worked so hard in his life. I also could hardly stand on my feet, but I was happy with our excursion which had allowed me to visit one of the most fertile areas in Australia where Italian immigrants could settle and prosper.

In Denmark, as Mr Tompson told me, 100 to 120 acres would be sufficient for our peasant farmers. They could not comfortably handle any more owing to the quite literally intensive nature of cultivation. Vegetables (cabbages, onions, potatoes) and fruit (apples, pears, plums, cherries, apricots and grapes) would probably be the most successful crops. The district would also be ideal for cultivated pasture to serve the needs of dairy cattle and pigs. Raising sheep, apart from providing meat for the settlers, is not advisable because in this district they suffer from a disease of the hooves, known as 'rotten sock,' caused by the excessive humidity in the soil.

Mr Tompson assured me that land cultivated for fruit and vegetables would earn a profit of between £50 and £100 per acre and often more; less if turned into pasture but, all in all, the farmer would have a magnificent return, unimaginable in other countries. The only difficulty is the removal of the bush. On the company's land, as I have already noted, the largest trees have already been cut and removed, eliminating much of the problem. Huge stumps remain but these can be blasted out with dynamite. The newly grown bush can be easily removed by burning at the end of summer. Clearing on the company's land would probably cost between £8 and £10 an acre; elsewhere, where the tall trees are still growing, it could cost up to £20.

Because of the nature of their lumber and the thickness of their trunks, trees which cannot be burnt down are uprooted by a special method. Usually, cables are attached to the first fork in the branches which are then pulled by several teams of horses or oxen. Recently a new gadget called a tree-puller, which needs less animal power, has been tried and seems to have been effective. In this district, however, the bush is rarely completely destroyed. The biggest trees, after they dry up, are left standing; like this, they make no shade nor do they absorb the moisture from the soil and therefore do not impede the harvest or the pastures around them.

I have already noted elsewhere that for some time the government of Western Australia has had a policy of buying back the land from private owners who have not cultivated it and then selling it by tender to settlers. Negotiations between the government and Millars were also under way in the Denmark area, the latter asking £100,000 initially for the land and railway but then dropping the price to £50,000. The government did not want to go to more than £40,000 and negotiations lapsed.

Our coming to Australia seemed to Mr Teesdale-Smith a good time to reopen the matter. Certainly he did not exclude the idea that, whether directly or indirectly, he might sell the land to our settlers; but more than likely he saw our visit as a chance to spark further negotiations with the government.

In fact it is well known that the government wants to have all immigration matters under its direct control. Thus our visit, and the good impression which doubtless we have made, may, apart from the possibility of an agreement between the Italian government and

Millars, see the emergence of an entrepreneur or firm who might buy the enterprise, an eventuality not relished by the Western Australian government which had tried strenuously to buy it itself. The purchase of the Denmark parcel of land, which is relatively small, indeed tiny compared to that held by the Midland Company, would be favourable to the government. Moreover, Millars, to avoid any delay in realising the sale (our immigrants would have to pay by instalment over a long period) had to give preference to the government.

However, as I said, the idea of dealing with us was not totally rejected by Millars because, in the final analysis, like the Midland Company, it was in their best interests to sell off some of their land to hardworking families. In any event, if the negotiations were to be put on the table, we would have to obtain from Millars the same conditions which the Australian government was prepared to offer. The only point on which we might be persuaded to be lenient would be with respect to the price of the land, 20 to 30 shillings per acre instead of 10 shillings. The debt shouldered by the settler would be greater only on paper because in the Denmark area the amount of land needed would be considerably less than in other parts.

Certainly it would be difficult to find land as fertile and well-situated elsewhere. There is also the enormous advantage of having a railway right in the heart of the district, or rather the town, whose population would most likely become Italian in origin. On the lake near the township wharves could be built for the loading and unloading of goods. The lake itself, teeming with fish, would be a source of considerable income for the settlers. One hundred and twenty houses are already habitable, some of which could easily be taken apart and transported to individual holdings.

However, despite the favourable conditions, I would not advise sending all the families to Denmark. Some ought to go to the central districts and, perhaps, a small group to northern areas. In this way several small nuclei of Italians would be scattered about, which is preferable to having large concentrations in one area. But I shall discuss this matter later.

In Albany we were at the southernmost point of the state; from east to west, along the coast, there are no railways. Unfortunately, our time being limited, there was no alternative but to turn back the way we came. We travelled again on the Great Southern Railway to Katanning where we cut across the country to Bridgetown, the southern terminus of the other railway which runs parallel to the west coast of the state.

Chapter Thirteen

Tambellup—The Polletti Farm—A Socialist Senator—
Travelling in the Bush—An Australian Hyde Park—
The Effect of Cultivation on the Climate—Kojonup—
'Poison Land'—A Farming Mayor—The Stephens'
Farm—Paddocks and Blackboys—Land for Italians—
A Zoological Garden—The Blackwood—
Lost in the Forest?—Bridgetown.

October 12. The first stage of our return journey was to Tambellup which is situated at the northern-most point of the Albany district. We stopped there to visit the farm of an Italian, a certain Polletti, who lives in the area. Beforehand we went to restore ourselves at the local hotel, which was an awful weatherboard building, and were served a most revolting meal which we found hard to swallow. The now customary buggy ride helped digest it as we bumped over the stony road. We still had some time to spare and decided that we would visit the farm of the local guide. The soil, the usual reddish clay, did not seem the best to me, particularly because of the brick-like texture it develops in the sun. The wheat was not bad but the pastures were of very poor quality.

Our fellow countryman's property presented a different picture; the soil was grey, very soft and of excellent quality although a bit sandy in parts. Fruit trees grew very well there; even vines were prolific producers. We tried the wine which resembled a burgundy somewhat, with a certain pleasant tang.

Large numbers of sheep are raised in the Tambellup district. The richness of the pasture can be seen in the fact that, according to Polletti, 1000 acres of ringbarked land runs 1000 sheep. And he went on to state that each sheep brings in between 15s and 20s a year. These sums seemed somewhat exaggerated to me. The glimpse of the paddocks on our guide's farm made me somewhat sceptical about such claims.

The average rainfall is $16\frac{1}{2}$ inches. Wheat, which is affected by the height above sea-level and the sketchy rainfall, yields between 10 and

12 bushels per acre. I was told that thirty-three miles to the east at Broome Hill, the next station on the railway line to Perth, there was excellent soil for cereal crops and pasture. These areas will be served by the projected Broome Hill–Ravensthorpe railway. The entire population of Tambellup amounts to no more than one hundred and fifty.

October 13. We left Tambellup at ten in the morning. We shall not easily forget this singularly unattractive hamlet, scorched by the sun, nor its hotel which, although comfortable enough, was filled with chronic drunkards who made our stay very unpleasant. A two hour train ride from Tambellup brought us to Katanning from where we would cut across country to Bridgetown.

On the way I made the acquaintance of Mr Pearce, one of the six senators representing Western Australia in the federal parliament. Still quite young, he is reputed to be one of the most able politicians in the state. He is very intelligent and, although he is a member of the Labour Party, which like our Socialist Party is intransigent in its ideology, he holds moderate views. Perhaps it is because he is an intelligent man that he is also a moderate one. While he was in Melbourne he had heard about our mission and the colonization project but only in vague terms. He now asked me for a good deal of information and detail to which he listened with much interest.

I explained to him in clear terms the origins and scope of the project, based as it is on the wish to avoid any and every cause for dissent between local workers and Italians. I told him there was no intention whatsoever to send in wage earners as immigrants. The settlers (and this is the wish of both governments) must, from the moment they disembark, be land owners and thus assure Australians that they present no competition on the labour market. Our plan will bring nothing but benefit to Australia, which will gain a strong, healthy and hardworking group of people who are much needed to develop the resources of the land and form the basis of a defence against future outside threats. I explained that our government is in favour of the scheme not in the wish to exert any undue interference in the country, but to create and stimulate links with the southern continent.

This brings us to another subject of current concern. All the country's newspapers have reported that Queensland had gained the consent of the Italian government to import several thousand workers to work on sugar plantations. Previously, the planters had employed Kanakas, blacks from the Pacific Islands, but they were deported when federal legislation prohibited so-called 'coloured' labour. Steps were taken to replace them with German workers but, it is understood, nothing eventuated. Now Italians were being considered and no one here doubted that the Italian government would give its consent.

Without hesitation I told my travelling companion that he could be quite certain that the Italian government would never approve enlisting workers in this way. In fact, it is unacceptable that Italians take the place of the deported Kanakas only to find themselves treated on the same level as blacks or Chinese. I added that I was not unaware of the hostile and offensive comments contained in this newspaper report which had been widely circulated and which had heaped discredit upon Italians who unfortunately, for whatever the reason, were already held in contempt.

Australia has some of the largest tracts of unoccupied land. It is thus in a position to offer our immigrants ownership of land and to involve them in the progress and development of the country. Why therefore create a group of wage earners in competition with local workers when one can have a population of small independent farmers? Why run the risk of repeating the sad story of the Brazilian fazendas or the Louisiana plantations, the memory of which makes the heart of every Italian tremble with shame?[1] It is absolutely essential that Italians go to Australia with the dignity of free and independent citizens. The ownership of land, the basic requirement for our agricultural immigrants, as far as I am concerned, must be assured by those we deal with, whether from the private or government sector. The planned covenant between the Italian and the Western Australian governments is based precisely on this principle, and such a principle should be adhered to by Queensland should it wish to avail itself of our valuable workforce.

We spoke at length about a number of issues relative to Australia and particularly about those concerning social problems. I respected my fellow traveller not only for the depth of his intelligence but also for his uncommonly broad point of view. He told me that, as he was now fully apprised of the nature of our project, should any prejudice emerge to hinder our immigration, he would do no less than to declare his full support and he assured me that the Labour Party would also share his opinion.

I must say, with respect to this conversation, that, never having previously met Mr Pearce, I believed right up to the end that I was

---

1 Translators' note: Zunini was referring to unsuccessful attempts to settle Italian farmers in the southern United States after the Civil War. See R. Brandfon, 'The End of Immigration to the Cottonfields', *Mississippi Valley Historical Review*, 50, 1964, pp. 596–610.

merely talking with an influential friendly Labourite, but not so. When he gave me his card and I read the name of a very well-known politician I experienced a sense of amazement mixed with satisfaction. I hoped that the favourable impression gained by the worthy gentleman might have its repercussions on the Labour Party all over Australia.

Before leaving, Mr Pearce kindly invited me to go to Melbourne where he would introduce me to Mr Watson, once Prime Minister of Australia and now leader of the Australian Labour Party. He was sure such a visit would be fruitful and increase popular support for our project.

We stopped at Katanning only long enough to have lunch. We found the vehicles which would convey us across country already waiting. Thus we were able to leave without delay. We must give the indefatigable Mr Ranford the praise he deserves for the care and attention he has taken in organizing the details of the expedition. Every day he has sent at least half a dozen telegrams to places along the route we will be following the next day in order to give the necessary instructions. The only time his arrangements let him down was the disastrous evening when we arrived in Tenterden, which upset him considerably.

We set off about midday in tropical heat. The idea of leaving the monotonous railway and cutting across country delighted everybody. We felt as if we, too, had become explorers. But, really, journeying through the Australian bush in this section is not at all heroic because the track between Katanning and Bridgetown, which runs for 110 miles, was quite trafficable. For about ten miles the road crossed land which appeared to be very fertile and, almost everywhere, we saw tracts that had been cleared and cultivated.

Further on a magnificent area, untouched by the hand of man, came into view. The trees, of medium size, were set some distance from one another and the earth was covered by a thick green carpet. The traveller could believe he had been transported to Hyde Park in London, but this Hyde Park continues for tens of miles and its inhabitants are not European. Flocks of brilliant emerald green parrots rose up often in our path, their strident cries shattering the silence of the bush. Here and there, we saw kangaroos scampering like shadows, and Mr Ranford assured me that, before long, we would see some brumbies. The countryside was really splendid and we were thoroughly aroused by it.

WESTERN AUSTRALIA AS IT IS TODAY, 1906

Turning off the established track we came to a farm belonging to several fellow countrymen—Tiraboschi, Ferrari and the Abbadini brothers—who, having previously worked as miners, had found the change to agriculture worth while. They had begun with a few pounds capital and were now the owners of a farm worth at least £5000. The Agricultural Bank had been a great help to them because, without its loans, they would have had trouble getting things started. They grow mainly wheat (12 to 14 bushels to the acre) but they also raise a good number of sheep.

Our fine settler friends were something of an exception in their class in Australia. None was married and their house looked like a monastery. It was easy to see that the domestic arrangements lacked the comforting touch of a woman. We asked Abbadini to accompany us as far as Kojonup. The next day being Sunday he needed little persuasion.

The countryside through which we travelled continued to impress. I was particularly taken with the luxuriance of the extremely green grass, even though there was no sign of the trees being ringbarked. I attributed it to the heavy dews (the rainfall is moderate, about 18 inches) and the fact that the trees were sparse.

With respect to the rainfall, Abbadini told me that, on average in the vicinity of his property, prior to clearing and cultivating, it was 18 inches but now it has risen to 22 inches. I do not know if there is any connection between the two facts. In South Australia the opposite would be found to be true. Some areas that have been cultivated have been abandoned because the rainfall became insufficient, although in that area other, more complex, meteorological factors perhaps came into play.

However, in the majority of cases, there is little doubt that, when man cultivates dry and uninhabited areas, the rainfall is stimulated. Near Kalgoorlie, the centre of mineral activity in Western Australia, where the rainfall is scant despite the existence of scrubby trees, there has been an increase in the rainfall after the construction of an aqueduct and the piping of water to gardens. The same phenomenon has been observed in Antofagasta and Iquique and other points along the Chilean coast, as well as in French possessions in the Sahara. Traces of cultivation found in the mountains along the Peruvian and Chilean coasts where the aridity is astounding (it is estimated in some of these areas it has only rained once in the last thirty or forty years) appear to confirm what I have said. All the slopes appear to have been terraced, held in place by dry walls like those in our Ligurian mountains. For agriculture to flourish there needs to be an abundant rainfall, as water cannot be taken to the mountains which, in many cases, are very high. However, when the Spanish invaders ravaged the populace and condemned the few survivors to abandon the land and work in the mines, the atmospheric conditions were radically changed and total drought reigned over the land.

The track ran aimlessly across a gently rolling section. The undulations gradually became more defined and took on the look of hills covered with dense bush interspersed here and there with open glades. Finally we reached Kojonup, a pleasant little hamlet comprised of about thirty houses, spread picturesquely on the slopes of a steep hill. It had a charming aspect and reminded me in some ways of little villages in the high Appenines. In a similar manner, the houses here are mostly built of wood set in green fields and shaded by majestic trees. The air also is fresh and sparkling. Kojonup (altitude 1800 feet) is one of the earliest settled districts of the state. It is situated at the halfway point on the old road between Albany and Perth. A strong garrison was posted here to protect the town from incursions by the natives who, in the early days of settlement, were very numerous and fierce. Today, however, blacks have disappeared entirely from the surrounding areas and only rarely does one come across a poor, thin and sickly devil who no longer excites fear but rather pity. A railway, destined to breathe life into the region, is being constructed between Katanning and Kojonup. It will then continue to Bridgetown and thus will connect the southern sections of the state's main railways which are already linked in the north.

The land around Kojonup was excellent; the pasture, in particular, was good. The only problem was 'poison weed' which infects extensive areas further to the west. These areas were part of the so-called 'poison land' which the government was selling at the extremely low price of 9d an acre, payable over thirty years. The only condition was to eradicate the weed. As a result some enormous properties, such as that owned by Mr Piesse, which totalled more than 20,000 acres, were developed. Now, however, since it has became apparent that the weed can be easily eradicated, the sale of poison land at the forementioned prices has been suspended. The infested areas are actually sold at the same price and under the same conditions as any other Crown Land.

There are a number of different types of poison plants, the most common being York Road, box and heart leaf. Generally, the different species are not found in the same place, each occupying its own

Furthest point of the Katanning–Kojonup railway, near Kojonup
Battye Library, 20677P

distinct area. Thus, it is unlikely that all of any tract of land will be infested; clumps of poison weed, for the most part, are grouped in particular spots, especially on tops of ridges where there are iron nodules in the rock. The plants reach a maximum height of slightly more than one metre. The average farmer can recognise the weed and only a little experience is needed to identify it at first glance. The most common is the York Road, which has little pointy leaves similar to the olive and is bluish-green with yellowish veining.

The following system is used to clear the land of poison weed: one digs the soil around the roots to a depth of ten centimetres, then the plant is ripped out and either burnt or buried. Sometimes the roots shoot out anew and the land must be gone over again for the following three years to be on the safe side. On large tracts of land, even with a large workforce, it would be impossible to eradicate the weed completely all at once because some plants would be overlooked. So the land is divided into small lots of 100 to 200 acres and each is then worked over several times in every direction by lines of men.

The poisonous plants are not usually a danger because their leaves are very rough and farm animals, particularly sheep, are not attracted to them. The danger occurs when, after a bush fire, which occurs

Mr Clarke's farm near Kojonup
Battye Library, 20675P

Water reservoir for stock on Mr Clarke's farm near Kojonup
Battye Library, 20676P

frequently here, new shoots appear and are avidly devoured by both sheep and cattle. If sheep eat a fatal amount of the weed, they die without warning; if they have ingested only a little, they can be saved if allowed to rest and stopped from drinking. Cows run less risk and horses less still because they are accustomed to this food and quickly learn to avoid it. Brumbies or wild horses which live in the bush without any supervision never die of poisoning. Nor do any of the other wild herbivores such as kangaroos, rabbits etc. The cost of ridding the land of poisonous plants completely could be about three shillings per acre.

October 14. We went to visit Mr Clarke, once the mayor of Fremantle, now settled here in Kojonup and dedicating himself entirely to the country. He was particularly interested in pasturage. We had a long conversation on the matter. He showed me a book which he considers to be a classic and esteems greatly: *The Principles and Practice of the Australian Woolclasser*, by George Jeffrey, Adelaide. It ought to be the bible of the squatter. For actual farming he has *Farmer and Fruit Grower Guide*, by John Kidd of Sydney.

Thus we got around to talking about oenology. Mr Clarke had read an article in the *West Australian* giving an account of my visit to Mr Piesse's wine cellars in Katanning; my opinion was cited as that of an expert. Therefore, it was not surprising that my host, who intended to turn part of his property into vineyard, sought my opinion on the matter. I confessed to him that, frankly, my knowledge was not extensive. However I was of the opinion that, while almost all the agricultural regions of Western Australia were very well suited to the production of sweet and heavily fortified wines, areas suited to light table wines were few (for example, some centres in the south-west corner of the state); but to be on the safe side, the land selected should be on the slopes of the Stirling Ranges, which rise to a considerable height, and enjoy a very cool climate. There, the relative closeness of the sea saves the vines from fluctuations in temperature and night frosts which are fatal when the vines begin to shoot. In all instances it would be preferable to be on the northern slope, protected from the winds of the southern sea. The quality of the soil is excellent, composed of iron-stone mixed in some parts with an extremely light humus. With respect to the Kojonup district, I do not believe that, contrary to his opinion, the area is suitable for the production of table wine. Because of the very hot summer weather and the particular quality of the soil, it would produce the usual overly alcoholic clarets.

We would have chatted for goodness knows how long had not Mr Ranford reminded us that our dinner was getting cold at the hotel and, in such matters, the dictates of the good Mr Ranford are not to be taken lightly.

It was decided to go on to Bridgetown that same day, stopping at a farm about twenty miles out of Kojonup. However, the homestead was very small, two rooms, and the idea of us all sleeping in the one room was not very pleasant. Thus, we decided to send Ricci, the land agent and his assistant (who had offered to accompany us) on with the weaker horses which would find it difficult to cover eighty miles in a day. We would follow them the day after.

October 15. At four o'clock in the morning Mr Ranford knocked on my door. The horses had been waiting for half an hour and, after the indispensable refreshment, we set off. It is strange the ability some individuals have to eat at any hour of the day or night. Just to look at food at that hour of the morning revolts me. But Mr Ranford had a huge meal and Ruozi and Bottoni did their best to do likewise.

As I have already said the day's journey entailed covering about eighty miles. There were no towns or hotels along the way, only the occasional farm. I looked at the poor horses who were unaware of the work ahead of them. Ruozi, who had a deal of experience with horses, said it would be very difficult for them to last the distance. In this event we would camp in the bush; better in the open than cramped in a narrow little room.

The countryside changed as soon as we left Kojonup. There were no more tall hills, only large undulations. Even the quality of the soil changed and with it the vegetation. There were large tracts of iron-stone fragmented with patches of sand. The green carpet disappeared and under the trees spiky shrubs with yellow flowers, like broom, grew, as well as a large amount of York Road. The bush was not very dense and Mr Ranford told me that the cost of clearing would not be more than 25s to 30s per acre. The land we were passing through did not appear to be suitable either for pasture, cereals or root crops (tuberous plants) but only for vines and fruit. However, the cost of cultivation would be very high.

Like oases in the desert we came across large tracts of fertile soil; for example, twenty miles from Kojonup, where Mr Stephens has his farm, there was magnificent brown soil mixed with black loam. On the property we found our three friends who had preceded us the previous evening, rushing about with spades in every direction intent on sampling the soil.

Mr Stephens had been settled here for just two months. He was completely alone and somewhat elderly; we found it hard to understand how he bore the loneliness, without family or anyone else to help him. As well, while in South Africa, he had lost all the money he had saved to set himself up in an agricultural enterprise in Australia. His holding was thus in what one might like to call a virgin state.

Even I got hold of a spade to see the quality of the soil for myself. There was almost two feet of black humus everywhere or else red loam with clay underneath. A little garden plot near the house, the only bit of land cultivated, had a number of vegetables growing luxuriantly and testifying to the fertility of the soil.

Mr Stephens extended us every courtesy and placed his house and meagre provisions at our disposal. Before we left he wanted to take a photograph of us. Unfortunately the background was not very picturesque, comprising some trees that had been knocked down and some dry and bare survivors of ringbarking.

After an hour's rest we set off again. For a little while the land remained uneven with long-thorned shrubs. Then we came to the grassy flats in the valley of the Balgarrup, the main tributary of the Blackwood River. The trees were fewer there and the pasture was magnificent. Once again the soil was rocky with an iron-stone base and then, finally, there appeared before us the most splendid and beautiful land which I had ever seen in Western Australia.

There were wide green plains on which grew, at some distance from one another, many huge 'blackboys,' which are very strange tree-like shrubs, with a spongy, scaly trunk and decorated on the top with a tuft of wire-like leaves, somewhat resembling our aquatic reeds. When the blackboy is tall and vigorous and, particularly when the trunk is divided into three or four branches, it is without doubt a sign of the very fertile nature of the soil. Isolated hills, their steep sides covered in a mantle of emerald green, formed a backdrop. Thick clumps of enormous trees grew on the summit. The sight was at once strange and unforgettable.

The region in which we found ourselves was the valley of the Dinninup (the other branch of the Blackwood) which flows in a north-westerly direction parallel to the Balgarrup. Mr Ranford told me that, above these two streams, there were hundreds of thousands of acres of land of more or less the same quality as that through which we were then passing. It was here in this area that Mr Ranford suggested at least some of our settlers should be placed. The soil was very fertile, the bush extremely light, the rainfall was plentiful without being excessive (25 inches), which would favour any kind of crop except sheep farming. It was true that there were some poison plants dangerous to cattle growing in the area; but, as I have explained earlier, this problem is easily overcome.

I was of the same opinion as Mr Ranford, as were the delegates, who liked this area very much. Of course it would be necessary to undertake a minute examination of the location where the settlement might be established. This will be done in time, for now our task was limited to a survey of all prospective districts in the state.

Selecting land for a largish settlement which ideally will remain fairly close knit is not an easy undertaking in Western Australia. Most problems arise from the nature of the soil, which is patchy every-where. In a few square miles, one can locate four or five completely different types: almost snow-white sand; black sand mixed with humus; red, yellowy and grey loam; iron-stone etc. Sand appears almost everywhere; oases of fertile soil, however, are found close by. There are frequent outcrops of iron conglomerates or quartz. When such outcrops take the form of rather steep ridges one finds the humus to be very fertile along the little valleys created by the formation.

Given the nature of the soil it would be impossible to select fifty or one hundred thousand acres and then divide it up ideally into a number of uniform allotments. Instead it would be necessary, having decided upon the general area, to go on site and proceed to develop single lots, assigning to each a certain amount of first, second and third-grade land. It follows that such lots would be situated in diverse areas and would retain their irregular shape according to the diversity of the soil.

Another difficulty is finding the most suitable district. One can appreciate that a certain area, while having many advantages, also has some disadvantages. Thus, where wheat, which requires a moderate rainfall, does well, forage and vegetable crops are less successful; where pastures are luxuriant, the yield from cereals is poor. In some regions, because of the perfect climatic conditions, poisonous plants grow; where they do not appear, one encounters enormous trees which cost a great deal to get rid of. However, it appears that such matters are not confined exclusively to Western Australia but recur to a greater or lesser degree in all countries with large expanses. Of course this wide range of types is very marked here; however, the country has many advantages which far outweigh the few problems one encounters.

Beyond the district just described the road left the plain and ran along the hills. The soil now became stony; we were once again in iron-stone country. The countryside reminded me of the Darling Range and Mount Barker areas. The sight of four or five gigantic kangaroos bounding away through a valley astounded my men; they were the first of such stature they had seen. These giants took off at high speed and quickly disappeared from view.

It is strange, even grotesque, the way in which these animals move. They use only their hind legs and their tail which they deploy as a kind of lever. There is no relationship between their highly developed and muscular hind legs and their fore legs, which are short and slender and which have razor-sharp nails that are a useful weapon against their enemies (which are confined to men and dogs). The kangaroo will not strike first but, if attacked, will defend itself with fury. The very tall ones, 'old men,' sometimes as tall as a young bull, are extremely dangerous. If they get their backs up against a tree and are in a sitting position on their hind legs, then beware any man or dog who gets near them; they are immediately grabbed and ripped open by a razor-like talon. The tail of some very developed individuals can reach two metres in length and sometimes is more than ten centimetres in diameter. It makes a delicious meal.

We also noticed a herd of wild horses, which paused to look at us for a moment, then galloped off at a great pace. Today was really our lucky day; as we went through a clearing, just in front of us there appeared two huge emus, or Australian ostriches, with greyish-yellow feathers. They are slightly shorter than their African counterparts; their meat is rather good, especially the drumsticks, although it has a somewhat rancid flavour. Unfortunately, they have become somewhat rare in this district. Mr Ranford told me that, here in the south, years go by without seeing one.

Bottoni and Ruozi were immediately entranced by this zoological display. Only poor Ricci, who was following behind in another vehicle, saw nothing because the frightened animals fled from us. He found it hard to believe what we told him and thought we were making fun of him.

We continued to cross the hilly area. Here the soil ought to have been good for fruit and vines but the cost of clearing would not be less than £3 per acre. The horses were beginning to show some signs of tiredness although they had borne up splendidly. These Australian horses are a race apart! They have proved themselves with the English army in India and in South Africa during the Boer War.

The track was descending once more. We had crossed a range of hills which ran between the Dinninup and Blackwood rivers. Another huge valley came into view; it was that of the Blackwood, one of the most important rivers in the southern section of Western Australia, and at this point wide and deep and crossed by a wooden bridge. It was already four o'clock in the afternoon and the pangs of hunger were biting so we decided to make camp.

Anyone who travels in the Australian bush must learn to do everything with their own two hands and look after themselves. It is a strict rule that everyone on an expedition must pitch in and help each other. Anyone who remains with their arms folded is looked upon poorly and loses the respect of his companions. Ruozi groomed the horses and I took them to water, then gathered dry branches to start a fire. Bottoni puffed and blew like a bellows, his eyes soon streaming from the smoke. They others busied themselves cooking and, in one way or another, everyone did something. The table was soon ready; table by any other name, for it consisted of a simple cloth spread on the ground on which we arranged the provisions. The more delicate seated themselves on cushions taken out of the vehicles while others stretched on the grass. It could have been a repast of the ancient Romans, only the couches were less soft!

We were on the land of a Mr Lee Steere, whose father was the Speaker, that is, the president of the Legislative Council or, better, the Senate. His holding is extensive; the main road runs across it for at least ten miles. We went to call and found him installed in the shearing shed in the midst of the shearers who had just started work. The famous Australian hospitality was lacking and he seemed irritated by our visit and barely replied to the questions I asked him. We pleased him by leaving immediately.

Mr Ranford told me that Mr Lee Steere owned 10,000 sheep; he had had many more but had sold a good number at a high profit. His property was ideal for pasture and any other kind of agriculture. It had the great advantage of being situated only twenty miles from Bridgetown which was the terminus of the coastal railway.

The countryside was beautiful for miles. In some place the grass was perfect, a truly green carpet and the blackboys gave the impression of palms. It was like being in Nice or San Remo.

The horses were very frisky after their rest, despite the sixty miles they had travelled; their pace was quick and lively and we hoped that, in spite of Ruozi's gloomy prediction, we would reach our destination safely. Along the track we met up with two young English immigrants who had been in Australia only seven months. They were very happy with their new country and full of hopes for the future.

The Blackwood River marks the boundary between the less dense and most dense bush which extends west from the river towards the coast. What immense trees! They are mainly jarrahs and red gums, little different in size from those in Denmark. The road had become a narrow track winding through dense forest. There were no shrubs or grass but a layer of leaves at the feet of the giant columns.

The sun had already set and dusk was falling beneath the thick mantle of foliage. The silence was absolute and a strange feeling of fear assailed me. We were frightened of losing our way and wandering in the dense and unknown bush. But Mr Ranford was a confident and expert guide who knew the country like the back of his hand. In fact, after a steep descent through dense undergrowth, the roofs of Bridgetown appeared in the valley below. It was our hoped-for destination and we breathed a sigh of relief.

The small township was excellently situated. Wedged between very high and steep hills it had the look of an alpine village. The surrounding bush had been largely cleared and had been replaced by pasture, orchards and vegetable gardens. Numerous herds of dairy cattle grazing on the green slopes gave the countryside a decidedly Swiss aspect. The area appeared to be extremely fertile. Water was plentiful everywhere and, even in smaller valleys, there were permanent streams. The high moisture content of the soil together with a relatively warm summer climate explained the luxuriance of the vegetation.

We descended to Farmers Hotel, the best of the four existing in the town. During dinner it was clear that we were in a different agricultural area from those we had just passed through. There was a profusion of vegetables and in particular a very fresh salad, which was a relief to our stomachs that had laboured for many days on a meat only diet.

Before I go on to describe our visit to the Bridgetown district, allow me to make some observations about the district we have just left, that is, Kojonup. The term district, however, is something of a misnomer because Kojonup is not a separate sector but part of Katanning to which I have already referred in Chapter Eight. Nevertheless the region is so big and important that I believe it warrants a separate description. The district, let us not forget, holds a special interest for us, given the proposal to settle some of our immigrants there.

The whole area has the tremendous advantage of being abundantly supplied with water, both in terms of rainfall and permanent watercourses. The rainfall varies from 20 inches on the eastern side to between 25 and 30 inches towards the west. It is drained by several rivers including the Carrolup, Balgarrup, Beaufort and Kojonup etc. There are also many small freshwater lakes and springs. The terrain is generally undulating and composed of very fertile reddish loam; here and there sandy tracts are noticeable. The land around Kojonup in a radius of thirty miles is almost all taken up, as is that along the railway line which is under construction.

However, to the west, towards Bridgetown, there is still magnificent Crown Land. As I have already mentioned one could negotiate to send some of our settlers here, where the government has already set aside some 200,000 acres to serve the needs of future rural immigration.

Wheat yields an average of 12 bushels to the acre in the district and oats between 15 and 20 bushels. Potatoes and barley also do well. Clover is the best suited forage for the area. The country has a great future in dairy farming. Fruit growing has been successful. Clearing costs between £1 and £2 an acre, sometimes less, and fencing costs £26 per mile.

The Minister for Agriculture has estimated the costs involved in the preparation of a four mile square allotment for sheep raising of 2560 acres (about 1000 hectares) as follows: twelve miles of internal and external fencing (the internal fence would divide the property into four sections) at £26 per mile—£312; four dams—£120; ringbarking in the region of 1s per acre—£128. Allowing a sum for unforeseen costs, the total is £600.

Of course the land would not be turned into first-class pasture at these prices but would set a basis for improvement. As noted, the major cost is always fencing which, as far as sheep farming is concerned, is necessary whether the land is improved or left in its natural state.

The virgin land in the Kojonup district can run 300 sheep to every 1000 acres and three times the number after rinkbarking. The best breed, whether in terms of its wool or meat, is the Shropshire whose lambs grow and fatten very rapidly. Raising horses is also very successful.

Chapter Fourteen

The Balbarrup District—The Giant Forest Continues —The South-West Corner of the State— The Timber Industry—Tree Oils—The Bridgetown District—Greenbushes—Sardinian Type Railways— Balingup —Donnybrook—An Australian 'Emilia'— The Settlement of Hamel—Arrival in Perth after the Great Inspection Tour.

October 16. Early in the morning we set out on the customary tour of the surrounding district. We reached Balbarrup, which is situated about twenty miles to the south. The area is linked to Bridgetown by telegraph and telephone but the place itself has few residents; besides the post office there was not a house to be seen. There are, however, many farms scattered about the area. Balbarrup is about halfway between Bridgetown and the Warren, a big river which flows into the Southern Ocean. It is flanked by very fertile land, although the dense forest there constitutes a considerable obstacle to settlement.

My discussion with the guide who accompanied us went something like this:

'What is the annual rainfall?'

'About 33 inches in Bridgetown, 35 in Balbarrup and 40 on the Warren.'

'What is the cost of clearing?'

'From £10 to £12 per acre if by the usual method, that is, dragging the tree out of the ground by means of chains around the trunk pulled by eight or ten pair of oxen. Trees of any size can be rooted out by this method. Gelignite has been used recently to clear the bush; this method, without doubt, is quicker and more economic. The tree is blown out of the ground with cartridges placed under the roots, then, once flattened, it is broken up further by smaller explosives. Time is saved in this way, and costs are reduced by about £3 per acre.'

Along the route we noticed the composition and quality of the soil in the roadside embankments. It was dark red loam, two or three feet deep, covered with several centimetres of very dark humus; its extra-ordinary fertility, which is said to be among the best in the state, was apparent to me. The trees, which were already very big in Bridgetown and vicinity, were bigger still the further south we went. We saw some enormous trees like those in Denmark. The forest was very dense and Mr Ranford estimated that there were at least fifty trees per acre.

We saw several farms at intervals along the way but the extent of cultivation was limited and testified to the work needed to clear the bush. We crossed some open grassy plains where there were few trees, only blackboys. The soil there is very fertile but the area is limited in size.

We finally arrived at our destination and camped in a large clearing under the shade of an enormous red gum. Its trunk was blackened to a height of several metres on one side, evidence of earlier campfires. In Australia, in common with other sparsely inhabited parts of the world, journeys always follow a path best suited to camping, both in terms of the soil, the proximity of a spring or stream and the availability of firewood etc.

The traveller often takes advantage of the work of those who have gone the same way beforehand and, in turn, is careful to leave everything in order for those who come after. Thus we found a pile of branches and a tripod from which to hang our 'billy,' the little pot used to make the tea. In short order the fire blazed, the water boiled and we were soon sipping the fragrant brew stretched out as usual on rugs laid on the ground.

We then decided to take a brief stroll around the place. Little grass grew around the big trees, only a few shrubs, particularly the common hovea (*Hovea trispermum*) laden with magnificent violet flowers. I noticed several tracts of land covered with innumerable kinds of ferns. I was told that they are one of the most serious obstacles to clearing the land.

The forest is overpowering and man feels dwarfed and almost smothered. My peasant farmers looked at these giants with amazement and one could read discouragement in the faces of Ruozi and Bottoni. Human means could never clear such a forest, they said. However Ricci was more optimistic and believed that even here our fellow countrymen would be able to prosper.

This was the area where Mr Mitchell envisaged some of our settlers would be placed. The south has the advantage of a cool climate, abundant rainfall and very fertile soil, all factors ensuring success for mixed farming and particularly for so-called dairy products. It is the ideal spot for raising dairy cattle, growing potatoes, all kinds of vegetables and even fruit. A settler in this southern district, as I have already said, could produce that which Western Australia lacks and which has to be imported from elsewhere at enormous cost.

However, an examination of the area convinced me that the establishment of a settlement in this district for our immigrants should be undertaken with the utmost caution. The objections raised by Mr Brown against the extreme south (see Chapter Nine) are not without foundation. The clearing of the forest, even when feasible, involves considerable time and expense and is a major obstacle. It would take a man a month to clear just one acre, working on the assumption that a family has two able-bodied adult workers. In a year they would not have more than 15 to 20 acres ready for seeding (for three or four months in winter, work is necessarily suspended). Certainly, compared to central and northern areas, these lands appear to be more productive; but is this productivity proportionate to the increased costs involved? The answer is in doubt.

One must not forget that we Italians are very impressionable. It could happen that one of our families, finding itself battling against such a formidable forest, might become discouraged and leave the country, putting in jeopardy the enterprise upon which so many hopes were pinned. But there is something else. The population of Western Australia is concentrated in the central region, where the land is quickly cleared and where, after eight months, settlers can reap their first harvest. Few in Western Australia know the real conditions that confront agriculture in the south. Should it be noticed that it took Italians two or three years to get their farms in production, it could fuel the belief that we are less industrious than local farmers. And one needs to be very careful of public opinion in this country.

The extreme south is comparable to Gippsland in Victoria, once covered by impenetrable forest and now, for the most part, transformed into a garden. Without doubt, the soil is the most fertile in Victoria but the clearing costs weighed heavily there and often it was not the first settlers who reaped the profit. However, there is no doubt that all the obstacles would vanish if the land is selected with circumspection.

I had already expressed my reservations about the area to the Minister of Agriculture who replied that families destined for the far south would never be placed in areas of dense forest but rather in parts where clearing would be relatively easy. Bear in mind, he said to me, that along the coast are vast grassy tracts where there are no trees at all and where cultivation is very easy. The blocks would be apportioned in such a way that each family would be assigned some bush and some open land. Once a centre was established, it would, little by little, spread out and the area would gradually be cleared, as the needs and the means of the settlers dictated. Bearing in mind the enormous advantages that a settlement in the far south would afford our immigrants, as I mentioned in Chapter Seven, the idea of settling in this district should not be discarded. However, every care should be taken.

Returning by a different route we had the opportunity of examining the huge expanses of land given over to pasture. These areas are strange to behold. As far as the eye could see there stretched a mass of huge trees, no longer green and flourishing but dried up and for the most part burnt and blackened. They were the remnants of a forest of karri which had been ringbarked and then burnt. But the fire had done little more than blacken the trunk, casting a funereal pall over the landscape. Only the branches remained white, standing out against the cloudless blue sky. Beneath, grass grew tall and luxuriant, watered here and there by little streams. Herds of cattle grazed peacefully all over the place, wending their way through the labyrinth created by the dead forest. It was the eternal contrast between life and death, the endless struggle for the survival of the fittest.

We left the skeletal forest behind and, with a sigh of relief, returned to that which was still living. Almost involuntarily, one feels a sense of dislike for a pygmy mankind which dares lay hand to things that, in the final analysis, are themselves living entities which enrich our world with their beauty and symmetry. The countryside, magnificent while its forest is intact, loses all its attractiveness as soon as the trees are cut down. Harmonious and pleasant forms give way to the sharp and irregular contours of a denuded land. I do not know who it was who said that the tree is man's best friend but the reverse is also true. One feels this love most strongly in countries where nature is still in its virgin state and reigns supreme, until man comes to destroy it.

But, unfortunately, we do not live in a world of poetic idylls and clearing the bush is a necessity in Australia, covered as it is by an endless forest. In fact, until recently, this forest was regarded by the colonists as a natural enemy; it was difficult to see a single tree even in areas where their destruction was not warranted, such as beside the road or near houses. For some time, however, clearing has been carried out with more sensitivity and, I will say, humaneness. They are leaving trees near townships, sparing the most majestic specimens, and they are retaining those which will provide shade for their flocks in summer. Previously the forest was knocked down and everything was relentlessly burnt. Now some settlers are beginning to utilize the wood in sawmills, driven by petrol or animal power, or else cutting the timber by hand for railway sleepers and other purposes.

Even the government is concerned about the immense damage to the state's economy that has been wrought by the senseless destruction of valuable timber, particularly in the southern districts. It is estimated in Western Australia, that commercially suitable timber alone is worth about £125,000,000.

The government has levied a tax on, and withdrawn from sale for the purposes of settlement, large tracts of land which it has placed under the jurisdiction of a special department, thus preventing the destruction of timber. According to the stipulations of the law, bushland may not be granted to settlers, but only leased to those who intend to use it by setting up a sawmill.

There are some thirty-five such establishments in the state, with a total working capital amounting to £2,180,000. Some are owned by a single individual but most are run by companies, Millars being the oldest and most important. It began some years ago with a capital of £500,000 and now, having merged with smaller companies (popularly known as a 'combine'), operates with a capital of £1.5 million. It leases some 813,070 acres of land from the state and in some places owns the land freehold (in Denmark, for example, it has 30,000 acres).

Other companies, in order of importance, are the Timber Corporation of Greenbushes with 54,400 acres; the Collie Co-operative, 19,000 acres and the Western Australian Jarrah etc., 5760 acres.

The timber industry requires considerable capital if it is to be developed. Besides the costs of machinery, buildings etc., one must bear in mind those of constructing a rail network to make use of the more remote areas. Nor must it be forgotten that the wages paid to workers in Western Australia in this industry are very high, ranging from 8s to 10s per day.

The question of wages, which the companies believe are excessive and drain the owners' profits, has recently been the cause of dissent between labour and management and led to a strike which lasted several months, a rare occurrence in Australia where arbitration is compulsory. The strike was finally resolved through concessions on both sides and the government reducing the rates for rail transport. The sawmills use all types of timber found in the southern forests, but particularly jarrah. In passing, it should be noted that Western

Australia has an abundance of timber oils or essences; however, most belong to the large eucalyptus family. Each essence usually occurs in a particular location; at most two or three are found together.

The most important varieties of timber are: jarrah, which covers an area of 8,000,000 acres; wandoo, 7,000,000; sandalwood, 4,000,000; karri 1,200,000, and tuart 200,000. They are followed by the yate and blackbutt, and (less used for industrial purposes) the red gum, white gum, the morrel, wattle, blackberry, raspberry, jam, and banksia (which has very strange long cylinder-shaped flowers like huge pine cones).

Jarrah holds first place for its strength and imperviousness and the beauty of its grain. It is used for railway sleepers, piles and paving etc. It lasts indefinitely even under the most unfavourable conditions, for example when it is left exposed to humidity or dryness. I took a sample of a sleeper, given to me by the Western Australian government, to Italy. It had been in use for twenty years and was not altered in appearance; obviously these sleepers will last thirty years, whereas ours made of oak survive some ten years. Jarrah lasts even longer when left in the water or completely dry. In Port Adelaide there are wharf pylons, sunk in 1868, which are still intact. This wood also has the distinction of being immune to the attack of termites, or white ants, which destroy timber in tropical or semi-tropical areas. I recall having seen the ruins of a church near Kojonup which had been built of softwood and whose walls crumbled to dust at the touch of a finger; only the outside layer of the wood had remained intact, inside all had been reduced to powder by termites.

Karri is also renowned for its hardness; a vessel built forty years ago is still in a perfect state of preservation. However, it cannot be compared with jarrah if it is exposed to the elements, though it is excellent for covered constructions or those submerged in water. The karri is the giant of the Australian forest; sometimes these trees reach 300 feet in height with a circumference of 32 feet. The trunk is smooth and straight, almost a single column which can reach a height of 180 feet before the first branches. The tuart (150 feet in height and 27 feet in circumference) is the heaviest and strongest of all. It is used for wheels, wagons, bridges etc. The sandalwood is a small tree which just reaches 18 feet; its wood is highly perfumed and much sought by the Chinese who burn it like incense and use it to make little statuettes. It has an annual export value of between £40,000 and £50,000 per year. The value of timber exported from Western Australia in 1903 totalled £660,000.

We arrived at Bridgetown as dusk was falling. The sluggishness of our horses, which had irritated us in the morning, was no better on the return journey; even Mr Ranford lost his customary aplomb. We had just time to stop for a few minutes to inspect a small but well-kept orchard situated a couple of miles out of town. The trees growing in that fertile soil were extraordinarily vigorous. All, with the exception of the peaches, fruited very well. Four acres had been set aside for apples; the trees were seven years old and last year yielded a nett product worth £200.

October 17. We reluctantly left Bridgetown which is probably the most picturesque town in Western Australia. Although situated only 580 feet above sea-level, the high rocky mountains which surround it, as I have already said, give it a look something akin to Switzerland, and very different from the usual aspect of the country which is monotonous and uniform.

Bridgetown has less than 500 inhabitants, although it has a certain importance given that it is the southernmost point of the coastal railway and thus a centre for products from the southern region not yet served by the railway. The town is situated 174 miles from Perth, a distance usually covered in eleven hours by the one daily train.

The district, of which it is the main centre, is mountainous and covered almost uniformly with dense forest. The climate is moderate, however the nights are very brisk and there are often frosts. The average rainfall is 35 inches. Clearing costs are between £6 and £18 per acre. Fencing costs £30 a mile. In 1903 there were some 3000 acres under cultivation; wheat yielded an average of 8 bushels; oats, 16.6 bushels; potatoes, 3 tons. The land in the district lends itself well to the cultivation of fruit, but the consumer markets are distant; orchards occupy 750 acres.

We travelled along the Bridgetown–Perth railway. About ten a.m. we reached Greenbushes, the highest point on the line (947 feet) and a centre of very rich tin mines. The land continued to be uneven. I was told that near the town there were very fertile tracts where fine forage was grown, particularly *erba medica*. The rainfall in this area is plentiful; between 32 and 49 inches. Clearing is always very expensive, from between £6 to £20 per acre. A large amount of timber, which is used for railway sleepers, is cut down by private individuals. The wood is hewn with an adze in such a way as to render its logs stronger than those sawn by machine which often cannot follow the grain of the wood.

The railway in this part of the country followed the incline of the land; for the sake of economy there were no embellishments, no trenches, no tunnels and few bridges. We were travelling on a line similar to those in use in Sardinia to which I have referred earlier in the text. Going uphill the train puffed and panted and was awfully slow, to the extent that some travellers got off and followed it on foot. I noticed a fireman happily stop off to gather flowers which he offered to a lady. However, it made up lost time on the downward section which it covered at breakneck speed.

The mountains were imperceptibly flattening out, giving way to the more common undulating country. We were at Balingup, 306 feet above sea-level and blessed with a very fertile soil, and clearing costs that were relatively cheap; in fact the timber was lighter and sparser. At two o'clock the train stopped for a few moments at Donnybrook, the main town of the district, where gold was discovered some years ago. German capital had been invested to develop the enterprise. I remember travelling from Genoa to Fremantle with the director of the company who had come especially to inspect this undertaking; the good fellow who, between you and me, was very full of his own importance, floated the idea of employing Italian labourers at the mine, who would be paid partly by means of land grants. He forgot that the Western Australian government would give land away for practically nothing without any obligation to work off the cost. The mine was not a success and the government resumed the vast tracts of land it had granted. The population of Donnybrook is 400. The district has a plentiful rainfall of between 29 and 37 inches. There is no shortage of good land suitable for fruit growing. The forest here is also very dense and clearing costs between £6 and £18.

From Boyanup a branch of the main line runs to the port of Busselton, situated on the Indian Ocean at the end of Geographe Bay. In the vicinity of Busselton there are a number of caves with splendid examples of stalactites which are visited by tourists from all over Australia. At Picton, another branch line links Bunbury (a most important port on the west coast) to the line on which we were travelling.

We entered a section of magnificent, well-cultivated country. The forest had all but disappeared and the wide plain was divided up into large rectangular paddocks. To our right rose the Darling Ranges which run parallel to the sea for a distance of some thirty to forty miles. Scattered about on the spur of the hills, which were already cleared and cultivated, were picturesque small farmhouses. On the flat, the land was cultivated alternately with wheat and forage. The wheat had been already harvested and on the limitless plains innumerable sheep grazed.

The aspect of the land gave the countryside the look of the fertile plains of Lombardy and Emilia. Ruozi said it reminded him of the surroundings of Reggio and he was quite carried away—Ah! If only we could settle down here! he exclaimed. But it was a vain wish because all the land in the area was already in private hands. The prospective immigrant can pay no more than 10s an acre, whereas here it can reach £10 or more. My companions despaired as they looked with envious eyes at the strata of rich loam visible on the edges of the road, sometimes four or five feet deep, and the luxuriant vegetation it supported. The rainfall here is one of the highest, between 37 and 40 inches.

Later on we passed close by the Harvey River, the scene of our first excursion after arriving in Australia. The orange trees were now in bloom and bathed the air about with their perfume. It was already dark when we arrived at Pinjarra, an important station in the central agricultural district. Six miles to the west is Mandurah, a favourite spot for amateur fishermen, situated on an inlet of the ocean; there you can find excellent hotels with all modern conveniences. There are also fish canning factories established in the district.

Before Pinjarra the train passed through Hamel, the area where the government had tried to set up a subsidised settlement drawn from the ranks of dissatisfied miners. The attempt, as anticipated, failed, adding strength to the adage, which, in Italian, means 'the right man for the right job.'[1] It was late at night when the electric lights of Perth station appeared in the distance. For a month we had lived in the bush and our eyes were almost blinded by them. Our first fact finding mission was over.

---

1 Translators' note: A footnote by Zunini gives the translation of *ognuno al suo mestiere* as 'The right man in the right place,' which he attributes to Shakespeare, but with no further details.

Chapter Fifteen

*Journey to Moora—Gingin and the Cultivation
of Oranges—The Midland Railway Company
Land—Berkshire Valley—The Benedictine Abbey—
An Automobile Adventure—An Ideal Pasture—
The Advantage of a Special Train—Return to Perth.*

October 18. We had sent a telegram to Mr Gardiner, the representative of the Midland Railway, to let him know that we would be available on the Thursday to undertake a trip north to inspect the land which the company owns along the Perth-Geraldton line. I have mentioned this company earlier and noted how it finds itself in possession of about three million acres of excellent land, and how it has decided to sell it off gradually. I also commented that Mr Gardiner had shown himself to be most anxious to enter into negotiations with us in the hope that at least some of our farmers would settle on that land. He assured me that the company was ready to sell us an area alongside the railway and would construct a railway station for our exclusive use, as well as provide all the other facilities which an important settlement would require.

I also referred to the fact that Mr Gardiner believed that, before entering into any negotiations, it was preferable we visit the area to see for ourselves its excellent location and ascertain the fertility of the soil, and I noted that I had willingly accepted his invitation but without any obligation. It would afford an opportunity to visit the northern districts which had been omitted from the ministerial itinerary because the majority of the land there did not belong to the state.

We all wanted to visit the area having heard it spoken of in most glowing terms everywhere. The region's climate and soil, its geographical position and the means of communication were represented to us as absolutely marvellous. If the land had not been settled before this, it was the fault of the company which had hitherto taken no interest in it, being engaged in negotiations with the government for the sale of the land and railway.

The agricultural, timber and mineral resources of the region had already been remarked on many years ago by engineers engaged in the preliminary work for the construction of the railway. This is how Messrs Bond and Smith described the area in their report:

> Leaving the proposed line to our left we turned towards Dongara, we passed through magnificent pastoral country. In the virgin forest wild oats waved in the breeze like ripe wheat. The land in the cleared areas is most fertile, wheat yields between 16 and 25 bushels per acre and barley 30 bushels. These yields are ensured by the regular nature of the rainfall. We travelled for some 18 or 20 miles across this section which comprises thousands and thousands of acres. Similarly in the Yarrogadea area, the country is uniformly rich; we noticed herds of splendid cattle looking as if they had been fattened expressly to be put on show.
>
> There is no doubt that all the railway land is suitable for cultivation. It would be hard to find better crops of wheat, barley and oats in any other colony. The country is destined surely to become a granary *par excellence*. There are abundant jarrah forests from which excellent timber may be obtained. Sandalwood is plentiful. There are many deposits of copper, lead, iron and coal; copper, particularly, may be worked very profitably, as soon as the road is opened. Gold has been found near New Norcia and other areas. The climate in the region is very healthy; there is never any shortage of rain which falls regularly throughout the year. And in any case water can be found everywhere at a depth of about 20 feet. The goods to be carried on the line include wool, wheat, hay, cattle, horses, timber, construction materials etc. As well, it will carry exclusively, all the goods etc., destined for the Murchison goldfields area.

Thus the report from the Midland Company's engineers; now let us turn to our expedition.

The three delegates would have liked to have accompanied me. However, because Mr Ranford decided to come also, even though his mission was accomplished, and brought a Mr Smith, one of the railway directors, with him, there was room for only one of them. Wanting to be fair, I suggested they draw lots for the place. However, Ricci, who was by nature passionate and convivial and could not resign himself to staying home, put pressure on Ruozi and Bottoni who voluntarily gave up their chance of going.

We left Perth at five p.m. We had seats in a most luxurious compartment used by the management of the company. We travelled on the state line as far as Midland Junction (twelve miles from Perth) after which we used the Midland Company line. From Perth to Midland Junction there was the usual white sandy soil common to Perth and surroundings. The Guildford area, however, was the exception, a real oasis of very fertile, well-cultivated soil. After Midland Junction there were miles and miles of semi-sandy soil covered with stunted vegetation. There was very little cultivation and extensive pasture holdings predominated. Here and there we saw small freshwater lakes. The land gradually improved and at Gingin (329 feet above sea-level), an important centre of orange growing, it was once more of top quality.

The train stopped there for about ten minutes. We all took the opportunity to get off and buy cases of delicious fruit. Here in the north it was harvest time and they loaded up entire wagons with the produce. There were baskets full to the brim everywhere, peel was strewn all over the ground and on the line, and an acrid smell wafted through the air.

The train moved off but it was already dark and I was unable to see the countryside through which we were passing. However, Mr Gardiner cheered me up saying that it would be daylight on our return journey. It was after ten o'clock when we arrived at Moora, our destination. It is one of the company's most important centres; a few years ago it did not exist, now it is of considerable significance. It owes, if not its origins, at least its recent development to the push for settlement initiated by the company through the gradual selling off of its lands. Mr Gardiner told me that the average rainfall here is between 19 and 23 inches, the soil is very fertile and suited to the cultivation of cereals, examples of which we would see tomorrow.

October 19. Rising bright and early we found Messrs Gardiner and Smith ready and waiting. I joined Gardiner in a light rig drawn by two magnificent horses which, as is the usual custom in Australia, were harnessed one behind the other. Our companions followed us in a big buggy, which is a sort of cart cum coach. The climate in Moora was much hotter than Perth (not forgetting that we were several degrees further north); however it was tempered by a breeze from the Indian Ocean which is about fifty miles away.

We travelled along a straight track through a forest of jams and white eucalypts. The trees were few and far between and not very big. Two or three miles on we came to a vast expanse of sand which, however, was fairly shallow and had the customary clay soil underneath. In summer, these sandy plains are covered by a grass which is particularly nutritious for sheep; given the scarcity of fodder during the hot dry months these flats are much sought after by squatters in the vicinity who lease them at high prices.

We came to the celebrated Berkshire Valley, the soils of which are famous throughout the state for their extraordinary fertility. The valley is crossed by the Moore River which, like many others in Australia, does not flow permanently, but consists of a series or chain of ponds and lakes which last all summer and provide excellent water for animals and domestic use.

In the centre of the valley there is a branch of the famous New Norcia abbey, founded in 1846 by the Benedictine Dom (later Archbishop) Salvado to civilize the Aborigines. A lack of time prevented us from visiting the main abbey which is situated about forty miles from Berkshire. I learned on our return to Perth that the abbot had been ready waiting to receive us with all due ceremony; he was very disappointed not to have met us.

The Berkshire abbey comprised a number of large buildings, some of which were used for accommodation, others as a granary and still others as wool stores. I was somewhat shocked to see that the church was little more than a room furnished with very simple religious motifs. It was explained to me that the buildings had not been erected by the Benedictines but had been purchased from a squatter who had gone to live in Perth.

The monks' main crop was wheat (20 to 25 bushels per acre). They also raised sheep (more than 11,000). We admired some magnificent vegetables in the garden, lettuces, huge cabbages, peas, chick peas etc. Chick peas are a rarity in Australia and I do not recall having seen them anywhere except on this property The olive and the vine are also grown at New Norcia. The brothers, who are Spanish for the most part, have all the European crops here to help them bear more readily the separation from their native land.

As I said, we were received with great cordiality. The superior, who very rarely had the opportunity to speak in his native tongue, was very happy to exchange a few words in Spanish with me. He offered us some excellent fruit and beer which the monks brew themselves but which was not the best. Mr Ranford was dying to taste it. However, being a teetotaller, alcoholic beverages were forbidden him. Only after the abbot assured him that fermentation had not yet taken place did he decide to drink some of it. But I don't think even he was very impressed.

Besides the monks, we saw a number of secular priests. The reason for their presence was quite strange. Not everyone in Australia follows

Mr Ranford's good example of abstinence nor is the clergy completely free from sin in this respect. However, I hasten to add that the clergy, who are almost all Irish, are in general very sober and diligent in their duties, to the extent that they hardly ever give cause for criticism or backbiting. But there seems to be something in the Irish nature which fatally attracts them to beer or whisky which they are unable to resist. And so, when the bishop learns that a priest is given to drunkenness, he sends him to the brothers where, because they are of Latin stock and thus very sober, he will be free from temptation and danger. Here the culprit is closely watched. He is provided with excellent food, even wine with the meal (a bottle a day) but no spirits or beer. This kind of spiritual exercise lasts for one or two years. Usually the offender comes out a new man. The temptation is strong however, and once outside he often succumbs again. Then there is no other course but to expel him from the priesthood.

On the road once more we soon found ourselves in a superb area most suited to raising cattle. The grass, which was extremely nutritious and tasty, was thick and luxuriant with the result that the beasts fattened astonishingly. Here we noticed a very strange phenomenon. Underneath the white eucalypts the grass had not sprouted at all, whereas it was thick under the jams and other varieties. I do not know whether this demarcation is so clear in other parts of Western Australia. We met with droves of kangaroos who are the best judges of the quality of the pasture. We also saw many wild turkeys but unfortunately none of us had a rifle.

After the section under pasture we crossed into an agricultural area (that is, a potential agricultural area, because it was still completely covered by bush). The soil was dark red and very deep, and seemed to be uniformly good. We had travelled in a wide circle: having left the railway line near Moora we had then cut across it again twelve miles further north. This was the spot where Mr Gardiner envisaged an Italian settlement. The land was first class and suited either to agriculture or rearing stock. However, cultivation would have to be large scale; the same products and methods used around Kellerberrin would apply but there the rainfall is only 12 inches whereas here it sometimes reaches 23 inches, ensuring a big difference both to the size and certainty of the harvest.

We stopped a while for refreshments, having already had lunch in the Berkshire Valley, and returned to Moora following the railway line. I noticed that the good soil was inland whereas sandy plains predominated along the line. We arrived at Moora about three o'clock where a surprise awaited us. We saw two cars parked in front of the hotel. Mr Gardiner had had them come from Perth especially for us. It was quite an event for Moora, given that these were the first automobiles ever seen in the town. We were very grateful to Mr Gardiner for his kind thought. Unfortunately none of us could have foreseen the trouble these wretched vehicles would cause.

It was decided to make a quick trip to the south of Moora before dark to examine the wheat growing area. I got into the larger vehicle, a four-seater, 16 horse-power De Dion. Ricci and Gardiner were with me and we were driven by a chauffeur from Perth. Ranford, always the unlucky one, got in the smaller two-seater car which Smith proposed to drive. His knowledge of the subject, however, was not extensive; he had only had three lessons. The small car moved off, slowly zig-zagging like a drunken person. Momentarily it was in danger of leaving the road and crashing horribly in the ditches on either side. Thank God, finally it straightened up and then suddenly took off at high speed and in a short while had disappeared from sight.

Our chauffeur was most able but his car was not, or rather his tyres were no good. After about seven or eight miles we heard an explosion to the left; the inner-tube had blown out and we were left stranded in the middle of the road. We got out and all set about fixing the problem which took us about two hours. We moved off again but ten minutes later the car broke down again. Worried as we were by our own bad luck, how our friends were faring with a 'chauffeur' of the calibre of Mr Smith gave equal cause for concern. What if something similar had happened to them! Without doubt they would have surely overturned.

Several carts passed by as well as persons on horseback who looked at us pityingly with a smile on their lips. We started to panic. Finally, however, we managed to get the car going but, at a turn in the road, we were confronted by a sad yet funny sight. What had been foreseen had indeed come to pass; the poor little car lay half overturned against a parapet and the passengers sat with their arms folded, unable to think of a saint who might intercede, and looking veritable pictures of pain and despair. We could not help but burst out laughing. Smith's prowess as a driver would be the subject of our jibes for days afterwards. Luckily no one was hurt. Ranford was not too sure on this point and kept feeling himself all over, repeating for the hundredth time, give me a horse, any old nag, and keep your automobiles. He will not stop complaining for many a long day. It would take too long to describe the vicissitudes of the return trip, save to say that we left at three o'clock and got back home at about nine o'clock having covered fully sixteen miles.

We found the town in an uproar: a grand ball had been organised and, as everyone knows, Australians are mad about such diversions. Young men and women from up to sixty miles away flock to them. We were sent complimentary tickets and Gardiner, Smith and Ricci attended. I preferred to go to bed early but there was no chance of getting any sleep. They danced all night in the Town Hall and in the hotel they drank till morning, the drunkards making the loudest din possible.

October 20. I arose next morning after a completely sleepless night. Our programme for the day entailed a visit to the farm of Mr Roberts. I thought I would find the horse-drawn vehicles in front of the hotel but alas, no, the two automobiles were already awaiting us. The faith that Mr Roberts and the chauffeur placed in these machines seemed completely exaggerated to me. I registered some objections but Mr Dean (the chauffeur) assured me that they were now in excellent condition. I looked at friend Ranford and saw his face had clouded over; no doubt his mind was full of sad forebodings. And, unfortunately, who could blame him?

The farm (or better still the station, it being mostly given over to grazing) was twenty-eight miles out of Moora. As was so often the case, Mr Roberts had started out without a penny and now owned an enormous property whose grazing land was the best in the state. He buys scrawny cattle from the Kimberley area, where they have to walk thousands of miles to market and arrive in an emaciated state, then fattens them up here and sells them. He makes a huge profit from the exercise.

All went well on the outward journey and, strange to say, the automobiles ran smoothly. The countryside through which we travelled was somewhat barren at the outset but, ten miles on, became more fertile than ever. Vast expanses were covered with tall luxuriant grass. In some places, for as far as the eye could see, there were countless bushes of smoke-grass, a shrub whose small leaves and flowers are covered with a white down. It was as if there had been a heavy snowfall. Here and there amid the pristine carpet were patches of pink of various hues; they were entire fields of everlastings, then in full bloom.

We passed through many stations which, like all properties given over to raising cattle, were very extensive. The gates, which every few miles blocked the way, hindered our progress. It would be a heavy burden for the owners to fence their land, even along the road, so the government allows them instead to close off access, a practice which frankly contributes little to rapid communications. Here we were in an area of do-it-yourself, of ingenious, roughly built gates, often made of iron, which opened and closed automatically with the flick of a catch easily operated by a man on horseback or in a vehicle.

The countryside now was magnificent; the rises were more marked, although the slopes continued to be gentle. Reaching the summit of one of the undulations unexpectedly one's glance roved over an immense open space. The whiteness disappeared from the landscape and we found ourselves in a sea of emerald green dotted everywhere with brightly coloured flowers.

We travelled through the countryside at high speed without stopping because Yatheroo, Mr Robert's station, was quite a distance off and we wanted to be back in Moora by evening. At last a splendid valley loomed in front of us. We gave three cheers and in a few minutes we were in front of the house. It was a large one-storeyed building, its walls hidden by the dense foliage of creepers and grapevine shoots. We met the owner of the house, a fine figure of an old gentleman. He greeted us with open arms and begged us to make ourselves at home. His welcome was not exaggerated, for quite literally he put his home at our disposal.

The Roberts family, as is customary in Australia, is completely patriarchal, numbering about twenty, between children, in-laws and grandchildren. At lunch the conversation was general, Mr Roberts speaking almost exclusively about agriculture and cattle raising. This did not surprise me for what else is as interesting to an honest squatter as these matters? However, I noticed that our host was extremely knowledgeable and full of common sense and good humour. We died of laughter at his jokes. He had also travelled widely and spoke enthusiastically about Italy, which he knew quite well.

With lunch over, he took us to survey his property. 'Look,' he said, 'here I produce what could be described as all my family's needs. I bring very little in from outside; only salt and sugar besides clothes.' We visited the sections where they made butter and cheese; further on was the place where they cured ham and bacon, an indispensable food as far as the British are concerned. Then we saw the mill, the abattoir etc. We inspected stables housing magnificent harness and riding horses; nearby, a marvellous machine for chopping up hay had been installed. Then we went to the groves where I was surprised by the extraordinary number of fig trees; the delicious sweet fruit, believe it or not, was destined as fodder for the pigs. Such a diet, they assured me, fattened the hogs to perfection. There were also many oranges. What a wealth of delicious fruit! They were all of the Washington navel variety which produces huge fruit here and is most prized for its taste and aroma. Mr Roberts, notwithstanding his sixty-five years, scaled the trees with agility and sent down a rain of fruit.

We got in the buggies again; Mr Roberts, for whom the years had dimmed neither vim nor vigour, drove, taking us to spots where I would not have believed it possible for a vehicle to remain upright. He went along banks so steep that I feared any minute we would be plunged into the streams below; we went over steep rises; we got to the top of a hill and down we went at high speed and up the opposite side; there were watercourses in deep ravines which were forded with a huzzah of encouragement, if necessary with a hard shove and certainly with a great din.

Finally we arrived at the land which was the pride and joy of the old squatter. It was a vast, undulating expanse covered in soft succulent grass about a metre high. There was plenty of water and grass, a condition near and dear to the heart of every Australian. Here the presence of water and grass, barring other problems with the land, means it is possible for the fortunate owner to raise an indeterminate number of sheep and cattle with considerable profit.

Yatheroo, in this respect, was one of the places most favoured by Mother Nature; there were streams and springs everywhere; the grass was so luxuriant that Ricci was surprised that it was not regularly mown. Mr Roberts laughed and said it was hardly worth while given that a labourer cost eight shillings day. The sub-soil was rich in calcareous matter. This, according to those in the know, gives a certain natural warmth to the soil which produces very nourishing pasture. In fact, the herds we saw at Yatheroo were in superb condition. Mr Roberts was keen for us to leave the vehicles and go into the paddocks to inspect the animals at close range. Then they became no longer cattle but joints of meat. There were some there that weighed more than a ton and a half. Their owner knew them all one by one, he stroked and caressed them and called them by name. We were amazed to see how meek and mild the bulls were. I was told this is common in Australia and was the result of their being left completely free to roam.

We returned to the homestead about five o'clock. Tea was taken and we made ready to return to Moora. We begged Mr Roberts to come with us. He had never been in an automobile and was persuaded to do so by his desire to experience this new form of transport. Poor fellow! He, too, would be part of our mishap.

I shall spare the reader a chronicle of our vicissitudes, save to say that the troubles we experienced the previous day were repeated to the letter. Ranford kept up his string of complaints and Roberts suddenly lost his penchant for newfangled things. We decided to abandon the cars on the road and to proceed on foot to a nearby farm and seek out some horses and carriages. Old style carriages, that is, said Roberts. The farm was some way off and the track was tedious because of the heat and the insufferable sticky flies which clung to one's hands, face and eyes, preferring to be squashed rather than go away. It was almost dark when we got there. They had only two horses and a small cart which would not hold all of us. Think of it, we were more than twenty miles out of Moora! It would be a long way to go on foot! Mr Ranford, accomplished bushman that he was, suggested that we camp in the open. It was pointed out to him that we had no blankets and that, if the worst came to the worst, we could ask to stay overnight at the farm.

Luckily Mr Dean saved us from such an embarrassing situation. He had gone back to the scene of our misfortune and after closely re-examining the automobiles had been able to repair one of them and returned in it triumphantly. Three persons could be accommodated and the others could easily fit in the horse-drawn vehicle. I decided to go with the chauffeur, in whom I had complete trust. He was as able as his machines were not. It was at this point that his skills were truly made manifest. The road was extremely narrow and it was a very dark night. Straining my eyes I could not see more than two metres ahead, and yet the automobile ran along at high speed. If only the track had been straight! But no such luck! There were continuous curves almost at right angles; I was aware of this from watching the steering wheel. We scraped huge tree-trunks, branches lashed our faces but still we pressed on. I could not help but admire Mr Dean and praised him for his skill and, particularly, for his sharp eyesight. He replied that it was simply a question of experience and know-how. The breakneck run continued. We were going downhill and literally flew over the road. I thought that a catastrophe was a distinct possibility but I put myself in the hands of fortune. I could not imagine what was whirling about in the mind of Mr Ranford, who had decided to come with us, and I did not dare ask. Suddenly, thank God, we saw the outskirts of Moora. The automobile arrived safe and sound and we parked in front of the hotel. We had travelled the twenty miles in a little over half an hour.

October 21. Mr Gardiner had an important appointment in Perth on the Monday and had planned to catch the train on Saturday evening, there being no service on Sunday. The automobiles had decided otherwise but Gardiner was not put out on their account. We were in the domain of the Midland Company and the railway, no less the material means, were at our disposal. A simple telegram to Perth and we would be honoured with a special train.

We left about two o'clock. Ricci took the opportunity of the wait to organise his collection of plants and animals; he had gathered all four kinds of kangaroo paws, green, red and green, yellow and black. All of Yatheroo was covered with the green variety which produced a very odd effect. There are few green flowers in Europe and Ricci was pleased to possess such a rarity. Gardiner had offered us a bunch of the black variety which, even in Australia, is rare and grows only in remote northerly areas.

We helped load the automobiles on the train. That morning, at a very early hour, the chauffeur had returned to the site of our troubles and had managed to get the other automobile going and brought it back to town. I would quite seriously advise any travellers or explorers in Australia never to use automobiles unless they have first-class machines and tyres. Otherwise they should follow Mr Ranford's advice and stick to the old but sure forms of transport, namely a good buggy and two pair of first-class horses. There is no shortage of horses and carts in Australia even in the more isolated districts. With them one is sure to arrive at one's destination.

We took our places in the saloon car. I noticed something which had escaped me on the outward journey which had taken place at night. The carriage had large windows, even at the rear, and we were able to enjoy the view of the countryside on all sides while seated, with the exception of course of the forward view. One had to agree that it was very pleasant to have a special train at one's disposal. We halted when we wished and went out into the countryside as we pleased, stopping and starting at will. At one spot we saw a flock of splendid turkeys. Mr Smith immediately gave orders to stop the engine. The fireman, a real marksman, got off and, crouching behind some shrubs, managed a shot. The birds rose in unison, we heard a bang and a magnificent bird fell heavily to the ground. Gardiner courteously offered it to me.

We travelled along the same line as previously. However, in daylight, we were able to observe closely that part of the country we had passed through earlier in complete darkness. There was nothing very noteworthy about it. The land was quite fertile up to the outskirts of Gingin but lightly cultivated. Herds of cattle could be seen here and there and there were also some flocks of sheep, then sandy flats with stunted vegetation. We arrived at Midland Junction and again saw the oasis of Guildford, followed by the white sandy outskirts of Perth and on to the city itself. We had arrived and the second and last phase of our journey through the agricultural districts of Western Australia was complete. However, the trips were over only for the delegates, for, as far as I was concerned, I anticipated that I would soon be off on new journeys and new explorations.

Chapter Sixteen

The Delegates' Impressions—Where to put our Settlements?—The Departure of the Delegates for Italy —The Beginning of Negotiations with the Western Australian Government—The Blackwood Region—My Arrival in Kojonup—English Society — On the Balgarrup—Journey into the Unknown— The Swamps —Aboriginal Camp—An Unfortunate Hunter—A Wonderful Country—The Dinninup River.

The delegates would willingly have stayed longer in Australia. They were fond of the place and viewed their imminent departure with some gloom. However, I realized that any extension of their stay would be costly, something which the local government would probably be loath to accept, to say nothing of the Emigration Commission. From the time of the negotiations with Mr James in London it had been envisaged that the trip would be for three months and no more. The delegates conceded the point, but with some reluctance. Ricci, in particular, could not resign himself to the idea of returning to Italy.

However, before they left, I felt it would be useful to have an explicit statement from them, above all if the impression gained by them during the tour of Western Australia was entirely favourable. The delegates confirmed what they had already intimated to me several times during our journey. They believed that Western Australia, in general, would prove a fertile field for our peasant farmers. The thing that had struck them most was the fact that no Italian farmer, of those already established, had met with failure; the climatic conditions they felt were superb. Ricci was most enthusiastic, the other two, though more conservative in expressing their sentiments, agreed completely with the idea of settling Italians in the state.

I also needed to elicit another, most important, declaration from them. Roughly speaking, which area or areas did they feel would be most suitable for settlers? Their opinions would serve me as a basis for my forthcoming negotiations with the Australian government.

Ruozi and Bottoni would have preferred the northern grain growing region where the timber is thin and where, after a year or even less, one could count on a harvest. However, I reminded them of the problems and the dangers of establishing numbers of farmers in an area dependent upon one crop. The opinion of knowledgeable persons left little doubt about the matter; the land is very good and easy to cultivate, but it is suitable only for those who already have a certain amount of capital. Thus, the most preferable areas are those where mixed farming is possible. One needs to select a place where the climatic and soil conditions and ease of clearing the bush are favourable.

One area seemed to unite all these prerequisites: the central part of the Kojonup district, which marks the transition from the almost arid sector to the east of the Great Southern Railway and the rainy area to the west of the Blackwood. The land in this area has been blessed by nature. The amount of rain (25 inches), while it still allows wheat to be grown, is admirably suited to other agricultural products. The land in general is very fertile, and the timber is not very thick, so that the cost of clearing is not more than £4 per acre.

This region is bounded on the west by the Blackwood River (thereafter the forest is gigantic), in the south by the Kojonup–Bridgetown road, to the east by the Kojonup River, to the north by the junction of the Blackwood and the Balgarrup rivers. However, in this direction, it extends beyond these two watercourses along the Arthur River.

One of the advantages of this area is that it is watered by numerous rivers along which abundant fresh water is always found. We had passed through the southern part of the country, as noted in the entry for October 15, and had all been struck by the apparent fertility of the soil and the freshness and luxuriance of the vegetation. The Western Australian government has also indicated that this region is very well suited to large scale settlement and, to prove it, has set aside 200,000 acres for the purpose.

The delegates agreed that this was definitely the preferred area. However, given that both the Australian government and I felt it wiser to establish two separate settlements, instead of one comprised of one hundred families, it was necessary to select a second area.

As I have already noted, the local government wanted at least some of the Italians to be involved exclusively with dairy products and market gardening. The area in the far south is about the only district which lends itself entirely to this kind of undertaking. Thus, we must turn to this area in order to find a spot for the second portion of our colony.

The delegates were most impressed with Denmark and would have willingly given their vote to that district. However, it was not certain whether agreement could be reached with Millars. If this were not possible, they said, they would have no objection to more southern parts, if the land was something like that around Denmark, that is, a less dense forest or, if that could not be found, land which had at least been partially cleared.

We agreed on these main points and I was at pains to reiterate that, in accordance with the agreement between me and the Western Australian government, I would, together with the Minister for Agriculture or his representative (in any event an expert in the field), make a definite decision before the settlement of farmers took place. It goes without saying that such a selection would be as close as possible to the areas suggested by the delegates. Having decided on the location of the two settlements, the allocation of allotments and the building of houses etc., could then take place so that the families would find everything ready on their arrival.

The delegates left on October 24 on the *Gera*, the same vessel that had brought us to Australia. I accompanied my friends on board and it was with real sadness that I said goodbye to them. I had become fond of them and, having lived together with them for a month, I had had the opportunity to appreciate their fine qualities. Ruozi and Bottoni, although most unassuming, showed themselves to be well versed in agriculture; everybody who had occasion to discuss the subject with them was of the same opinion. Ricci, besides his practical know-how, also possessed a wealth of theoretical knowledge.[1] However, what I most admired in him was his warm, genuine enthusiasm which swept the most reluctant before it. It was certainly an important factor in the success of everything we did.

According to the instructions given me by the Commission, I had to stay on in Australia for some time in order to reach agreement with the local government on the conditions and terms applicable to our settlement. It was not the most pleasant of tasks because, as I have already noted, such an undertaking was beset by a number of serious difficulties. For the Western Australian government it meant putting in place new immigration policies. However, such initiatives, until recently,

---

1 Translators' note: Back in Italy, Ricci wrote a detailed report on his journey which was published under the auspices of the Emigration Commission. See Bibliography.

had been tolerated in Australia rather than encouraged. The Italian government, for its part, had to bear in mind the special conditions under which its citizens would take up residence and to agree to conditions which were essentially quite different from those in effect in other emigration cases, thus it, too, ventured on to an untrodden path.

I have previously remarked that the preliminary negotiations, conducted between myself, as a representative of the Emigration Commission, and the Western Australian Agent-General in London, had accepted the principle of a settlement which would be assisted and subsidised by both governments. This clause resolved an otherwise insoluble problem in that it eliminated the need for primary capital essential for a farmer who might wish to settle down there. At the same time the scheme seemed to be reasonable and fair; both nations were, in fact, interested in the undertaking. Italy, to open up new avenues and establish some influence in a country where, one could almost say, at the moment it has none; Australia, because it would add worth to its natural resources and, with the increase in population, act as a buffer against the much feared 'yellow peril.' Both parties, sharing in these benefits, must also assume the responsibilities.

Following the departure of the delegates, I had several discussions with the Minister for Agriculture, Mr Mitchell, in order to clarify the main points of the agreement. It was, however, merely an exchange of views because I wanted to wait for the return of Mr James from London, expected halfway through December. Mr James, who had been closely involved in the development of the project, and who had always displayed a very favourable attitude towards our country, could turn out to be of vital help to me. His keen mind and perfect understanding of local legislation assured me that I would have in him a reliable guide and counsellor.

Other concerns also persuaded me to put off negotiations to a later date. There were several important matters of a financial and agricultural nature under discussion in parliament which I wanted to see resolved, as their approval could have had certain repercussions on the agreement. The construction of a new railway line across the agricultural sector was proposed, as well as changes in the law concerning the Agricultural Bank and a loan of 30 million francs, to be spent almost entirely for the benefit of agriculture etc.; clearly, all were projects of the utmost importance. We were almost at the beginning of 1907.

*   *   *

I must go back a day or two. One evening, while strolling through the somewhat deserted streets of Perth, I met an all-agog Mr Ranford. 'I must give you some interesting news,' he said. 'The railway between Katanning and Kojonup is almost finished; the government has decided to push hard for the settlement of lands crossed by the new railway. Quite a few settlers are leaving this evening for the area in order to select their allotments and I have been assigned to guide them; you must come with us. As soon as we have fixed up the settlers' business, we will have the opportunity of visiting the land that the government has assigned to the Italians. We will travel the length and breadth of it. Such an opportune occasion will never present itself again.'

I willingly accepted his suggestion. I quickly returned to the hotel, packed my bags and once again found myself 'on the road,' as they say in Australia. We were accompanied by Mr Kittel, an official from the Lands Department, entrusted on this occasion with the job of photographer. He was a fine person, very lively and a great travelling companion. The young Piesse fellow, whom I had met previously in Katanning, was also in our carriage. His presence proved most useful in that he made up a four for a game of bridge. Thus the night passed without us realising it and early morning we found ourselves in Katanning. It was Sunday and we devoted the day to rest.

Travelling in the customary buggies we arrived at Kojonup the next day where we met up with a half dozen settlers who had gone ahead of us. Mr Ranford was employed to pilot them about the district and I tacked myself on to the group. I will not annoy the reader with a description of these jaunts, being much the same as those undertaken earlier of which I have already spoken.

In the days that followed more new settlers arrived and further visits to the surrounding country ensued. I became impatient. I thought our trip to the little-known Blackwood region would have taken place immediately, but instead Mr Ranford was continually detained in Kojonup by his duties as chief guide. We stayed there until late Thursday. It was not a complete waste of time for me, however, in that it enabled me to examine the land in the surrounding areas more closely. I met up with the good Mr Clarke and his family again. I met Mr Vanzuilcom, Mr Ranford's father-in-law and one of the earliest settlers in the district. He comes from a very good family; his father was a captain in the British navy but a reversal of fortune reduced him to poverty. Mr Vanzuilcom came to Australia and settled in the Kojonup district which was then completely uninhabited with the exception of a few houses in the town and, with a tenacity without peer, he hurled himself into work. He invited us to his home, a huge bungalow. 'Look,' he said to us, 'all built with my own hands; I have been bricklayer, carpenter and blacksmith.' Now, however, Mr Vanzuilcom is quite elderly and the desire to see again the wonders of the civilized world assails him. He has several sons but it seemed to me that his place was not that prosperous. And yet the farm is splendid; there are extensive wheat fields, the best pastures in the district and, moreover, a magnificent orchard. Mr Ranford told me that what it needed was a more energetic management.

There are enormous tracts of still vacant land near the Vanzuilcom farm. In the afternoon the group went to one of the so-called 'ten thousand blocks,' that is, a property composed of ten thousand acres owned by an English company which did poorly there and have now put the land up for sale. I have rarely seen a soil more barren and unsuitable for pasture (which was the aim of the company) nor one as thickly covered with poison plants, which in some places were so dense as to impede passage. The failure must be attributed to those inexperienced individuals who were sent here without the faintest idea about how to choose a suitable area, and who managed only to spend enormous sums of money senselessly.

It appears that such examples of English enterprise, which in Western Australia have often fared badly, are not unusual to the extent that it is common to hear that such and such an undertaking had failed, but it was not surprising given that the management is in London. The present visit to the 'ten thousand blocks' gave me pause: we often speak of the English genius and the ability with which Anglo-Saxons conduct their affairs and succeed in all their undertakings; we wallow in admiration and consider Italy to be a country composed of perfect imbeciles. How many times have I heard the same refrain: yes, the matter of which you speak appears sound but don't you think that, if things are really like this, the English will not have already cornered the market? All the same, I can say from personal experience, I believe that these able geniuses frequently get things very wrong, often leaving themselves open to swindlers, with the result that they lose huge sums of money in outlandish deals; and, more importantly, in their own colonies they often have no concept of business which, if exploited as it should be, would bring handsome returns.

Of course the English can pride themselves on great successes but one must never forget that they are privileged. Almost all the world, politically speaking, is theirs. They have limitless money and they have been able to create a financial monopoly when competition from other nations in the industrial or commercial fields was non-existent or negligible. But show me an Englishman and an Italian with the same opportunity and means; I don't know if our Anglo-Saxon friend would be necessarily superior.

I have allowed myself this outburst because it is necessary to get rid of a misconception which damages our interests and results in us crawling into our shell and rejecting any overseas undertakings. We need to persuade ourselves that, in this world, anybody can succeed, whatever their nationality, provided that they are intelligent, honest and have a spirit of initiative and some capital.

We spent the night in Mr Vanzuilcom's hospitable home and the next day visited several farms in the vicinity. We spent all afternoon at one property belonging to a recently established settler. He was an old gentleman, formerly the manager of a bank in Sydney. He, too, had made bad investments and lost everything and was now trying to recoup his fortune in Western Australia. He had his wife and two children with him, and it was sad to see a person of refinement, used to an easy and comfortable life, now forced to do the rough and heavy work of the pioneer in the virgin bush. How much pain, bitterness and disappointment lie hidden in the endless forests of this continent which, if it offers wealth and success to the young and strong, is often a premature tomb for those who have lost the strength to face the struggle for life!

Mr Ranford told me that he had to go back to Perth urgently and would return in a day or so. So as not to waste time I decided to make the journey across the Blackwood area without him. I took Norrish with me. He is the district guide, a very practical man and held to be one of the most able persons around, both in terms of agriculture and the bush. Mr Kittel asked me if he could be part of the group and said that he would bring his camera with him. I accepted willingly.

The area to be crossed was almost completely uninhabited. Therefore it would be difficult to find hotels or houses along the way where we could obtain board and lodging. We took a big tent and all the necessary provisions with us. On long trips these latter consist basically of tea, sugar, flour, salt and some tins of jam, with the choice reduced to the absolute minimum in order not to be overburdened. Our trip, however, was to be of short duration and, having a large vehicle at our disposal, it was possible to think about some delicacies for the table.

The local grocer provided everything needed: tinned meats, salted beef and lamb tongues, tinned peaches, condensed milk, jam, biscuits, vegetables, sugar, tea etc. Speaking of tea, I would never have believed that I could get used to having this beverage with meals; and yet, in semi-tropical climes, after a long trek, with nothing more than turbid, muddy water at one's disposal, a good cup of tea is a real pleasure, although too much of it can be monotonous. No traveller in Australia sets out without the indispensable billy, or small tin can, and a good supply of tea and sugar; add some flour and salt and he is not afraid to shut himself away for weeks, even months, in the wilderness. We remembered to bring arms and ammunition upon which we would rely to provide us with fresh meat.

December 28. We left early in the morning travelling, for part of the way, along the road from Kojonup to Bridgetown which we had traversed a month earlier. Our plan was to reach the Balgarrup River and follow its course northwards to where it joined the Blackwood. Then we would return southwards, crossing diagonally the parallelogram formed by the Kojonup–Bridgetown road and the Balgarrup and Blackwood rivers. Meeting up with the latter watercourse in the south-west, we would follow it northwards to its confluence with the Arthur River, and go on still further north, turn then to the east and reach the Kojonup creek and follow it to the town of the same name. It was a very interesting trip because, as I said, we would be going through a little-known area where there was hardly any settlement. The few settlers that there were spoke of it enthusiastically, extolling its amazing fertility.

We got to the Marredup pool at about ten o'clock. There we left the made road and were quickly swallowed up by the dense bush. Mr Kittel wanted to photograph the pond whose water, by the way, was excellent and very fresh. I have already explained that, with the exception of the very dense forest in the far south, there are few areas in Australia which cannot be crossed in a cart. Our trip therefore would not be very difficult as we could rely on this comfortable means of transport for our entire time in the bush. We walked only to stretch our legs, or when we came to a dangerous section.

As soon as we left the Marredup pool we were confronted with a fence that ran as far as the eye could see; for about ten metres on either side of it the bush had been razed to the ground. We were on the boundary of Mr Piesse's vast block of about 20,000 acres. I did not think the land was so very fertile; there were quartz outcrops here and there, some of which appeared like small hills. We got down and, using hammers, made a quick check of the rock, or as they say here, we 'prospected.' It could be said that there is no quartz rock in the Central district which does not bear gold in large or small quantity but in the south the metal is almost completely absent so that our prospecting was fruitless.

We finally got to the Balgarrup whose bed was dry. There were only little pools here and there where water remains all the year round. Now the soil had changed its composition and was first class, a reddish deep loam.

At noon we camped in a very narrow valley. A fire was lit and in a short while lunch, which we devoured with gusto, was ready. Then we stretched out happily on the turf gazing at the blue sky through the leaves of the trees. The air was pure, a fresh breeze tempered the heat of the sun. A deep peace reigned everywhere. How lovely and magical are these Australian wildernesses with their wonderful weather.

The sharp ear of our guide, used to picking up the tiniest noise in the bush, had noticed a far off sound which had passed us by unnoticed. It was the melancholy cooing of doves in love. The wild species, known as bronzina from the colour of their wings, abound in this district. Norrish got up all at once and, like a squirrel, slunk from tree to tree hoping to get a good shot which would provide us with fresh meat. Instead, he came back crestfallen. The birds had fled and we would have to be content with tinned meat that evening.

We set off once more, flanking the river all the while. The soil was still excellent and Norrish told me it was like this for two or three miles either side of the watercourse. We came across the Piesse property's fence again and noticed several kangaroos running along it. As I have already noted, these animals do not possess sufficient intelligence to turn around or take another path when they are confronted with an obstacle, but follow it until it ends. However, it was impossible in the cart to catch up with such fast runners and we had to wait for another opportunity to get a good shot at them.

We were now on very uneven ground. There were steep and craggy granite hills, which the fence crossed in a relentlessly straight line. Then, there was a dense copse of mallet trees, from whose bark tannin is extracted; then grassy flats, more hills covered in poison bushes over a metre high, and at last the Balgarrup with its fertile plains. It was by now six o'clock and we decided to camp; we had covered twenty-seven miles that day, quite a distance when one considers that it had been through bush without any sign of a made track.

Both Norrish and Kittel showed themselves to be accomplished bushmen. The pegs were cut and set in the ground; small saplings, their branches neatly removed, served as support poles and in a few minutes our tent was ready. We used the lush crest of the blackboy as a carpet and also as a mattress. We ate, and after some chatting we each retired to our 'apartment,' but, gracious me, only then did we realize we had forgotten an absolute essential! We had but two blankets and needed at least six. Kittel thought the hotel keeper had given the extra ones to me and I thought vice versa . . . whereas, in fact, we had left them in Kojonup. It was not a trivial matter because in this area the night cold is piercing and there are frequent frosts. Lying as close to each other as possible we did the best we could to cover ourselves with the two blankets.

December 29. In the short term we slept; but after a few hours we were terribly cold; the thin canvas did not protect us at all from the outside temperature and I felt frozen to the bone. The moon was very bright and I looked at my watch; it was barely two o'clock in the morning. I tried to go back to sleep but it was impossible. I spent another hour, my teeth chattering, then I jumped up and ran madly around in the open air away from the camp. Little by little I began to get a bit warmer and only then did I slow down my steps. So as not to get lost I walked alongside the fence for miles and miles and returned to camp after dawn had broken. Kittel and Norrish were already up and had lit a big fire. They were already concerned about me, fearing that I had perhaps become lost, which is one of the easiest things to happen in the Australian bush which is so uniform that it is hard to tell one bit from another. They had fired off a couple of shots, but the height of the land between us had prevented me from hearing them.

Before taking down the tent Kittel took a photograph of it. He insisted that I sit on the ground in front of it with a rifle between my legs; thus, I would give the appearance of a great hunter. I felt a bit remorseful about faking things in this way because, since we left, I had observed the fifth commandment to the letter.

We got going about nine o'clock. The countryside was beautiful, little timber but very many-branched blackboys which, as I have said, was a sign of great fertility. In an hour we reached Mr Briggs' farm. It comprised first-class land but was poorly cultivated and the pastures were very neglected. The fence was falling to pieces and in several places the wires were broken. The land had been 'overstocked,' that is, an enormous flock had been put to graze there with adverse effects on the pasture; the soil in places appeared to be completely denuded. The owner is elderly and does not attend carefully to the running of his property. If he were to get rid of it, it would, without doubt, be a bargain. Who would not buy if they had enough capital? It would be an excellent proposition which, with little outlay, could be brought up to standard. Mr Briggs told me that wheat yields eight bushels to the acre but, with the right fertilizer, it would, without doubt, yield much more. In any event, in this area, I would advise the investor to go in for sheep raising, that is, for both wool and meat; the profit would be quite considerable.

We then went back to the Balgarrup from which we had diverted in order to visit Mr Briggs' property. We reached close to its junction with the Blackwood and decided to return, as planned, in a south-westerly direction crossing diagonally across a huge triangle, or as I said earlier, a parallelogram. It was a little-known area and the fever of the unknown took hold of us all.

We found ourselves, at first, in a magnificent area. The trees were of medium size but widely set apart. The ground was flat and covered with thick grass which gave the scene the appearance of endless parkland. Behind us, to our right, lay the chain of gently sloping, picturesque green hills which we had skirted for several miles. Gradually the land became more hilly; in some spots there were thorny shrubs and iron-stone; the bush was more dense and appeared wilder and the trees had become enormous. We were in an area of jarrah which usually is found in arid land. The cart proceeded with difficulty and the frequent hard bumps bounced us about in our seats; occasionally we ran the risk of being overturned by huge boulders or fallen timber. Innumerable little parrots, about as big as sparrows, swarmed in the forest; they flew continually through the bush like a green cloud, their strident call deafening us.

We came out of the jarrah forest and before us was a stretch of country like a large valley in the centre of which was a vast swamp which, in the rainy months, is probably transformed into a lake. The swamp does not appear on the map, which is completely blank for this area. Since leaving Mr Briggs' property we had not seen any sort of water; the horses were very thirsty and tired. We pulled them up on the edge of the swamp. Norrish stepped gingerly on to the less-than-firm earth and managed to fill up a little can of water which did not look too promising but boiling would purify it and kill off any microbes. We could slake our thirst with a cup of tea but the horses, unfortunately, would not have anything to drink. The guide did not think it advisable to give them what was possibly bad water. The poor animals were so tired that we decided to stop here and let them rest for an hour or so.

We took advantage of the stop to scour the surroundings of the swamp for game. We each took a different path. All at once a wallaby, which is a kind of medium-sized kangaroo, jumped in front of me for a moment, then disappeared. I saw several wild horses but, even if I had had a shot, they would not be suitable game. I had to be content with killing several rosellas, beautiful, brightly plumed parrots, mainly red in colour; they are found always in pairs whereas the other varieties live in flocks. I returned to camp to discover that Norrish had wreaked havoc among the parrots and doves. It was an odd thing that no-one had found any water birds even though we were close to a swamp. I believe they are completely absent from this area.

Norrish had found an abandoned Aboriginal camp. I went to look at it. There were several huts of branches, in a manner of speaking, being simple, semicircular, slightly raised hedge-like structures. More than a protection from the rain or sun, they serve to shield the occupant from the wind. In fact the English call them wind-breaks. We noticed traces of large fires near the huts.

We moved off again about four o'clock. For a while the bush continued to be very thick. Suddenly a big mob of kangaroos appeared in front of us. Some five or six of them stopped to stare curiously at us. In the less inhabited areas these animals do not flee from man but sit awkwardly on their hind legs and look at him. If the man does not move they remain in their position for a long time. It seemed as if the sight of us had hypnotised them. Norrish handed me the carbine which I carefully aimed at the biggest animal in the group, only about fifty metres away from me. However, I was so overcome with emotion at the sight of such a magnificent wild animal that the rifle shook in my hands. I fired but did not hit it and instantly the whole flock disappeared. I felt angry and disgusted at my lack of nerve which I found difficult to come to terms with. But both Norrish and Kittel reassured me saying that, even in Australia, these things happen to hunters making their first attempt at a shot.

The further we went the more fertile the soil appeared. The grass was very high and the vegetation was comprised almost exclusively of jams and many-branched blackboys. It was an enchanting sight. Hills succeeded hills and plains, plains but with a variation of aspect and character that continued to surprise. The blackboys were so tall they looked like palms in the distance. There was no shortage of animal life, even ants. There were parrots, wild turkeys and mobs of kangaroos everywhere. What a paradise for the hunter! However, we were out of luck. The shell-case of a cartridge had become jammed in the barrel of the rifle and it was impossible to get it out having lost the proper piece of wire. The other two rifles were small calibre ('pea guns'—in truth little more than children's toys) which were absolutely useless for big game. We had to be content, particularly Norrish who was an obdurate hunter, with looking longingly at all God's gifts passing in front of us, without being able to take a shot.

Towards evening we stopped in front of a fence. Obviously we were in an inhabited area or at least one already occupied by a squatter. Unfortunately the gate was locked and we were at a loss as to how to proceed. To knock down a fence to allow the cart to pass is viewed very unfavourably here in Australia. However, we could not stop indefinitely. Fortunately one of my keys opened the lock and we were able to pass through. It was the first time I had seen such a practice in Australia and to put the inhospitable owner in his place we left the padlock open.

We thought we had kept a straight path heading south, or slightly south-west and, according to our calculations, we should have found ourselves once more on the Kojonup–Bridgetown Road. However, we realized that we had trekked west and had reached the Dinninup River. Actually we had intended to visit this area but we thought that the lay of the land would require us to make a wide circle in order to reach it. So we thanked providence that the distance had been thus shortened. We were now in the midst of very high rocky hills, one of which grabbed our attention. It was the Darling, a real mountain, the like of which is rarely found in Western Australia. The countryside here was oddly similar to that of the Apennines.

There were four or five farms at this spot on the Dinninup. The soil here is generally very good and the farmers are well off and pleased with their situation. We were invited to take refreshments by a Mrs Lilly Draper. Her dining room was filled with a number of small personages. 'These are my children,' she announced proudly. I counted eleven of them and the woman was just thirty-two years old! The population of Western Australia may be sparse, but its people seem to be working very hard to remedy the situation.

The Dinninup at this point was not far from its junction with the Blackwood. We decided to push the horses a bit harder in order to reach the larger river before evening and make camp. However, it was quite late when we finally arrived. We came to rest in a magnificent grassy area surrounded by a thick screen of trees which would protect us from the cold night breeze. The tent was set up in a few minutes and soon a welcoming fire glowed in the darkness and we warmed our numb limbs. It was my job to make the tea, a new task which I carried out quite well.

We had hoped that further west the temperature would be milder and that it would not be necessary to borrow blankets from the farmers in Dinninup. We were quite mistaken. I was obliged once more to jog about before dawn in order to prevent myself from literally freezing. My companions, lucky things, being less affected by the drop in temperature, slept peacefully all night.

Chapter Seventeen

Along the Blackwood—The Stewart Property—
Ants and Ant-hills—The Bush Maze—Norrish's
Resourcefulness—The Popularity of the Italian
Consul—The Agricultural Development of
Western Australia.

December 30. I woke them up at six o'clock; my excursion on foot had convinced me that the land in this area was not very fertile. Conversely the river was very rich in fish and shell-fish, particularly freshwater crayfish and crabs.

We intended that day to flank the Blackwood as far as its confluence with the Arthur River. We were now in partly settled country and the track was fairly good. Thus, it would be possible to cover greater distances than in previous days. The river at a certain point flowed in a wide semicircle; to save time we took a short-cut across the arc. We could see that the land here was also not of a high standard, being very often composed of quartz, rock and iron nodules; in the side valleys there was the usual reddish earth. After an hour spent travelling across uneven country we met again with the Blackwood. The track continued to run alongside it but went up and down because of the rocky hills through which the river flowed. The view was most attractive in some sections. Kittel could not help himself and stopped the carriage to photograph the landscape from this height. These photos probably turned out to be the best of those taken.

We crossed the river about eleven o'clock. We were now on Mr Stewart's holding which was comprised of some fifteen thousand acres. Today it would be difficult for anyone without capital to acquire such extensive lands. However, at the time, Mr Stewart had been able to avail himself of the now-defunct law respecting 'poison land' to which I referred in Chapter Thirteen. He had recently fulfilled all the necessary conditions, the construction of fences, the eradication of poison grasses etc., and shortly the freehold title to the land will be transferred to him by the government. However, now he needs the capital to purchase the necessary stock. At present only 600 sheep graze on his 15,000 acres which could support ten times this number.

One section of the land near the house had been ploughed and cultivated; its yields were extraordinary. A small vineyard, about a half-acre in size, had so many bunches of grapes it seemed as if the vines would break under the weight. On one plant alone I counted at least forty bunches.

Nowhere else is it as difficult to gauge the worth of the soil at first glance than in Western Australia. When it is still uncultivated and virgin the rains which beat down on it wash away the top-soil leaving what seems to be quartz gravel or iron nodules which are frequently mixed with the vegetable matter here. It could be said that at first glance some land appears to be absolutely barren. However, scratching around in the soil soon disproves this. We were also fooled. We believed Mr Stewart's land to be of poor quality; the entire property seemed to us to be one huge expanse of sand and gravel. The magnificent recently ploughed soil in the vineyard and garden proved to us the error of our first impression.

The attachment which Mr Stewart had for his land is difficult to describe. Even though it was too big for the means he had at his disposal no price on earth would persuade him to give it up. Even in the remote wilderness of Australia, where the land mass is beyond the colonizing capacity of the populace, the passion to own and expand one's possession of land beyond that with which an individual could be expected to cope, is common. An individual will never say it is enough! The fever is contagious and anyone moving about the country feels himself unconsciously infected. The passion for land, so well described by Zola, which may seem to be a sickness afflicting only very developed countries with high density populations, is, instead, common to all humanity and demonstrates once again that, where there is need, mankind's passions are the same, irrespective of the race to which he belongs or the country in which he lives.

We continued our journey northwards. The path was not easy, nevertheless we travelled quite quickly. The countryside was somewhat monotonous and the road dusty. To fob off boredom and fatigue I took to driving the horses. Kittel, who had broken his arm some weeks ago as the result of an accident, looked at me with some misgivings. We arrived at the junction of the Arthur and the Black-wood and stopped for lunch. The sun was shining in a cloudless sky, but a fresh, in fact cold, wind was blowing which made the stop somewhat uncomfortable. We sheltered behind a building which served as a school and forced ourselves to cook our meal. It was no easy task because the wind was determined to blow out the fire and fill our eyes with smoke.

We followed the Arthur for four or five miles along its left bank. We then crossed over and turned south-east. Initially we encountered several farms growing wheat and later others given over to pasture. The grass was dry and yellow everywhere. The soil, which was not bad, was very compacted and in some places had the consistency of a brick. The tepid water in the rivers and pools did little to slake our thirst. We knocked at nearby houses in the hope of buying a bottle of beer or wine but no one answered.

I advise anyone who travels in the inland of this country to carry with them, if not a supply of beer or wine, which may be bulky, at least a bottle of cognac or whisky with which, as they say, to clear the water. Tea, which is appreciated at the beginning, becomes tiresome after a while and it is difficult for the European stomach to get used to it.

The architecture of homes in the bush was the same everywhere: single storey with a verandah all around. And, everywhere, the same hatred on the part of the Australian farmer for greenery: the trees are scrupulously cut down near the houses; no grapevines or creepers, no greenery that might give shade. We were in a countryside with a Roman severity of aspect.

We soon left the farms behind and again entered virgin country. What a delicious part of the world! Once more the grass was very high, there were jams and blackboys and green foliage on the trees, cool shade, the forest undefiled by mankind. We were now in an extremely fertile district whose lands had been set aside by the government for future group settlement. The land was gently undulating and the track went off into the distance following the line of the hills. Ascents and descents were continuous. The valleys were enchanting, the timber was not too dense and the grass superb. At the highest point the forest became more dense; from up there the view was of a green sea that waved in the breeze like a field of wheat. Norrish estimated the size of this area to be about twenty-five square miles. Gradually the jams and blackboys disappeared giving way to a thick forest of white eucalypts. However, the soil continued to be excellent. It was black loam, slightly sandy, and probably better than that through which we had just passed. This second area was considerably larger than the first.

It was by then getting late and we decided to make camp. We stopped first at a pool whose banks were covered with innumerable red flowers; flocks of birds rose up at our approach. However, Norrish did not think the water was very good and advised us to press on to the nearby Kojonup creek. All along the two miles which separated the pool from the creek we encountered large numbers of kangaroos, but they were very shy and took off at such speed that we were unable to get in a shot, even though Norrish had repaired the carbine by then! We were completely out of luck! However, we hoped for revenge the next day and resolved to spend all morning hunting. Norrish assured us that game aplenty would fall to his aim.

The carriage stopped near a small lake full of very clear water; we were on the banks of the Kojonup. As we unloaded the cart calamity struck; we realized that we had lost the axe. This tool is essential for anybody who travels in the bush. Without it it is impossible to pitch a tent, cut wood etc. We would have to resign ourselves to sleeping in the open and go to bed without anything warm in our stomachs. Luckily we noticed another tent some way off. We called out but no one answered. Norrish said that it must belong to kangaroo hunters who were probably out searching for game. Without ado we went in and picked an axe from the many lying about on the ground. We will return it when we no longer have use for it or, better still, we will buy it.

The temperature that evening was extremely mild as the cold wind had died down. Nevertheless, the weather continued squally and a storm seemed in the offing. We hastened to get under the tent, but we were fated not to sleep that night, not because of the cold but because of a sickening stench that sprang up from goodness knows where. It was like being close to a rotting carcass. It was pitch dark and impossible for us to change our location. Norrish, who was unable to stand it, went out with a lantern to investigate and finally found the cause of the stink; it was the putrefied body of a huge sheep that had been tied up to a sapling by one leg and lay half-submerged in the pond about two or three metres away from us. Obviously it had been left there by the kangaroo hunters to attract the crabs. Norrish gallantly dragged it a hundred or so yards further off. There was torrential rain all night. The tent was not in very good condition and the water dripped through quite merrily. Thus we got an early bath.

December 31. We woke up in the morning to superb weather; the air was shining and clear. Only along the river was there a wisp of bluish fog which gradually dissipated under the sun's rays. The heavy rain of the previous night had perked up the leaves on the trees and the grass beneath; everything appeared luxuriant and full of life.

The scrub around the lake was populated by innumerable large blue, red and green parrots known as twenty-eights because of their particular cry. Like the black variety of parrot they are considered to make excellent eating. Kittel and I targeted them with our pea-guns and killed several. Norrish had leapt into the saddle as soon as he had got up and armed with the carbine had gone off in search of kangaroos. I filled in time strolling around the environs of the camp. The soil was really very good; it was not the common chocolate or reddish-brown type which, albeit fertile, has the tendency to go very hard in the sun after it has been wet by rain. This, instead, was a very black light and friable humus that would be exceptionally suitable for all kinds of cultivation. Norrish was of the exact same opinion. He estimated the annual rainfall here to be between 25 and 27 inches which made an ideal blend of soil and climatic conditions; it would be a perfect spot for our settlement.

During my brief stroll I had noticed a large number of ant-hills which varied considerably in shape and height in accordance with the many species of inhabitant. Some very small, almost microscopic, ants built cylinders of what seemed like rammed earth which quickly took on the texture of stone. Others built little mountains of stalks and twigs, shaky structures which could be easily kicked down. The largest hills were constructed by sergeant ants, also called bull-ants. These are the largest of the species, some individuals reaching to a length of three centimetres. Their offensive weapons are formidable, comprised of strong jaws and a long proboscis whose sting is extremely painful. They are very aggressive and without fear; a sergeant ant, even on its own, will not hesitate to attack any animal that it perceives as a threat. I have seen many launch themselves against me, jaws open and in a challenging position. With their heads raised they followed my every movement with close attention. It might be said they have been blessed with a quite intelligent expression. When they attack they never give up and they would rather be squashed than retreat. When camping it is essential to ensure one does not disturb their nests. Otherwise one must take off at speed. Strange to say, the leech is the one creature that scares them. I had been told this and wanted to prove it for myself. We filled up an empty milk tin with these disgusting little creatures, which swarm in these freshwater pools, and poured them on to the top of an ant-hill whose inhabitants we had previously disturbed with sticks. We saw the ants hurl themselves on the intruders but, as soon as they got whiff of them, they retreated in all haste. Regarding ants, it is an odd fact that, here in Australia, not only sergeant ants, but most other varieties also, are furnished with a sting.

Norrish arrived downcast; he had not located any game. He had, however, made up his mind not to return to Kojonup empty handed. So he went to borrow a dog from one of our neighbours who obliged and offered to accompany him. They all mounted their horses and disappeared into the dense bush. Before long we heard a shot and shouts of joy; it was the hunters returning in triumph with their kill. It was a medium sized kangaroo whose meat, I was assured, would be succulent.

It was just after ten o'clock and the indefatigable Norrish invited me to go with him on a new raid, this time for parrots. It was not too onerous; all about was absolutely swarming with the squawking birds. We walked together for a short way along the track, then he left me to pursue a large flock while I continued in the opposite direction. I did not want to go too far away for I was well aware how easy it was to lose oneself in the bush. Experience quickly showed me that my fears were well-founded. A quarter of an hour went by, then half an hour and still the guide had not returned. I began to feel anxious and called to him a few times without result. I fired my rifle but no one answered. I thought the best thing to do was to sit down and wait. Wandering about achieves nothing other than to separate one from the other even more. After a long fruitless wait I decided to head towards the camp which I was sure was northwards. After walking for ten minutes I saw Norrish who was returning laden with game. I asked him if I had been heading in the right direction. 'Right direction?' he asked in astonishment, 'Certainly not, my dear fellow, exactly the opposite; the camp is behind you.' The incident convinced me more than ever of the difficulty, in fact the impossibility, for anyone who is not a bushman, experienced in the true sense of the word, to find his way in this Australian bush, the aspect of which is unchanging for hundreds of miles.

As I have already noted there are many cases of persons becoming lost, even close to town, often with fatal results. The lack of water and very cold nights can kill a poor soul in a few days. Several months ago the body of a young man was found in a stretch of bush which ran between two tracks which converged close by. The spot where he lay was no more than five miles from either road and yet he perished, unable to extricate himself from the labyrinth. His tracks showed that

A group of prospective settlers inspecting land
Battye Library, 4045B/19

Consul Zunini's camp near the Balgarrup river
Battye Library, 20658P

for days he had wandered about in a very restricted space going round and round in big concentric circles.

Back in camp we cooked our prey while the camera recorded the important event. Before setting out once more Norrish wanted to show me his ability and resourcefulness as a bushman. We had spoken about people who were lost dying of thirst in the inland where there is usually a total lack of water. Norrish told me that they would run no such risk if they were equipped with an axe. He showed me how to survive: selecting a young sapling he cut it off close to the ground, and then snapped it close to the top-most leafy branches. Keeping the sapling upright he bent the top branches over and placed a small container under the break. In an hour it was filled with very clear, good drinking water.

We left about two o'clock to return to Kojonup. The country we passed through was a little less fertile than formerly. Our camp was nineteen miles from Kojonup but all the land in a ten mile radius was already taken up. Even so we found the district to be almost un-inhabited. Settlement on agricultural land in the last few years has proceeded at an amazing pace, and it is certain that before long it will be difficult for newcomers to obtain Crown Land. One will need to have recourse to private sellers and pay the prices they feel like asking.

We came to large paddocks covered entirely with blackboys. They were even growing in the middle of the track making it difficult for the buggy to get through: the wheels continually struck their spongy trunks. One had to get down and remove the obstacle with an axe. Norrish took advantage of this to let me taste one of the delicacies of the bush. He cut off a blackboy at the point where the leaves join the trunk and offered me what I would call the tender part of their roots. It was really delicious, with a flavour somewhere between celery and almonds. This guide is really an able man; his help on a long trek would be invaluable. I mentioned how he obtained water from the trees. Taking advantage of a brief stop he showed me how to light a fire without matches as the Aborigines do by rubbing together two pieces of wood.

We arrived at Kojonup at five in the afternoon and, without ado, indulged our long dreamed-of desire to down a few bottles of cold beer. We were fed up with the eternal tea and hot muddy water from the swamps!

A telegram was awaiting us in Kojonup from Mr Ranford who said that that evening he would arrive with a group of settlers. I began to feel somewhat concerned, fearing that space would be limited and that our people would no longer be able easily to find a spot. Of course the number of newcomers is not overwhelming because, as I said, only farmers with means can establish themselves here. However it must be borne in mind that in Western Australia farming is generally carried on alongside grazing and, as a result, much more land is needed by the farmer. Genuine settlers apart, one has to fear more the speculators and profiteers who buy up the land for the sole purpose of selling it, thus taking it away from those who really want to cultivate it, or else artificially pushing up the price.

Mr Ranford arrived about ten o'clock that evening with his cohort of farmers; there were Australians, English and Maltese. I had arranged to go back to Perth the next day. However, he was so insistent he persuaded me to stay another day in order to accompany him on the following day's excursion.

January 1, 1907. We went to Mr Vanzuilcom's property, which I had already seen ten days earlier, and then on to another farm ten miles out of Kojonup belonging to a gentleman whose name escapes me. As soon as we went inside he introduced me to his wife with these words: 'Here he is at last! The Italian Consul about whom we've heard so much and who we were so anxious to meet!' I met this warm reception everywhere more or less. I was pleased about it because I realized that our nation was becoming better known and the name of Italians held in greater respect. The atmosphere was becoming decidedly more favourable although there was still considerable prejudice against us. It was, as I have repeated ad nauseum, the product of ignorance, which needs to be refuted by calm and effective means. One must battle against it continually with energy and renewed enthusiasm.

Many times, I must admit, I was demoralized. What was the use of all the work I have done here when our people show total indifference to this country and its resources and fail to develop profitable relations based on mutual self-interest?

Chapter Eighteen

Journey to Geraldton—Its Surroundings—
The Government Farm at Chapman—Erin Farm—
Paradise—Newmaracarra—Glengarry—
Dongara—The Phillips Farm—An Australian
Sunset—The Salt Lake—Arrival in Perth.

I returned to Perth and resumed negotiations with the government on the agreement. However, I shall discuss this later. For now, given I am in the mood, I shall talk about my trip to Geraldton which was the last in chronological order.

The Minister for Agriculture had decided to inspect the model farm which the state owns at Chapman Valley near Geraldton. Grave doubts about the functioning of this enterprise had arisen in government circles and an on-the-spot investigation was needed to ascertain the true situation. The Minister would be accompanied by his private secretary, Kealy, the under-secretary for Agriculture, Despeissis, and the editor of the *West Australian*, Mr Dryer. The Minister insisted that I accompany them. He said it was a golden opportunity for me to visit the northernmost part of the agricultural district which, until then, had been outside the scope of our travels. In his company I would have every opportunity to familiarise myself with all aspects of the area. Besides, the country we would cross was of particular interest because, as far as the fertility of the soil was concerned, some sections of it were equal to any in Australia. I also thought the occasion was most propitious. I thanked the Minister effusively for his kind thought and told him that I accepted the invitation with pleasure.

We left Perth on the evening of February 21, taking our places in the ministerial compartment which was coupled to the Geraldton express. The Western Australian government has a number of these carriages which are used for the frequent tours of the state made by members of the cabinet and by the governor. They are most elegant and furnished with every modern convenience. They usually comprise four compartments, a lounge and dining room, bedroom, kitchen and luggage space.

We travelled as far as Moora along the route we had taken three months earlier. At every stop our compartment was crowded with people coming and going to pay their respects to the Minister. There were also on board several other members of parliament and senators who were returning to their homes, the current session of parliament having ended that day. Mr Mitchell had courteously invited them to share our compartment. Among them I noticed Mr Brown, a member, and Senator Stone, both of whom then joined us for most of the trip.

We arrived at Geraldton (population 2500) the next day about noon. It is situated about 287 miles from Perth. Its port, which is the third most important in the state, is the natural outlet for the mineral region known as the Murchison, as well as the rich agricultural and grazing area of the Victoria Plains. Steamers, which link the ports of the north-west with Fremantle and Singapore, call there regularly. Geraldton is connected with the state's main centres by railway. The southern line, along which we travelled, puts it in touch with Perth and thus with all the central and southern rail network. The Nannine line (318 miles) ties it to the very important Murchison mineral area while the line to Northampton (33 miles) reaches the northern extremity of the agricultural zone.

There was a large crowd of people at the station to greet the minister. We were taken to a reception at the Town Hall. I was seated at the official table and had the pleasure of sitting next to Mr Drew, a minister in the Daglish (Labour Party) cabinet. A number of speeches were made; the local representatives, as is usual on such occasions, expressed their needs and their hopes. They would like easy credit terms for developing the export market. All were concerned with the wheat crisis because the price had dropped recently to two shillings per bushel no less! The price had hit 'bed-rock,' to the use the expressive English phrase.

The Mayor had organised several vehicles to take us to see the outskirts of the town. He wanted to show the Minister the work being done to bring drinking water to the town centre. Like Albany and Fremantle, Geraldton has been built in the middle of a sandy area. As soon as one leaves the circle of houses one finds oneself in a real desert. This sort of landform, surrounding Western Australia's most important ports as it does, has done incalculable harm to the state in that it gives strangers the impression that all of Western Australia is comprised of barren land. It needed the discovery of the Kalgoorlie goldmines to put paid to that myth. The newcomers who had occasion to travel in the inland saw with their own eyes that the sandy section was very limited and that beyond were fertile lands.

We reached the site of the works. Deep wells had been dug near existing springs of fresh water which, by means of pumps, will be brought to town. However, it is a sandy area and the water always tastes slightly salty. For Geraldton, the problem of drinking water is one of the most difficult to resolve because inland there is a total lack of rivers or permanent creeks.

Back in town we went to the club where a reception, at which I was treated with great cordiality, was held in our honour. In his speech at the Town Hall Mr Mitchell had referred most courteously to my mission saying that he was greatly interested in the project. An official statement of this kind from the Minister certainly makes a favourable impact on public opinion.

During the brief time I was in Geraldton I struck up a friendship with the good Mr Brown, the member for the district. He belongs to the Labour Party but he is a moderate and enjoys the respect of all for his equanimity and good nature.

We left Geraldton immediately after our visit to the club. It was arranged that we should follow the railway to Northampton as far as Oakabella and from there proceed by buggy to the government farm at Chapman. The Geraldton–Northampton railway, the first in Western Australia, was opened in 1879. Its purpose was to link the port with the very rich mineral sector (lead and copper) which extends in a great arc, ten to fifteen miles wide and a hundred miles long, to the north and north-east of Geraldton. Now it also serves agricultural interests. However, the railway was constructed in the stupidest manner. The developers received a set sum from the government on a per mile basis which resulted in an inordinately long line but one with little attention to the quality of construction. Given the easiness of the terrain, it is hard to conceive how the builders managed to incorporate so many curves, elbow bends, zig-zags and ups and downs. The line is now in a deplorable state and needs to be completely reconstructed as trains continually run the risk of derailment.

A few miles out of Geraldton the sand gave way to an excellent, very friable, red clay soil which continued as far as Oakabella. This area, however, was only slightly cultivated, the district being neglected these past years. And yet it was well-endowed by nature: wheat yields 20 or more bushels to the acre; the rainfall is regular at between 18 and

21 inches. Even though water is scarce on the surface, one has only to dig a well a few feet deep to obtain excellent and abundant supplies. The timber is light and would not cost more than £1 to £2 per acre to clear. The area can, without doubt, look forward to a great future.

Carriages, which belonged to a Mr Jupp, a wealthy landowner of the district who was engaged to show us around, were waiting at the Oakabella station. We travelled through undulating country where the trees were sparse and of medium height, and in half an hour arrived at Mr Burges' property where we were right royally received. The farm, known as The Bowes, is one of the biggest and most fertile in the state. It is comprised of 132,000 acres, 12,000 of which were fully owned and the rest conditionally. (When one buys land from the state, ownership remains conditional until the purchaser fulfils the requirements set by the law after which ownership is full and absolute.) The Bowes River, which flows in a deep valley just near the house, crosses the entire length of the property, considerably enhancing its value. A permanent water supply is, in fact, like money in the bank for the squatter.

Mr Burges was engaged almost exclusively in grazing to the exclusion of agriculture. Only 200 acres of his vast holding was cultivated, whereas he had 32,000 sheep, 300 cattle and 100 horses. He reaped huge profits as a result of buying, fattening up and re-selling flocks of extremely emaciated sheep which had been driven hundreds of miles on foot from the north-west to be loaded on ships for export. His scheme for sheep was similar to that practised by Mr Roberts with cattle at Yatheroo.

We reached the government farm, which was situated in the middle of a wide plain, towards evening. We were met by the manager, Mr Reys, who immediately took us to visit various areas. The buildings, used to house the students, staff and management personnel, were extensive, while further off were the stables, granaries and machinery workshops etc. Like the other government farm at Narrogin, here they experiment with different crops and raise the best breeds of cattle. However, we postponed a general inspection of the farm until tomorrow.

Mr Mitchell and I were assigned to the same room, the best in the house. It belonged to the manager who moved out for the occasion. I had also occupied the same compartment in the train as Mr Mitchell. But while it was certainly an honour for me I could not get used to the early morning habits of his excellency; he was always up before daybreak. His extraordinary energy did not allow him to rest for more than a few hours.

The next morning we enjoyed the 'country life' under the guidance of the manager. Mr Mitchell took note of every minute detail. He wanted specific information about the earnings of the farm, the costs, the methods of farming etc. He did not seem very pleased. He was not prepared to believe that such a fertile property, upon which the government had lavished money, could be in debt. In any event we saw some magnificent wheat fields and splendid breeds of sheep.

The nutritive content of the northern pastures was amazing; the grass dries up completely during the summer months, and yet the sheep manage to find adequate food to keep meat on their bones. We were close to one paddock which was about fifty acres in size. Noting that the grass had been completely dried up almost to a powder by the sun, I asked the manager if that section of land could carry more than two or three sheep. 'Two or three,' he exclaimed in amazement, 'Don't you know that more than a hundred have grazed there the entire summer?' We went into the paddock and the manager grabbed a handful of soil; mixed with the dust were a large number of oily seeds —the secret of fattening up the sheep without grass was explained. However, besides these seeds, a good supply of water, not lacking at Chapman, is indispensable.

On the farm there were also experimental paddocks for pasture grasses. We noted with interest a planting of salt-bush, an excellent fodder which grows in the more barren and sandy areas. It gets its name from the salty taste of its leaves which all stock find utterly delicious. There are five or six varieties. Some form a low scrub only a few centimetres high, others are more than a metre high. I sent some seeds of this plant to the director of the faculty of agriculture at Rimini, who had asked me for them to see if they could be acclimatised in the sandy area along the Adriatic coast. I am unaware of the results obtained.

After several hours touring around we returned to the school. Mr Mitchell gathered the students together in a large hall; the manager, teachers and ourselves were present. Without ado he told them that he was not at all satisfied with his visit. The property was in debt, the students did little work and were poorly disciplined, the farm machinery was antiquated and working cattle numbers were insufficient. It was not his intention to criticize the manager, who had drawn his attention to the problems and had done everything to try to overcome them. But he intended to see from now on that everything went smoothly. He wanted to restore order, upgrade the equipment, and ensure that the farm ran at a profit. The students, when their time came, would be farmers. Therefore, it was of primary importance that their education show them how a property could be well run. If this farm was a failure how could they have any faith in their teachers' methods?

Rarely had I heard a minister deliver such a frank and sensible speech. Mr Mitchell blurted out the truth without ceremony even though it concerned an institute which fell within the ambit of his own ministry and he had to reckon with the fact that strangers, including the representative of a foreign country, were present. I could not help but admire this and my estimation of him went up still further.

At long last we took our leave of the manager and departed to visit the area to the east of the coastal railway. Initially we crossed through the property known as Erin, formerly owned by Mr Lee Steere but subsequently bought by the government and sub-divided into smaller lots which were sold to farmers. Unfortunately, however, the government's plan to have the land cultivated did not eventuate. The land is still virgin and the existent pastures have not been expanded.

Mr Dryer believed that the present settlers in the Geraldton district were unsuited to develop the area, at least as far as the cultivation of the soil was concerned. They were the descendants of the first colonists who arrived in Australia a hundred or so years ago. They had come at a time when one person could easily obtain hundreds of square miles of land and make a living with little effort. The population did not grow, there was no struggle of the fittest and those who lived there became lazy and indifferent. New blood and energy are urgently needed to infuse new life into this people in order that they do justice to what is one of the most fertile areas in the whole of Australia.

Before we got to Erin we stopped for lunch at Paradise, which is the name of the property owned by Mr Jupp. He is one of the most bizarre, but at the same time one of the most likeable, persons I have ever met. He is very comfortably off now, although he came to Australia with nothing and worked at a number of jobs before turning to agriculture. An old feud existed between Mr Jupp and Mr Dryer and all through lunch there were continual colourful and acerbic exchanges between the two which we found highly amusing.

At Paradise we saw a magnificent orange grove which aroused the admiration of all the visitors. However, I noticed that the plants were suffering somewhat from the dryness. I am of the opinion that it would have been better to have chosen a more moist soil. Less than half an hour later we reached Erin Farm in the centre of which was the residence of a Mr Mehan (the house was formerly the homestead of the previous owner, Lee Steere). Mr Mehan had us stop for tea; the time-honoured social niceties are always observed in Australia.

We were travelling across splendid country. It was lightly timbered with only a few eucalypts; we noted some of the white variety in the valleys. Jam and banksia, with its conical flowers, abounded, as well as wattle, whose shiny long green leaves made it easy to identify. The road was very badly kept, in some places little more than a furrow gouged out by rain. Both Mr Jones and myself, in the same lightweight, two-wheeled gig, had to hang on tightly so as not to be thrown out.

We finally reached the fences of Newmaracarra. It was a magnificent property considered to be the most outstanding in the agricultural sector both because of its size and the fact that it was owned outright. This is a rare thing in Western Australia where most of the land (that is, the large farms) are rented or owned conditionally.

The bush has been cut down in many places and ringbarked in others but there was no sign of cultivation, the land being given over entirely to pasture. We then passed through a section characterised by fine deep sand. The vehicles became bogged on the sandy road and the horses were unable to proceed. We were forced to get down and do the remaining two or three miles on foot which was not the most pleasant thing.

Suddenly we found ourselves in front of the gates of a sort of palace, a huge yet simple construction but not without architectural taste. The overseer met us and informed us that the owners, the Grant brothers, were away. However, one of them was at Glengarry, another part of the property, situated many miles away. We would see him tomorrow as we would pass by Glengarry on our return journey. The overseer invited us in and, without ado, told us to make ourselves at home.

We quickly realized that it was the home of a wealthy and cultured family. The rooms were richly decorated and there were a number of paintings and statues rarely found in Australia, where the artistic sense is not well developed. However, in the present situation, art was of little interest even to us. We were quite literally dying of hunger. Luckily there was a good cook on the staff, a Japanese who earned our undying thanks for the delicious meal he provided. An appreciation of art reasserted itself, but on a full stomach. We played music all evening and would have danced but for the complete absence of the fair sex.

The following morning we visited some of the outbuildings, in particular the huge shearing shed (there are some 30,000 sheep on the property). Large scale turkey farming was also carried on at Newmaracarra and we noted countless numbers of the birds. The overseer furnished us with some interesting data with respect to the property. It is about eighteen miles from Geraldton and crossed by the Murchison railway line. It comprises more than 100,000 acres, of which 40,000 are of good quality, 40,000 mediocre and 10,000 sand. The land is generally undulating but in some places the inclines become hills, several of which are extremely rocky. The entire property is enclosed by a seven-wire fence and sub-divided into 53 enclosures ranging in size from 200 to 2500 acres each. £55,000 had been spent in improvements, including £7500 for the eradication of poisonous plants. The present value of the property is more than £150,000.

Messrs Stone and Brown had left us the previous evening to return directly to Geraldton. However, we still planned to visit Glengarry, the Greenough plains and then link up with the railway at Walkaway, south of Geraldton. The overseer offered to accompany us to Glengarry and drove the carriage in which I travelled. I have rarely met anyone more reckless and indifferent to danger. He whipped the horses along at a furious pace which was all right on the flat and going uphill, but absolutely chilling when we got to the top and found the track went straight down the other side. The path was very steep and I realized that the horses were no longer responding to the reins. The brakes were not working and the carriage tumbled at breakneck speed down the slope. I thought I was about to breathe my last, and, grabbing the bar in front of the seat, I awaited the final catastrophe. It happened half way along the track that luck intervened and the buggy collided with a tree and came to rest. We emerged with only psychological damage.

We finally reached Glengarry. The homestead was situated atop a high ridge at whose base flowed the Greenough River. We were met by Mr David Grant who, having been informed of our coming, was waiting for us. Although still quite young he is an expert on pastures and completely dedicated to his work. He and his brothers live the lives of country gentlemen spending all year on their own land. Really, when one is the owner of such immense and profitable lands it is worth while becoming a peasant; one makes a so much greater profit than many other professions! The good Dave was also very keen on horses and his stock was among the most esteemed in the district. There was an enormous circular building near the homestead. In times past Glengarry raised horses for the British army in India and the building served, then as now, as a riding school.

The overseer went back with his carriages. Mr Grant took us himself to Walkaway. The road was better and the driver more expert, or at least more prudent, given that nothing further untoward occurred. We followed the course of the Greenough River, flanked by its rich plains which are renowned all over Australia for their fertility. Glengarry holds the higher up lands, whereas the valley section is sub-divided into smallholdings. It is a pity that agriculture is completely ignored at Glengarry because the magnificent soil, if cultivated, would yield splendid produce. A judicious combination of grazing and agriculture could also raise present flock numbers.

We were now on the southern bank of the river. The earth, which was completely cleared and cultivated, was of a light brownish colour and very fertile. Here also the populace is very lazy and, despite the excellent conditions, there was relatively little produce. By three o'clock in the afternoon we reached the railway at Walkaway. Our special carriage was ready and without further ado we seated ourselves. The train moved off and in a short while we were at Dongara.

The train stopped here for about an hour; the Minister's brother lived in the town and he decided to go and say hello to him. We were off to Mr Phillips' property and planned to link up with the train at a station further south. Dongara, which is also a sea-port, is a small centre with about one hundred inhabitants. The surrounding land was very fertile and well cultivated, the soil a mixture of clay, iron-oxide and calcareous debris, greyish in colour and in some place tending towards red. The populace was very energetic and, given the favourable nature of the climate, agriculture and grazing were well developed.

We went by buggy to the home of Mr Phillips, one of the most important land owners in Dongara. His holdings, situated on the banks of the Irwin River, were magnificently cultivated. The bush had disappeared completely with only a few of the biggest trees remaining. We admired several head of cattle to which the owner drew our attention. They were splendid animals, so fat that they could hardly move. They rivalled those owned by Mr Roberts.

We picked up the train at a small siding south of Dongara. We travelled quickly across the Arrino and Three Springs area which was largely owned by the Midland Company. The country was still covered by virgin bush but, given its fertility and the entrepreneurship of the company, it was destined to become a very important agricultural centre.

The countryside was magnificent; the sun had already set and the sky was tinged with a dark pink which quickly changed into violet. On either side of the line the bush closed in. In the dusk we could still make out tall, thin, column-like trees close by us; the dense foliage on their umbrella-like branches stood out blackly against the sky. Further off they marked out a dark and uneven line which faded into the immensity of the horizon. Suddenly the half-light was broken by a whitish patch of light. We were crossing the dried bed of a huge salt lake. All around, as far as the eye could see, it looked as if the earth had been blanketed by a huge snowfall, but a strange sort of snow which did not melt at a temperature of 25 degrees.

We left the lake behind. Night was well and truly upon us and we were no longer able to take note of the surrounding countryside. We left the outside observation platform and went back to our compartments. We supped pleasantly, had a few hands of cards, chatted and went to bed. Without realising it, we passed through Moora and the other stations, waking in the morning at Midland Junction. A few minutes later we were in Perth.

* * *

My narrative has almost come to its end. Mr James arrived back from Europe and, with the passage of the new agricultural laws, I began negotiations in earnest to draw up an agreement. These negotiations, which had extended over January and early February, and had been interrupted during our trip to Geraldton, were now renewed. I had thought the matter would have reached a satisfactory conclusion in a few weeks but I was mistaken. Difficulties, particularly those of a legal nature (mainly that of reconciling the clauses of the agreement with the existent legislation, given that the Australian government did not wish to be seen to favour foreigners), sprang up continually despite the good will of all, particularly that of Mr James and Mr Mitchell whose support was invaluable. Accord seemed a long way off.

My sojourn in Australia was necessarily extended, so I took advantage of the time to intensify, if that were possible, my work of publicising the advantages of our settlement and of Italy in general.

I had proof on a number of occasions that my efforts had not been in vain. The opposition of the radical wing of the Labour Party had become very subdued, while the more moderate section, not less the Liberal Party, were decidedly in favour. I am not referring to the government, which openly supported the project. Mr Mitchell was particularly enthusiastic about it. In fact, he told me that he intended to go to Italy to take part in selecting the families and be responsible for their welfare at the point of departure. Such a journey, he believed, would also provide an opportunity to forge friendly relations between the two countries and encourage reciprocal trade. The good man was keen to see if Italy could become a market for Australian products such as wool, frozen meat, wheat, timber, etc. Our country, for its part, would be able to export a wide range of its products to the southern continent, presently overlooked by us in commercial terms. However, neither visit could come to fruition until the Italian government sanctioned the project.

The disposition of the Western Australian government towards Italy and towards Italians in general was very cordial at the time. They never failed to show me, as a representative of a friendly power, courtesy and respect. I cite the following incident as an example.

On March 18, Mr Deakin, the Prime Minister of the Commonwealth, passed through Perth on his way to the Colonial Conference in London. The government of Western Australia gave a banquet in his honour. Ministers in office, ex-prime ministers, the President of the House of Representatives and the Senate, as well as Mr Deakin's entourage were invited. I was the only other person invited besides this group, a distinction not without significance. After dinner Mr Deakin came to congratulate me for my efforts with respect to the immigration of farmers to Australia. He told me that he agreed entirely with the project and he hoped that it would soon be approved. That his words reflected the sentiments of a large part of public opinion in the rest of Australia was borne out by the number of invitations I received from Chambers of Commerce and other officials from the vast states of the Commonwealth (Queensland and New Zealand in particular) to visit them and exchange ideas concerning the possibility of settlement in their region.

An unfortunate incident, which luckily ended on a happy note, occurred at this time and helped cement the good relations between Australians and Italians and served also to demonstrate the good will of the Western Australian government towards our countrymen. I believe it is worth mentioning, it having had repercussions throughout the Commonwealth.

Following torrential rains which fell in late March, a stream of water suddenly broke through into a mine near Coolgardie filling up the shafts and galleries in a few minutes. Most of the workers managed to get out, with the exception of one of our countryman, a certain

Modesto Varischetti, who, at the time of the disaster, was at the lowest level of the mine, about 800 feet below the surface.

All believed that the poor fellow was unquestionably lost, assuming he had drowned in the torrent. Everyone was completely stunned when regular rappings were heard indicating that he was still alive! The particular shape of the gallery, like an up-turned siphon closed at one end, had saved him. The column of water had poured down violently but the pressure of air had prevented it reaching the upper section where Varischetti had managed to secrete himself. His position, whichever way one looked at it, was desperate, imprisoned as he was in a very small space, lacking food and light, and separated from help by a barrier of rock and water hundreds of metres deep. Draining the mine would take at least ten days and, in the meantime, the prisoner would be dead from hunger and fear. There was nothing for it but to attempt to rescue him with divers. Several brave persons volunteered.

The government, as soon as it was apprised of the calamity, quickly took the necessary measures. The Minister for Mines, Mr Gregory, who assumed charge of operations, proved to be tireless and beyond mere words of praise. He organised a special train to leave Perth immediately, loaded with all the necessary equipment and with three divers from Fremantle aboard. He gave orders that everything humanly possible must be done to save Varischetti without regard to expense. The good man also remembered to telephone me every few hours to keep me informed about the rescue operations.

The riskiest part of the operation—reaching the spot where Varischetti was trapped—was assigned to diver Hughes. The man who undertook the task must have had a heart of steel for he showed no respect for his own life. It was not a case of dropping down in the open sea, but in narrow shafts, in galleries half filled up with detritus dragged in by the force of the water and full of thick mud and cloudy muddy water. Added to this the divers were hampered by the need to carry air hoses, electric cables and food for the prisoner. After numerous descents and eight days of continual draining of the mine, Varischetti, helped by Hughes (the water still reached chest height) was finally rescued from his tomb.

The news of the disaster, the efforts of the government and the heroism of the divers (the other two also undertook risky descents) spread like lightning throughout the Commonwealth. Extra editions of newspapers and special bulletins sold like hot cakes. There was a continual crush of people at newspaper offices and many made regular trips to the site of the calamity. Enthusiasm for the divers reached delirium and, by extension, compassion for the victim ran deep. The Australian populace, apparently cool, calm and collected, has actually the ardour and exuberance of southerners. In fact the country they live in is southern, if by southern one means a hot or at least temperate climate. As with our people, Australians have sudden outbursts and their passions, good or bad as they may be, are violent and cannot be held back. The entire Italian community was instantly identified with the victim and all our countrymen enjoyed the good will and friendship of the Australian people. Such a moving and sincere moment had never happened before.

As is the custom here, appreciation of the divers was expressed through expensive gifts. To this end a subscription was opened all over Western Australia, and other states contributed generously. Nor was Varischetti forgotten. The Italian community showed its gratitude to Hughes by presenting him with a splendid gold medal and a purse of money. The occasion was celebrated by a very nice party in Kalgoorlie.

However, the main honouring of the divers took place in Perth, with the government and the entire populace taking part. The Town Hall was chosen for the occasion; on the stage were the Governor, ministers, the Mayor, the Anglican archbishop, the divers, Varischetti, myself, as well as other notables. In the gallery and the stalls, a crowd, the likes of which had never been seen before, was assembled. There were a number of orations and I too spoke, to great applause. Such was the enthusiasm of the crowd that, when Varischetti was leaving, he was embraced and kissed indiscriminately by men and women, young and old. I was also treated to endless displays of good will.[1]

I shall conclude this digression and come back to the point. By the end of March the agreement was finally reached. *Only two or three points remained unresolved*, which, if required, could be finalized directly between the Commission and the Western Australian Agent-General in London, who would be furnished with full powers for the occasion. I must note at this point that, according to instructions received, the negotiations I conducted were *ad referendum*, in order that His Majesty's government could propose modifications if it saw fit.

---

1 I have been informed that His Majesty's government has accepted my suggestion that the title of Cavaliere be conferred upon Mr Gregory, and a medal for civilian bravery given to Hughes, as well as other lesser honours to those who distinguished themselves during the accident. The British government has also conferred honours.

I sent the text of the agreement to the Commission together with a memorandum compiled by Messers James and Mitchell which set out and explained the technical side of the document. I also included a special report I had prepared in which I traced the history of the negotiations, cleared up some points in the agreement which, without knowledge of the local legislation, were misleading, and I commented on the main clauses pointing out the reasons behind them.

I ended the report with the following words:

> In conclusion I believe I can say that, apart from some minor finishing touches, the project is sound and acceptable. The settlers, if chosen as they should be, are certain to succeed, and the Commission of Emigration is not likely to lose a cent or, at least, will run only a minimal risk. For my part, I have always maintained that this project was not one of concluding a rushed agreement but to begin, even with some small sacrifices, a flow of emigration that, if wisely directed and linked to relevant capital investment, could be of significant importance to our nation.

* * *

My mission could be said to be at an end. One important task, it is true, remained. I had already closely examined the Blackwood area and had found it to be suitable for the settlement of some of the families. About fifty families could be easily placed in this area; some near Darling Hill, some between the Arthur and the Kojonup River, on fertile land with plenty of rivers and springs. I now should have gone to inspect the second area in the extreme south, the eventual site for settling the rest of the families. The Minister for Agriculture had several times urged that we undertake this trip together.

However my return to Italy became necessary for a number of reasons. Firstly and above all, because the Emigration Commission wanted me to be present at discussions which the Commissioners intended having about the settlement project and the relevant agreement with the Western Australian government. Thus, I reluctantly had to decline what would have been a most interesting trip, hoping fervently that I shall be able to undertake it at a more propitious time.

Shortly before my departure I received a letter from Mr Mitchell, part of which I reproduce here.

Perth 26th May, 1907

To Cavaliere Zunini, Palace Hotel, Perth.

My dear Zunini,

I take this opportunity to wish you *bon voyage*, with the hope, nevertheless, that you will soon return.

I trust that, during your time in Italy, you will be able to bring the immigration project to a successful conclusion. Do not forget that I very much want to see Italian farmers settled in Western Australia; in fact, I hope that the first group (which I trust will arrive shortly) will be the forerunner of others to follow in the near future. There is no need to assure you of my utmost cooperation in the scheme. You know full well that I shall be most happy to interest myself in whatever way possible to ensure your fellow countrymen are allocated land to their liking.

I also think that your return to Italy could be very useful in other ways. Western Australia is most suited to private investment. Should your friends feel it opportune to invest some of their capital in this state I am sure they would reap a rich harvest from whatever sector they chose to involve themselves, whether it be in agriculture, cattle raising, the pearl industry, timber or minerals . . . The Kimberley region is wonderfully suited to cattle raising. Its importance is growing and is further enhanced by its proximity to European and Far Eastern markets. As you know we lease land, designated for grazing, for quite long periods at a nominal rent.

If any Italian liked to interest himself in this industry, you might, for example, point to the vast and exceptionally profitable properties in the area. The same applies to the North-West land where sheep are raised. It should be noted that the demand for sheep and lambs' wool is increasing continually. These products can be exported with great ease to Europe and all over the Far-East. I want to point out at this juncture that Western Australia has this advantage over Eastern Australia, in that drought here is scarcely known. For this reason our land is preferred by many . . .

We also have unlimited land suitable for pasture in the Eucla region across which the Trans-Australian railway will cross. At present it is almost completely unoccupied; there could be a great future there for sheep and cattle raising . . .

A number of your fellow-countrymen are already settled in different parts of our state. They have proved to be excellent settlers and a boon to this country. You can recommend Western Australia with confidence to those of your compatriots who are seeking 'new lands and fresh fields.'

Of the 40,000,000 acres referred to above, some 30,000,000 are still available and you know only too well the generous nature of our land policies . . . The Western Australian soil is extraordinarily fertile and can furnish any product needed by mankind. A lot of the land is suited to the type of intensive farming you practise in Italy.

Should you decide to recommend any of the aforementioned enterprises to your compatriots, you may be sure that I shall be only too pleased to help their efforts in whatever way I can.

Once again, wishing you a pleasant journey, I remain yours sincerely

James Mitchell, Minister for Agriculture

I arrived in Genoa at the end of June.[2]

---

2   In July the Emigration Commission approved the agreement in full. In December, after a lively debate, a majority of the Emigration Council, which had been called in to give a final opinion, also approved the scheme suggesting, however, several modifications.

Conclusions

I shall be as brief as possible in order not to repeat what has already been said throughout this work or what appears in the appendix which follows. Moreover, readers, who have had the patience to follow my narrative up to this point, will have had the opportunity to form their own firm opinion about the situation in Western Australia and of settling our farmers there. I hope that my conclusions will have the good fortune to coincide with theirs.

As far as I am concerned I can say honestly that a careful and impartial study of the situation has convinced me that Western Australia is presently most suitable for the project under discussion.

The land is very fertile. Of course I do not mean to imply that all of the two and a half million square kilometres of Western Australia are suitable for agriculture or grazing. There are large expanses of desert, and, in the agricultural area itself, there are tracts which are completely unusable. However, one cannot deny that the best land is such that it more than compensates for the more barren part.

The climate is superb. One can say without exaggeration that the climate of Western Australia, at least in the agricultural area, has no equal anywhere in the entire world. Frosts are practically unknown there (apart from some light hoar frosts during the winter months), while excessively hot days are very rare. Except for the extreme south, gale force winds are not common. Generally a light, pleasant fresh breeze prevails. It is like perpetual spring with clear, calm skies. The rainfall, which is very regular, varies from 10 to 54 inches a year, depending upon the area, and is sufficient to ensure growth of every kind of crop. The rainy season begins at the end of May and continues until the end of October. However, it is not characterised by the sad, dark and gloomy days to which we are accustomed in Europe. Rather, rain falls in heavy showers that last for half an hour, an hour, two hours at the most, and are followed by clear skies for several hours (note that the showers are more frequent at night). Drought is unknown in the agricultural areas, although it inflicts much irreparable damage in the eastern states of the continent. The grazing sector is often afflicted by the scourge but it never lasts for more than twenty months whereas in Victoria and New South Wales it has lasted for four years.

The agricultural areas are well-provided with running water or, when this is not available, by underground springs, found only a few feet down. Permanent watercourses are numerous in the far south. In the central and northern districts the rivers run only in winter. In summer they are transformed into a chain of pools and small lakes where the water is always excellent.

The agricultural laws in Western Australia are among the most generous and liberal in the entire world. The price of Crown Land is very low: 10 shillings an acre. For some time they have been asking slightly higher prices for the top quality land (however, it must be remembered that the first 160 acres are always free). The only condition imposed is that some improvements be made and, in some cases, that the recipient take up residence. To avoid the concentration of land in few hands and the formation of large estates, the law limits the amount of land one can purchase from the Crown to not more than 2000 acres per person. However, these restrictions are not always effective and there are a thousand ways of overcoming them.

Even though I have referred to the agrarian legislation in Western Australia, I will, for general information, give a list of the main classifications under the Land Act. It defines the following types of property and the method by which they may be acquired.

1. *Family farm (free homestead farm).* An area of between 10 and 110 acres; priced at £1 including legal costs. The settler must reside in person on the property for five years. He must build a habitable house with a minimum value of £30 and fence the property. A quarter of the land must be cleared and cultivated in the space of seven years.

2. *Conditional purchase land.* Areas of between 100 and 1000 acres, at 10s an acre. Other 1000 acre lots may be acquired in particular circumstances. The purchaser must reside on the site for five years. A tenth of the lot must be fenced within two years and the rest within five years. Improvements worth the value of the property must be effected within ten years. Land may be bought under this scheme without the residence proviso; however, in that case, the value of the improvement requirement is doubled.

3. *Land for orchards, vineyards and market gardens.* From 5 to 50 acres. Priced at 20s an acre or more, payable in three years. Improvements, including fencing, to be made within three years.

4. *Working men's blocks.* Anyone who does not possess Crown Land and who is head of a family, or is a male of eighteen years of age, may obtain a block of land of between one and five acres at the cost of £1 per acre payable by ten instalments. The holder must live on the property for six months of the year for five years and must undertake certain improvements.

The state not only sells land but also allows it to be rented. I have referred elsewhere to lands that were leased for grazing purposes. There are also areas rented for the regular felling of timber, in so-called 'timber leases,' under the following conditions. The maximum area is 75,000 acres, the price is £20 for every square mile (a square mile is about 640 acres) for a period of between one and twenty-five years. Within two years the lessee must erect a sawmill and cut a minimum amount of timber each month.

Special permits are also granted to individuals who intend to cut timber in smaller amounts for commercial purposes. The licence is valid for between one and twelve months and costs 5s to 10s per year. No licence is needed for those who cut wood for personal or family use.

The special terms under which the Land Act grants land to all settlers are as follows (noting only the main ones): 1) Half the cost of surveying and mapping the land is borne by the government. 2) Any *bona fide* person who travels to a district in search of land has the right to free travel on the railway, as well as free transportation and the assistance of a local guide on arrival. There are special rates for the transportation of families and their belongings. 3) All recent arrivals can obtain passage to Australia from Europe. 4) For their families settlers may borrow sums up to £500 per annum from the Agricultural Bank.

Public opinion in Australia is now very much in favour of the immigration of our farmers. I have spoken earlier of the xenophobia that existed in Australia years ago, which I found was very much alive when I first arrived there. I have also explained that this attitude originated in a fear of the 'yellow peril' which, given the proximity of populous Asian nations which are developing rapidly and posing a threat, is no myth. One can begin to understood that a state, which must be strong in order to defend itself, needs a population and that a state as vast as this needs a population even more. Such points are patently clear to us but, for the mass of Australians, they require a certain amount of time to sink in. But how to procure such a populace? To wait until the numbers reach the required level by natural increase would be foolish. It would take centuries, and many of them! It is, therefore, necessary to turn toward immigration; but from which countries? The White Australia Policy (which is a wise policy to which I subscribe wholeheartedly), the thrust of which rigorously seeks to exclude coloured races from Australia, necessarily entails an appeal to the people of continental Europe. British immigration alone cannot fill the need, because it is both small and comprised of labourers and tradesmen, whereas in Australia they need farmers.

These latter make for a stable populace with a love of country, ready to defend it against danger at whatever cost or sacrifice. Moreover, only farmers can develop the limitless, still virgin expanses, and create the real wealth of the country; the mines are destined to peter out but agriculture and grazing will always yield their fruit. The increase in the population produced by so-called workers is imaginary. They are nearly always unmarried, they come and go, and cannot be relied upon. Instead, the farmer brings his family with him, he is stable and is, indubitably, the creator of population in new nations.

Among farmers of different nationalities Italians are always distinguished for their intelligence, sobriety and industriousness. It is not surprising, therefore, that Australians are coming around to the idea that accepting a certain number of our fellow countrymen as settlers would be, from all accounts, of inestimable value. It is a well-known fact here, and one which the delegates and I observed for ourselves, that no Italian farmer has failed. On the one hand this proves the very favourable situation that exists in the country, while on the other it attests to the splendid personal qualities of our farmers.

I have said that public opinion is in favour. There is, to tell the truth, a remnant of opposition within the radical wing of the Labour Party, which fears that farmers may leave their lands and turn into workers competing on the labour market. However, these last flickers of hostility will disappear forever when the fine achievement of Italian farmers is seen in practice.

The time is at hand for the settlement of our farmers in Western Australia. The country has made gigantic progress following the discovery of gold. The population has grown so quickly as a result that local agricultural produce cannot satisfy demand. Only wheat has recently reached market saturation; but not so for other products. I noted earlier that at present they import about £40 million worth of goods which are directly or indirectly related to agriculture. Thus, the prices are very high and profitable. The central region and the far south are suited to mixed farming and are the most likely to produce that which Australia lacks at present; and so it is there, where they cannot fail to prosper, that we wish to settle our farmers.

The establishment of Italian agricultural settlements in Western Australia will be to the great advantage of not only the individuals who take part, but also for our country in general. I have already dealt with this matter in full but is worth while making the point again. Only by establishing groups of our people in Australia can we initiate links with this country which, from such modest beginnings, will rise to great heights, *using other suitable, agreed-upon means.*

Everybody knows that in South America and more recently in the United States our trade owes its origins to emigration. It began with the export of purely Italian consumer goods (those which the English call 'Italian delicacies' including oil, pasta, salami, wine etc.), and then, with the path open, the scope of business was enlarged leading to very important trade links. Without doubt, the same thing would repeat itself in Australia. Nor let us forget that, whereas in Latin countries the Italian element is rapidly absorbed with the local culture and lost to the motherland, in Australia, given the particular circumstances (the little or no contact with the local populace whose culture is completely different) our true national characteristics may be preserved for a longer time.

It is not a case of satisfying some platonic sentiment but knowing how to retain, by means of our settlements, the useful and reciprocal gains which disappear or diminish when our race becomes completely assimilated with an alien one. The scheme which I have outlined above concerning the development of our relations with the so-called new nations has, unfortunately, another side. Where the Italianness of our people (and I use the word 'Italianness' in the widest sense possible, that is language, usage, tastes, customs, love of the mother country etc.) has vanished because it has been absorbed into the local population and has had no infusion of new blood to keep it alive and functioning, our trade, albeit well established and prosperous, does not grow with the same intensity as in those countries where the Italianness of our people remains strong and vigorous. (It seems to me that there are two main reasons for this phenomenon: one is of a general nature, that is, national sentiment—which always prefers the products of the mother country to foreign goods—decreases relative to the situation; the other refers to our exports to so-called new nations; this continues, even after some time, to be confined mainly to goods consumed by our people. When this demand tapers off, because they have adopted the local tastes and customs, trade ceases.)

A case in point is Uruguay, where there has been no Italian immigration for some years. The old settlements have disappeared and been replaced by a generation where Italian exists in name only, having been completely assimilated into the Castilian culture. Thus in Uruguay our trade has suffered a rapid decline, as the following figures attest so eloquently.

	Exports to Uruguay (L.)	Imports to Italy (L.)	Total (L.)
1886	10,070,000	3,256,000	13,326,000
1887	11,243,000	2,442,000	13,775,000
1904	4,769,000	1,611,000	6,380,000
1905	5,528,000	823,000	6,351,000

The same phenomenon would, in all probability, be found in nations in the same situation as Uruguay. In any event our trade has to overcome long and difficult times, having to compete as it does with that of more favoured nations.

Despite all I have said up to now, I certainly do not want to argue that it is desirable that our settlers in Australia should never mix in with the local populace. Nevertheless, I maintain that, given the particular circumstances in the country, our national sentiments and customs will be preserved for longer, thus favouring our commercial dealings. Besides, the settlers' children will become fine Australians. Certainly one cannot deny that those born there will love Australia and consider it their homeland. To aim otherwise would be to go against the laws of nature. However, we can hope that the life force of our nation, the best part of the race, does not go only to enrich others, but also represents an advantage to us, if not in political terms (in the case in point this would be patently absurd), at least in a commercial sense. And the longer that may be, the better for us.

A number of objections to the scheme have emerged in Italy where most people know of it in only the most superficial way and largely misunderstand its aims. There are basically three points of contention.

1. It will encourage the emigration of farmers which, actually, needs to be stopped. The emigration of our peasants in such numbers is worrying and projects which give a new impetus to such an exodus should not be allowed.

It should be pointed out that, in the present situation, it is not a matter of augmenting existing numbers of emigrants but of directing a group (which, unfortunately, cannot be other than small) to areas where they might prosper admirably. Given that emigration exists and cannot be cancelled by the stroke of a pen, our task must be to create the most suitable outlets. In any case four or five hundred persons will not depopulate Italy, given that the selection of emigrants will take place in densely populated provinces which would hardly be affected at all. In the meantime, if the example of these few families serves to dissuade a section of our farmers from going to die of yellow fever in some countries or to be almost reduced to slavery in others, well and good—indeed, will not the whole project be of the utmost advantage to our country?

2. It will initiate colonization under state auspices. Presently, all Italian legislation affirms the principle of the absolute neutrality of the government in emigration matters. To be more precise, government intervention must be seen only in terms of protecting the emigrant, never of encouraging his departure. Acceptance of the scheme in question implies a renunciation, at least in Italy, of principles which are more or less universally accepted.

The critics forget that this is a very special case of an exceptional nature. As I have said elsewhere in my book, one needs to remember the particular circumstances in Australia, which has always been a closed shop, where, with very few exceptions, Italian farmers have been unable to gain a foothold. Only with the establishment of a settlement of our people will the barriers fall for our future settlers. In fact, the first group will act as a natural point of reference for those who follow, and who will thus find their way smoothed and be able to count upon friends and relatives. It might happen down there, as it has generally in Argentina and America, that the first to arrive form the core of many other flourishing settlements. But in Australia personal initiative is not enough. It is a case of breaking down barriers which have always appeared insurmountable; it is an undertaking beyond the ability of any individual.

The problem to be overcome, which the projected agreement will, without doubt, accomplish brilliantly, is to settle the first group. *Only on this occasion is the concurrence of the Commission of Emigration needed.* The flow of immigration which will follow will be of an independent nature and will have no need of outside help. It seems to me that in all these negotiations there is only one question to answer: is the projected enterprise in our best interests or not? If no, then let us abandon it forthwith; if yes (and I think there is no doubt about it) let us pursue it to the end, even if it entails some *momentary deviation* from the rigidity of certain theoretical principles.

3. The project will only benefit Australia. If they are really interested in having our farmers why do they not take on all the responsibilities of the undertaking? Even if its role is eventually reduced to the minimum, there is no need for the involvement of the Commission.

I do not believe that I have to repeat everything I have already said to prove there are considerable advantages for Italy if the project comes to fruition. However, I want to make one observation. Several of the so-called 'yellow' newspapers, as well as the radical wing of the Labour Party, maintain that the project will confer undue advantages upon our farmers; according to them, Australia would gain nothing; everything would accrue to us. It seems to me that such differences of opinion best illustrate the fact that the agreement distributes advantages and responsibilities equally between the two countries.

Some, even though they agree that it is useful to open up outlets for our agricultural immigrants in Australia, ask why this task cannot be assigned to a private company?

The answer is simple. A private company acts on the basis of profit, whereas, for a government, it is enough to believe that they have acted for the benefit of the country. Therefore, a company has to impose strict regulations on its settlers which often turns into a stranglehold. Unfortunately there is no shortage of relevant examples. Furthermore, as I have already noted, the Australian public has views on the matter which, I do not hesitate to declare, are very just. In Australia there is no reason why the farmer has to be exploited by the middle-man. This is why the Western Australian government is disposed towards generous terms, such as offering land at very low prices and extending credit to agriculture, in order that settlers may rise to the rank of owners as soon as they arrive without the need of those parasites who, in other countries, grow fat at the expense of the worker. Why, therefore, bother to deal with a company? What would be its function? Would it not mean a repetition of the pain such companies have inflicted on the history of settlement in other areas? If it is impossible for immigrants to come independently, is it not better that the two governments, acting in accord, make the way easier and thus prevent any exploitation? The principles outlined above are consonant with the semi-socialist tendencies of the Australian states, tendencies which, while they leave themselves open to criticism, have nevertheless brought considerable benefits to the country.

Others are against the project because they cannot easily understand why the immigrants are directed towards non-Latin countries. According to them, if the government and individuals want to develop any sort of a scheme with respect to immigration, it should aim only towards South America where it is easy for our emigrants to maintain their Italianness and where, for the most part, they can mingle with and strengthen peoples who are similar to the Italian race. There is no denying that South America is now seen, from many standpoints, as a fine destination for our emigrants and I would not totally disagree. But to see it as an ideal place in which Italians can retain their identity is a very grave error and shows little practical knowledge of the country on the part of those who hold this view. The fact is that, without a continual influx of new contingents from the mother country, Italianness would be submerged in a short time. In South America there is considerable affinity between their people and ours because the fusion between the two has taken place slowly and is not, it should be understood, to our advantage. Unfortunately, it is no secret that the Italian worker or peasant, and very often more educated individuals, having spent several years in America almost forget their native tongue or are ashamed to use it. It is also a fact that their children, who have been born there, are more American than the Americans themselves.

It therefore seems absurd to me to suggest that our emigration policy should be aimed at strengthening countries of Latin origin! We need to have more practical goals, to leave aside the usual empty idealism which is, unfortunately, an unenviable characteristic of our race. However, there is no reason for us, on account of unattainable goals or misplaced idealism, to overlook countries which, as I have already mentioned, offer considerable advantages, especially when our immigrants will find conditions in such countries more favourable from the point of view of retaining their Italianness than in many other places.

Radicals, in respect to emigration matters, who do not want to hear anything about Australia or America or any other country outside Italy, are always present. In the Roman countryside, the *Maremma* and in Sardinia, they say, we have huge expanses of land where it is possible to locate thousands of families and alleviate the emigration problem. I believe that in this regard we are labouring under a misapprehension. One example will be enough. Every year some 800,000 persons, a good proportion of whom are farmers, depart. For how long could the uncultivated inland areas be expected to absorb them before reaching saturation point even if such a stream were to be channelled in their direction? A few years perhaps, and then? The phenomenon of emigration would reappear exactly as before. Certainly the opportunity, or rather the necessity, of eliminating the desert wastes of central Italy is obvious. But the problem of emigration will be solved by firm and energetic action and not by means of internal migration. And, as long as this phenomenon exists, it will be necessary to seek the best terms for those citizens who emigrate and for the state which sees them go.

Even if well-directed, an emigrant stream will never bring great benefit to the mother country if she ignores capital investment in that country. I believe that the foregoing has demonstrated the desirability of promoting the emigration of farmers to Western Australia. However, it is pointless to delude oneself. Italy, by simply exporting labour, can never occupy an important position overseas (I refer in particular to nations in the New World) and build up investments as other countries, notably Germany, have been able to do. Even under the most favourable conditions, such as those outlined in the proposed agreement with the Western Australian government whereby individuals would settle as land owners, it takes many, many years before our emigrants are financially secure and confident enough to be a significant factor in the country in which they have settled.

Generally speaking, emigration, when separated from capital, goes back to the old story of the Jewish slaves who built the pyramids for the Pharaohs or, in modern parlance, of the exploiter and the exploited. And unfortunately only workers leave Italy. Our capitalists stay at home and are indifferent to what happens elsewhere. It is true that a financial crisis has beset Italy recently and that the times have not been the rosiest. But even when the state of our markets and stock exchanges starts to change, when the wounds begin to heal, confidence returns and capital begins to flow, do you think things will change? Certainly not; it will be as it always has been and we will let ourselves be discredited by foreigners and leave the development of a multitude of resources, in which we could have participated, to them.

We chatter a lot, we are intoxicated by words and we believe that Italy is important in world terms, perhaps because it represents Latin civilization, and that it is heir to the medieval republic and champion in the world of the principles of Roman law or whatever. We are completely mistaken; and it is well to realize that there are very few countries where Italy counts for anything. In Australia, for example, Italians are known as a proletarian rabble who go about begging for any kind of work. How else are we to be perceived when capital investment, either in the shape of shipping companies, commercial houses, banks or other developments, is a mirage that never material-izes? People believe in that which they can see, and they will never have respect for a country which seems so poverty ridden, even when, in fact, the opposite is true.

It is pointless to delude oneself at this time. Capital is needed for internal industrial development, although, unfortunately, our inertia is again evident and one sees many lucrative industries, many develop-ments in the heart of the most advanced cities (including my own Genoa), being exploited by foreigners. But even in acknowledging that capital is needed at home, is there not enough left to invest overseas to ensure that Italy's influence is not always negligible?

Take Germany for example: has it not built a colossal industrial base; has it not had to undergo the same crises as we have and, like us, had to set aside too much capital in its national industries? And yet, did it not find a way to establish a prime position overseas in terms of commerce and finance and compete with England in its own colonies? Would it not be possible also to reserve some of the capital that is presently at 'work' (I use the term in its stock-market sense), or it might be more exact to say 'squandered,' for this patriotic and profit-able cause?

Furthermore, with respect to Australia, we see how the English, Germans, French, Belgians and Swiss have been able to establish very important commercial links, set up industries and exploit the country's enormous resources. We, instead, have been content to take on the most menial jobs such as being pedlars, organ grinders, fishermen etc. The 'big-wigs' of our communities are fruiterers or restaurateurs of the lowest order! While there is no shortage of workers such as cooks, miners etc., who earn good wages, they remain persons who can never rise to a prominent position and will never be able to convey to the public at large any sense of the country from which they have come. And yet what a productive field of activity Australia would be for the energies of our clever capitalists! What vast resources to exploit, what commerce to initiate! Limiting my observations to Western Australia, which I know very well having lived there for four years, I can state that, from this point of view, the conditions are entirely favourable.

I deal with this matter in greater depth in my official report concerning trade in this region, a report which is published as an appendix and to which I recommend the reader. I will say only that Western Australia is presently at a crucial point in its economic life, such as when one passes from infancy to sturdy youth, and that this may well be the most propitious moment for us to invest some capital. Even with modest sums, judiciously placed, we might be able to secure a significant position which, in the future, could improve and increase markedly. At present all the signs are favourable (the settlement project, in the event that it comes to fruition, would give a fillip to the process); but if we let the occasion pass us by, will we ever have another chance? Others, more entrepreneurial than we, will have taken our place. I hope that that will never happen, but rather, that Italy will decide to take its rightful place in the new world. I would consider myself to be amply rewarded if my efforts led my fellow countrymen into new fields of endeavour and in this way contribute to the glory and prosperity of the beloved motherland.

APPENDIX

*Western Australian Commerce with notes
concerning Australasian trade*

*Report by Cavaliere L. Zunini,
Royal Consul at Perth
Published in 1907 by the Ministry of Agriculture,
Industry and Commerce*

The commercial development of Western Australia dates from 1890, the period in which gold deposits were discovered in Coolgardie and Kalgoorlie. Fifteen years ago the importance of the region was minimal. Suffice to say that, although the area of Western Australia was close to a million square miles, its population in 1891 numbered little more than 50,000. The trade figures amounted to only £2 million sterling. However, since that date, there has been extraordinary progress.

The following table demonstrates the total value (£ stg) of imports and exports from 1891 to 1905:

1891	2,079,559	1899	11,459,174
1892	2,273,257	1900	12,814,232
1893	2,412,585	1901	14,969,794
1894	3,365,820	1902	16,269,710
1895	5,107,505	1903	17,094,654
1896	8,143,783	1904	16,943,991
1897	10,358,663	1905	16,352,893
1898	10,201,971		

The increase in population was also most noteworthy; from 53,000 at the end of 1891 it grew to 250,000 at the end of 1901.

My survey of the commercial trends in Western Australia will examine, in particular, data for the four-year period 1901 to 1904 which is the most complete. However, where possible, I shall include data for 1905.

The overall worth of trade (expressed in £ stg) for the aforesaid period, divided between imports and exports, is as follows:

Year	Imports	Exports	Total
1901	6,454,171	8,515,623	14,969,794
1902	7,218,352	9,051,358	16,269,710
1903	6,769,922	10,314,732	17,094,654
1904	6,672,480	10,271,511	16,943,991

The value of trade per head of population is as follows:

1901	£79.9s.11d.
1902	£79.1s.6d.
1903	£77.5s.1d.
1904	£71.12s.10d.

Western Australia's trade is, for the most part, with Great Britain and with British possessions. Trade with foreign countries, *up to now*, as the following figures (£ stg) suggest, have been considered of little importance here:

Year	British Empire	Foreign countries
1901	13,692,462	1,277,332
1902	14,309,500	1,960,210
1903	15,502,269	1,592,385
1904	15,299,575	1,644,416

Even though the current ratio of trade is not such as to give British commercial interest cause for disquiet, one can not exclude the possibility that they may be in for an unpleasant surprise in the future. Indeed it is worth noting that in 1895 the total value of foreign trade amounted to only £58,442. The rapid growth of trade overall may be attributed to the establishment of superb steamship lines (mainly German) between Europe and Australia.

It is apparent from the import and export data cited above that the value of exports greatly exceeds that of imports. The difference, at first glance, seems inexplicable with respect to a new country which, until recently, had to import literally everything. The explanation is simple when one remembers that Western Australia is the third largest producer of gold in the world. This fact, however, is relevant only to trade with Britain. The opposite is the case with respect to trade with foreign countries where, as the following figures (£ stg) show, imports greatly exceed exports.

Year	Imports	Exports
1901	959,295	318,037
1902	1,363,038	597,172
1903	1,314,028	278,357
1904	1,223,237	421,178

The British producer would not be too pleased about the imbalance. Nevertheless, it must not be forgotten that the gold is almost all exported to England or to British possessions. Imports from Britain, even when the value of the gold is deducted, still greatly outweigh exports.

The above figures refer to trade between Western Australia, the British Empire and foreign countries. With respect to the above mentioned empire, I think the following table may be of interest, referring as it does to trade figures (expressed in £ stg) between Western Australia and the United Kingdom, the Commonwealth (Australian confederation), New Zealand (the only Australian state that is not part of the confederation) and other British possessions.

Country	1901	1902	1903	1904
United Kingdom	8,191,621	7,715,554	6,671,110	7,006,119
Commonwealth	3,133,642	2,845,451	3,407,975	3,009,606
New Zealand	133,965	279,717	197,337	90,819
Other British	2,233,234	3,468,778	5,225,847	5,193,031

We will now examine the relative importance of trade between Western Australia and foreign states between 1901 and 1903. The figures I cite give the value of exports from Western Australia, imports into each country and the total sum of imports and exports (all expressed in £ stg). The following table suggests, as I have already noted, that almost all the foreign countries are importers *par excellence*.

The figures, with respect to Italy, are not encouraging, being exceeded by most other European states. In 1903 little Switzerland and Belgium experienced five and four times more trade respectively, than we did. Only Holland, with trade totalling 12,680, Sweden 10,775, Spain 6901, Greece 5619, Austria 3001, and some other states with minimal trading figures are below us. In 1903, in terms of importance, Italy might be in sixth place among the European states, excluding Great Britain.

	1901			1902			1903		
State	*Exports*	*Imports*	*Totals*	*Exports*	*Imports*	*Totals*	*Exports*	*Imports*	*Totals*
Argentina	39,818		39,818		76	76		340	340
Belgium	4,102	104,506	108.608	41,194	17,481	58,675	28.356	38,410	66,766
China	11,841	2,027	13,868	36,803	27,627	64,430	21,639	20,966	42,605
Egypt	50,000	271	50,271	105,002	533	105,535		397	397
France	110	18,970	19,080	30	77,399	77,429	840	71,097	71,937
Germany	9,686	264,435	274,121	20,673	302,864	323,537	2,703	326,054	328,757
Japan	298	4,016	4,314	250,000	28,732	278,732	38	18,509	18,547
Italy	3	8,312	8,315	181	16,004	16,185	105	16,086	16,191
Norway	435	9,094	9,529		21,389	21,389		26,468	26,468
Sweden		17,575	17,575		9,980			10,775	10,775
Switzerland		2,160	2,160	5	66,213	66,218	2	84,750	84,752
U.S.A.	273	507,563	507,836	305	650,219	650,524	150	651,526	651,676

It is worth noting the large German trade figures bettered only by those of the United States and, as always, excluding those of Great Britain. When one remembers that in 1894 German trade amounted to only £2932, one can not help but admire a nation that has been able to make such gigantic strides. Unfortunately we have not been able to come anywhere near them.

Thus far we have examined Western Australian commerce in the most general terms; I would now like to examine it in more detail, looking initially at imports then exports.

Import Trade

I have already noted that for the period 1901–1904 the total value of imports (£ stg) was as follows:

1901	6,454,171
1902	7,218,352
1903	6,769,922
1904	6,672,480

These figures, relative to the various kinds of imports, are split up as follows (expressed in £ stg):

	Goods	1901	1902	1903	1904
1.	Precious metals (minted & unprocessed)	26,073	17,340	92	2,000
2.	Meat & fish (fresh,tinned)	118,833	146,263	212,401	219,674
3.	Spirits, beer, wine	219,780	289,271	236,384	236,472
4.	Tobacco, cigars, cigarettes	101,263	119, 525	169,167	137,385
5.	Livestock (sheep, horses, pigs)	251,780	277,591	263,895	218,608
6.	Bacon, ham, tongue, butter, cheese, eggs	522,112	650,684	631,278	607,677
7.	Preserved milk	"	"	"	"
8.	Sugar	132,539	143,758	159,930	187,517
9.	Clothes, textiles, hats, blankets, shoes, linen & cotton thread	777,192	996,276	940,938	957,340
10.	Timber, cement, furniture	232,133	173,344	209,885	226,440
11.	Ammunition, explosives	153,271	190,027	194,370	199,740
12.	Petroleum	122,435	81,494	101,009	104,114
13.	Machines, pumps, instruments	643,116	796,756	884,257	617,387
14.	Iron, steel, tools, metals, hardware	610,386	609,545	712,978	770,368
15.	Wheat, flour, oats, barley, bran, potatoes, onions	82,362	446,548	441,241	282,049
16.	Fruit & jam	117,920	119,797	127,364	155,288
17.	Tea	88,160	69,790	71,694	83,379
18.	Coal & coke	186,015	159,589	73,847	86,610
19.	Paper, books, etc.	108,167	133,161	156,097	172,326
20.	Cyanide (used in gold treatment plants)	144,819	161,191	170,646	108,084
21.	Jewellery, watches, fancy goods	65,406	85,216	93,204	96,066

Goods	1901	1902	1903	1904
22. Drugs, chemicals, medicines	59,716	65,210	82,062	96,133
23. Assorted goods	1,389,641	1,485,976	839,183	1,014,833

As the foregoing table indicates, the goods which have registered an increase are as follows: clothing, paper and books, watches, jewellery, drugs and medicines, sugar, jam, and edibles in general. For many of them, the increase has exceeded that of demand, a pointer to a growth in general affluence. The sharp increase in the category of ammunition and explosives and, until 1903, machinery, demonstrates the strong growth in the mining sector. By contrast, there has been a marked decrease in the importation of livestock, both cattle and sheep, and, since 1902, in bacon and hams (which are widely consumed in English countries), butter, cheese, eggs etc. Also, since 1902, a decrease in wheat, flour, oats, barley, onions etc.

The decrease may be explained by the rapid development of agriculture in recent years, cattle raising and allied industries. In some categories (e.g. wheat) the country is independent. There is still a lot to be done in this area, but the future is rosy for local production.

The drop in the importation of spirits, wine and beer is noteworthy. Other, more detailed, data suggests that the sharpest decrease has been in the area of beer and spirits. It is quite odd when one considers that Western Australia holds the world record for the consumption of these beverages, and that the amount increases every year. The apparent contradiction is easily explained bearing in mind that the country has also made giant strides in this area of industrial activity.

The decrease in the importation of wine is slight. Production has increased considerably in Western Australia but, until now, consumption has been confined almost exclusively to bottled wine. Beer and whisky continue to be the people's favourite drink; however, Western Australians are beginning to appreciate light table wine (claret).

The following is a list of the main products used in Western Australia in 1903. I have noted with an asterisk those products which Italy could supply at competitive prices. The table is set out as follows: name of the country which is the major supplier, the value in £ stg of the import and the customs regulations (which are the same for all states of the Australian confederation).[1]

---

1 It should be noted that, since the completion of this work, import duties have been increased, rumour has it, to the advantage of British goods.

List of goods imported into Western Australia in 1903

Type of Merchandise	Country of Origin	Value £ stg	Customs Duty
Vinegar	England	2,285	variable
	South Australia	324	
Mineral Water*	Germany	3,111	20%
	NSW	1,214	
	Victoria	730	
Towels, handkerchiefs	England	11,777	15%
Objets d'art*	England	1,787	
	NSW	261	
	Italy	2	
Paints & dyes	England	13,188	variable
	USA	3,604	
	Germany	608	
Beer (bottled)	England	53,379	1s 6d per gallon
	Germany	16,921	
	Victoria	3,133	
	USA	669	
Beer (in barrels)	England	4,387	1s per gallon
	Germany	353	
Orange & lemon peel	England	327	1d per pound
	Italy	183	
Butter	Victoria	261,668	3d per pound
	New Zealand	21,257	
	England	283	
Cotton socks	England	2,894	10%
	Germany	1,884	
Woollen socks	England	24,113	10%
Cameos & precious stones	Victoria	636	exempt
	England	441	
Candles*	USA	6,945	1d per pound
	Italy	18	
Straw & felt hats*	England	32,800	20%–30%
	Victoria	5,669	
	Belgium	1,550	
	Italy	1,464	
	Germany	846	
Salted meat & hams	Victoria	106,115	3d per hundred
	South Australia	18,030	
	England	4,834	
Frozen beef	Victoria	12,736	exempt
Frozen mutton	Victoria	35,222	exempt
Frozen pork	Victoria	22,542	exempt
Tinned meat	NSW	56,420	$1\frac{1}{2}$d per tin
	Victoria	19,178	
	New Zealand	8,278	
	Italy	14	
Stationery & office supplies*	England	20,718	25%
	Victoria	10,700	
	Germany	1,247	

Type of Merchandise	Country of Origin	Value £ stg	Customs Duty
Paper for adverts	England	1,651	3d per lb
	Victoria	972	
	NSW	802	
Paper bags	England	3,109	5s per cwt (50kg)
India rubber	England	12,210	15%
	Germany	4,453	
	USA	3,889	
	Italy	441	
Gelatine	England	338	exempt
	India	113	
Onions	Victoria	7,012	1s per cwt
	South Australia	1,826	
	India	308	
Fertilizers	England	13,149	exempt
	Victoria	7,577	
	NSW	6,043	
	India	1,751	
Fruit preserves	Tasmania	20,230	$1\frac{1}{2}$ d per lb
	Victoria	19,605	
	NSW	6,935	
	South Australia	4,245	
	England	1,736	
Raw hides	Victoria	12,676	
	NSW	9,295	
	South Australia	7,350	
	England	2,554	
Dressed hides	South Australia	4,608	
	Victoria	2,742	
	Italy	9	
Explosives (dynamite & gunpowder)*	England	96,289	exempt
	Germany	60,802	
Fancy goods	England	14,497	20%
	Germany	5,221	
	Italy	206	
Tools/hardware	England	180,330	various
	USA	44,864	
	Victoria	29,157	
	Germany	23,160	
	Italy	3	
Iron & steel (bars & unworked)	England	39,093	exempt
	USA	2,583	
	Germany	1,718	
	Victoria	1,004	
Iron (galvanised & sheets)	England	183,532	exempt
	South Australia	1,409	
Pig iron	England	15,441	exempt
Cheese	New Zealand	18,788	2d per lb
	Victoria	11,791	
	England	1,070	
	Italy	27	
Fruit & vegetables (tinned & bottled)	Victoria	13,762	duty according to size of container
	Tasmania	3,478	

Type of Merchandise	Country of Origin	Value £ stg	Customs Duty
	France	2,734	
	Germany	449	
	Italy	135	
Fresh fruit:			
Oranges & lemons	Italy	7,529	2s per cwt
	South Australia	4,026	
	NSW	928	
Apples	Tasmania	3,678	2s per cwt
	South Australia	1,832	
	Victoria	1,366	
Dried fruit:			
Almonds	South Australia	1,293	2d per lb
	Italy	611	
	England	402	
	Germany	145	
Raisins	Greece	4,448	2d per lb
	Turkey	713	
	Italy	25	
Sultanas*	South Australia	1,750	3d per lb
	Greece	816	
	USA	809	
	Italy	13	
Other	South Australia	1,339	3d per lb
	Tasmania	1,065	
	Italy	7	
Jewellery & costume jewellery	England	26,390	25%
	Victoria	10,249	
	NSW	4,398	
	Germany	2,290	
	France	31	
Leather & knitted gloves*	England	10,600	20%
	Germany	1,849	
	France	929	
Trimmings for hats & clothing	Victoria	846	15%
	Switzerland	558	
	France	527	
	Germany	500	
Electrical instruments	England	23,540	exempt
	Germany	7,295	
Musical instruments in general	Germany	1,067	15%
	England	860	
	USA	763	
	NSW	589	
	Italy	6	
Military band instruments	England	899	exempt
	Italy	2	
Instruments (organs, harmoniums & pianos)	German	12,773	20%
	England	2,373	
	USA	1,122	
	Italy	16	
Lard & animal fat	Victoria	4,782	$\frac{1}{2}$d per lb
	South Australia	3,206	

Type of Merchandise	Country of Origin	Value £ stg	Customs Duty
Condensed milk	USA	1,585	1d per lb
	Switzerland	74,527	
	Victoria	9,512	
	England	5,554	
	New Zealand	1,943	
	Belgium	1,481	
	Germany	1,411	
	Italy	17	
Books, publications, newspapers, sheet music etc.	England	30,581	exempt
	Victoria	5,040	
	Germany	153	
	Italy	91	
Macaroni & vermicelli	Victoria	1,135	1d per lb
	Italy	718	
	England	184	
Machinery (particularly for mining)	England	341,222	$12\frac{1}{2}$ %
	USA	90,045	
	Victoria	47,903	
	Germany	36,821	
Medicines	England	17,115	15%
	NSW	7,549	
	USA	5,104	
Marble blocks	Italy	599	10%
Marble (worked incl. headstones)	Italy	786	20–25%
	England	129	
	Germany	141	
Castor oil	India	6,607	6d per gallon
	England	311	
	Italy	14	
Cotton seed oil	USA	329	2s per gallon
Essential oils	England	697	exempt
	Italy	351	
Eucalyptus oil	Victoria	1,617	6d per gallon
Linseed oil	England	5,825	6d per gallon
	USA	1,422	
Lubricating oil	USA	10,619	3d per gallon
	Victoria	6,059	
	England	2,546	
Olive oil	Italy	112	1s 4d per gallon
	England	35	
	Greece	25	
Watches	England	7,782	
	Switzerland	2,231	
	Victoria	2,136	
	USA	1,793	
Umbrellas, parasols etc.	England	4,010	20%
	Victoria	1,299	
Smoked fish	Victoria	701	1d per lb
Tinned fish*	England	10,059	1d per lb
	Norway	2,600	
	France	1,316	
	Italy	10	

Type of Merchandise	Country of Origin	Value £ stg	Customs Duty
Pipes & cigarette cases	England	5,298	20%
	France	1,628	
Perfumes	England	4,320	20%
	USA	891	
	NSW	860	
	France	676	
	Japan	218	
	Germany	173	
Rails & related material	Belgium	21,360	$12\frac{1}{2}$%
	England	12,771	
	Germany	7,708	
Toilet soap etc.	England	2,635	3d per lb
	USA	2,593	
	Victoria	1,361	
Household soap	NSW	14,709	$\frac{1}{2}$d per lb
Cloth sacks & packing material	India	35,102	exempt
	England	276	
Sauces & pickles	England	9,631	2s per doz pint
	Victoria	7,175	jars or 1s 4d per
	USA	77	gallon
Shoes*	Victoria	48,583	30%
	England	26,511	
	South Australia	21,704	
	Italy	1	
Stearin (wax)	Victoria	7,123	$\frac{1}{2}$d per lb
	Germany	7,113	
	England	1,376	
	Belgium	1,375	
Lemon juice & other fruit juices	England	985	9d per gallon
	Victoria	478	
Tobacco (general)	Victoria	29,744	1s 6d per lb
	NSW	27,900	
	South Australia	7,030	
	England	4,072	
	Italy	1	
Tobacco (cigars)*	Victoria	3,986	variable between
	Switzerland	3,035	15% & 6s 3d per lb
	Philippines	2,823	
	NSW	2,427	
	Germany	1,906	
	England	853	
	Italy	29	
Tobacco (cigarettes)*	USA	23,057	6s 6d per lb
	NSW	12,662	
	Victoria	2,887	
	England	1,685	
Table covers	England	4,693	15%
Floor rugs	England	19,953	15%
Netting for veils & curtains	England	10,887	exempt
	India	860	
Pottery/earthenware*	England	6,023	20%
	Victoria	2,352	

Type of Merchandise	Country of Origin	Value £ stg	Customs Duty
	Germany	1,171	
Textiles, cotton & linen*	England	139,666	5%
	Victoria	4,084	
	Germany	2,352	
	Italy	141	
Silk or silk mix*	England	19,005	15%
	Japan	5,541	
	Victoria	4,404	
	France	2,762	
	China	1,835	
	Switzerland	1,022	
	Italy	326	
Velvet*	England	28,956	15%
	France	3,165	
	Germany	2,428	
	Switzerland	2,101	
	Victoria	1,766	
	Italy	239	
Wool*	England	85,423	15%
	France	9,263	
	Victoria	9,185	
	Germany	1,139	
Clothing (manufactured)*	England	10,443	15%
	Belgium	270	
	India	104	
Clothing (various items)*	England	150,125	25%
	Victoria	64,125	
	USA	7,664	
	Germany	6,616	
	Italy	20	
Varnish	England	4,245	1s 9d per gallon
Glass (objects, mirrors, panes)*	Germany	10,894	20% mirrors 5s,
	England	8,848	7s 6d & 10%
	Belgium	3,446	per foot according
	Italy	14	to size of pane
Sparkling wine	France	11,004	12s per gallon
	Victoria	1,070	
	Germany	488	
	Italy	–	
Bottled wine*	South Australia	4,005	between 8s &
	France	1,343	14s per bottle
	Spain	908	
	Victoria	820	
	England	408	
	Italy	–	
Wine (other)	South Australia	4,223	6s to 14s
	Spain	2,212	per gallon
	Portugal	776	
	England	615	
Wax matches	England	5,580	6d per gross
	Germany	2,949	(12 doz)
	Italy	1,539	

Type of Merchandise	Country of Origin	Value £ stg	Customs Duty
	Belgium	1,296	
Wooden matches	England	452	6d per gross
	Sweden	441	
	Germany	198	
Sulphur*	England	422	exempt
	Victoria	374	
	Italy	73	
Sugar	Australia	41,229	6s per cwt

Even a superficial examination of the list of imports into Western Australia gives our commerce little cause for comfort. Italy could compete successfully in many areas. However, our exporters are weighed down by some inexplicable inertia and ignore the existence of a market where they would be able to sell a quantity of our products easily.

A very important fact that one should bear in mind is that, in manufacturing of all kinds, our industry holds a privileged position compared to other countries, because of the relatively cheap labour available in Italy. I have had the opportunity, on many occasions, to speak with foreign commercial travellers all of whom confirm the fact. As an example, they point to our cotton cloth which, almost always, beats the competition on world markets. It is estimated that this product could be offered for sale in Australia at about 15 per cent less than a similar foreign cloth; the same applies to a range of other products. Even taking into account that wages are tending to rise in Italy, we still have a tremendous advantage. However, despite this, we see that Italian exports are very meagre and that many items are completely unavailable. Only citrus fruits (£7,528), wax matches (£1,535), straw and felt hats (£1,464), macaroni (£718), almonds (£611) and marble (£599) are significant. And even some of these figures could be easily increased. Take hats, for example. Not just our straw hats, but felt ones as well, could beat the competition not only from Britain but also from local manufacturers. The *Borsalino* hat, which has already acquired international repute, has begun to be very fashionable in the eastern states of Australia; in almost all the shops in Sydney and Melbourne one can see hats displaying the words 'Made in Italy,' meaning, a fine product and top price. In this regard, the market in Perth still needs to be developed because all the felt hats worn here come from either England or Melbourne. There would not be much competition because the Australian or English product sold here is of very poor quality and is also over-priced.

Our marble could also command much higher prices. The city is now undergoing transformation. They are pulling down the shacks of the colonial period and erecting stylish buildings in which our marble could be used to great effect.

However, I do not think there is much chance of increasing the figures for citrus fruit because they are imported from Italy in the off-season here. The quantity imported corresponds, more or less, to the amount of the fruit consumed when no local product is available. In fact, Italy is the only foreign country from which citrus are imported. Nevertheless, Italy must be careful not to lose its place. California and Spain could pose a grave threat to us.

Likewise there would be little chance of increasing our exports of pasta and edible oils; the foodstuffs eaten by the English are considerably different from ours. As can be seen, the trade in olive oil is minimal in Australia. It could be said that oil, in the culinary sense, is unknown. The same could be said for pastas. Sometimes one reads *Minestra di maccheroni* on some hotel menus, although it is hard to find a single piece of pasta in the broth. Oil and pasta are eaten, almost exclusively, by the Italian community.

There are three or four fellow countrymen who occasionally import these goods, but their trade is slight. Also, it should be taken into account that, when our workers go back to Italy (on their periodic trips), they always bring back a certain amount of pasta, oil, salami etc., so they can do a little business.

Now we come to those products where Italy is scarcely, or not, represented at all but where it could well compete.

First of all cotton fabric of all sorts ought to be imported (presently the trade is worth £14) as well as ready made clothing such as shirts, vests, underwear, handkerchiefs, socks etc., because it is almost impossible to make them here because of the very high cost of labour.

Woollen cloth and clothing would also find a ready market here, as well as silk goods for which Italy only has £326 worth of the market and £239 of that for velvets.

Anchovy paste, which is used everywhere in Australia, is wholly imported from England which, in turn, imports the raw material, known as Gorgona anchovies, from Italy. It seems to me that Italy could manufacture the paste from the raw material and export it directly to the consumer.

Italy, which is a first-class producer of sulphur, accounts for only £75 of the market while England accounts for £422 and Victoria £374 and neither is a producer of this mineral.

The figures for tobacco (£30) need to be looked into because con-sumption in Australia is considerable. Most of the tobacco products, especially cigars and cigarettes, sold as 'Italian,' actually come from Switzerland, despite their Italian labels.

A figure of £14 for glassware and assorted products is absolutely incomprehensible given that in Italy this industry is so organised and prosperous. But the most ridiculous figures relate to objets d'art. Their importation, however, needs to undertaken with care. It is advisable to restrict the value of any item in this category (paintings, bronzes, marble etc.) to no more than £5.

Italy does not figure at all in the paper and office supplies category, although it would also be easy to be competitive in this area.

Other items which could be imported include mineral water, shoes, candles, terracotta articles, anchovy sauce, sultanas etc.

Another area to be explored is that of explosives which, because of the mines, are heavily used here. An attempt might also be made in the area of spirits, such as whisky, gin, rum and cognac, £100,000 worth of which are imported. It might also be possible to introduce our own brands. The customs duty is 14s a gallon. Given the high duty on wine, Italy should limit itself to exporting fine wine in bottles.

Export Trade

We now come to a brief discussion about exports. Elsewhere, I have referred to the total figure for each year in the four year period 1901–1904. Below is the value for the main products (£ stg).

Goods	1901	1902	1903	1904
Gold (not minted)	3,941,797	3,318,958	4,061,767	3,965,095
Minted gold	2,807,481	4,149,869	4,556,192	4,563,537
Wool	378,135	458,078	443,743	419,395
Timber	572,354	500,593	619,705	654,949
Hides	86,559	111,456	128,625	126,672
Pearls and mother-of-pearl	130,730	178,699	224,322	164,505
Sandalwood	73,931	61,771	37,913	25,417
Copper	110,769	12,904	39,815	7,859
Tin	52,102	39,398	52,193	41,179
Various	261,462	361,405	218,602	162,517
Total	8,515,623	9,051,358	10,324,732	10,271,497

Gold is always the main item. It has superseded timber. Wool has a very promising future as well as copper and tin in the mineral sphere. Rich tin mines have recently been discovered.

Wool should be of particular interest to our businessmen. It is well known that Australia is a producer of exceptionally fine wool. The Geelong and Sydney markets supply the whole world.

In the course of my frequent journeys from Europe to Western Australia and from Western Australia to the eastern states (Victoria and New South Wales) I have often had the opportunity of meeting representatives of large British, Belgian, French and German firms who come to Australia at certain times of the year to buy wool. Yet I have never had the pleasure of meeting one Italian representative. I have asked why this is in Italy and, generally, I am told that not having a large turnover, there is no advantage in sending special representatives. It is easier to buy it in London which is the clearing house for wool in the world.

I must take the liberty of saying that our businessmen have very little initiative. I will concede that not every firm can afford the considerable expenses involved in sending a representative or commercial traveller, but why cannot they get together among themselves and form a co-operative, or better still establish an appropriate organisation empowered to buy wholesale and then sell it to our business concerns? The commissions which are currently paid to the English, French and Germans would then remain at home.

I think that an Italo–Australian import/export corporation, endowed with enough capital, would be able to negotiate successful deals.

Let us not overlook the pearl market, especially mother-of-pearl. The pearl beds of Western Australia are extremely rich. The two most important centres of pearl fishing are at Broome and Shark Bay. A commercial enterprise might find it useful to exploit the industry. It is, without doubt, very lucrative, especially when the price of mother-of-pearl is high. It was very high in 1903, but slumped badly in 1904, although it is again on the rise. There is a big difference between the price for mother-of-pearl fished in Broome and that in Shark Bay. It is reckoned that the price of the former is five times that of the latter.

The value of pearls varies greatly according to colour, size and shape. There are some that have sold for up to £6000. It is reckoned that every ton of oysters yields on the average £20 worth of pearls. The industry is generally carried on by those who own five to ten luggers.

The cost of building and equipping a lugger is estimated to cost £400 on average, and a diver's gear costs £150. The divers, who do most of the hard work, get paid about £22 a month, as well as board, and they are entitled to 20 lire per ton of the shell fished. It is estimated that a diver can recover half a ton a month.

A maximum depth of 18 fathoms (1 fathom = 6 feet) can be achieved in a diving suit. A colossal fortune awaits the person who discovers a way to reach even greater depths. It has been proved that rich pearling beds extend to a depth of 30 to 40 fathoms.

Western Australia, like all the continent, is covered with an immense eucalypt forest which includes many varieties. Jarrah is much esteemed, both for outdoor construction (it is resistant to termites, the scourge of all other timbers found in tropical countries), for jetty piles, and for use in areas where timber is exposed alternately to damp and dry conditions, such as railway sleepers. Our oak is good for eight to ten years in these conditions, whereas jarrah, even after thirty years, is little changed.

I recently took two examples of railway sleepers to Italy. One was new and the other had been buried for twenty years. There was hardly any difference between the two. The Indian and South African railways, as well as certain others in the East, use Australian timber exclusively. With the supply of oak steadily diminishing in Europe, especially in Italy, is it not time to consider seriously the feasibility of importing Australian timber? The cost, however, is very high because of the high price of labour and freight in Western Australia (the workers in this industry earn an average of 11s a day).

The railway sleepers from Karachi in India cost 6s 6d each on the spot, whereas the cost in Italy would be about 8s each. In Italy those made of oak presently cost something in the range of 5 lire. However, as I have said, one has to bear in mind that the life of a jarrah railway sleeper is three times that of ours.

One export which could offer excellent returns is the mineral copper, which exists in immense quantities in the state. Some very rich deposits were found recently in the North-West region (Pilbara). Experienced persons have assured me that, in order to melt it down, it would be better to export it to Europe by sailing ship because of the high cost of production in Australia. It would also be possible for someone to save a lot on the price if representatives were sent to deal directly with the mines scattered about the interior. Copper mines are generally small undertakings, worked in an essentially primitive manner, whose owners would be glad to find a well-established firm to which they could sell off their product at regular intervals.

An import/export company could also turn its attention to many other local products which could return good profits, such as lamb, kangaroo and possum skins (total export value for 1904 £102,000), and frozen meat and entrails. Rabbit skins could be obtained from other states of Australia, and, in particular, the fur of this rodent, which is largely used in the manufacture of felt.

Rabbits, which incidentally are the scourge of agriculture and the Australian pastoral industry, multiply by the millions. They have also given rise to a very lucrative export both for their skin and their meat (frozen).

At Whitecliffe, in Western Australia, as elsewhere, opals, perhaps the most beautiful in the world for their 'fire' (brilliant red, green and blue with amazing flashes) are quarried. These quarries are not owned by large companies but by individual miners. The price of this gem, at the point of origin, is at least two thirds less than in Italy. Even in this area Italy does not know how to look after its interests overseas, paying the usual commission to foreigners.

Before completing this examination of the import/export trade of Western Australia, I believe it would be opportune to provide a statistical picture of the main manufactured products of this state. The reader will thus be able to gain an understanding of the relationship which exists between trade and local production.

Products from Western Australia's principal manufacturers (excluding mining) for the years 1904 and 1905

Goods	Units	1904	1905
Tanned hides (horse and cattle)		19,267	20,396
Tanned hides (other animals)		8,636	2,560
Soap	Cwt (I)	27,854	28,005
Candles	Pounds	1,989,610	1,626,000
Bricks		50,332,190	44,045,355
Lime	Tons	214,799	148,873
Flour	Sacks	1,024,593	1,332,748
Sparkling waters	Dozens of bottles	1,377,064	1,552,509
Cordials	"	17,859	20,673
Beer	Gallons	5,424,474	5,144,050
Tobacco	Pounds	"	"
Cigars & Cigarettes	Number	649,700	587,200
Shoes	Pair	232,692	186,703
Gas	Cubic feet	58,561,000	64,764,800
Dressed timber	"	143,594,950	137,196,860

The total number of manufacturing firms in Western Australia was 793 in 1904 and 777 in 1905; the number of persons employed respectively was 13,427 and 13,481.

Notes concerning the commerce of Australasia

I believe I have, in the statement already tendered, presented a picture of the exports and imports of Western Australia with reasonable accuracy. Given that the Consulate in Perth has jurisdiction only for that state, I have had to limit myself to examining figures for there alone. It can be assumed, however, that the relative importance of the various foreign countries referred to above, to the trade of Western Australia is approximately the same as their trade with the Commonwealth as a whole.

In any event, I believe it would be useful to refer to some figures which might give a general idea of the trade of the different states of the Australian confederation, and of their economic importance. I will also refer to the relative figures for New Zealand which, as I have already noted, is not part of the said confederation.

First of all, let us examine the area and the population in different states for 1905.

	Area in square miles	Population
New South Wales	310,700	1,496,050
Queensland	668,690	528,048
South Australia	903,690	378,208
Tasmania	26,215	181,105
Victoria	87,884	1,218,571
Western Australia	975,920	254,779
New Zealand	107,751	882,462

As one can see, the most populous states are New South Wales, Victoria and New Zealand which were the first colonised. South Australia has a vast area, but, except for the south coast and the extreme north, is just desert. Western Australia, the last to be settled in chronological terms (development really only began about twenty years ago with the discovery of gold), is the state that has the greatest future both in terms of its mineral wealth and its possession of vast stretches of prime land suitable for agriculture and grazing.

Western Australia's most elementary advantage over the other states, namely that it is closer to European markets, cannot be overlooked.

The voyage from Genoa to Fremantle (the main port of Western Australia) takes about 25 or 26 days; from there it is another eight days to Melbourne and ten days to Sydney.

The commercial importance of Western Australia has also been recognised by the Italian government. In fact, the only other official Consulate, besides that in Melbourne, is the one in Perth.

Here now are the relative figures (£ stg) for imports and exports in the different states for 1905.

	Imports		Exports	
	Total	*for each inhabitant*	*Total*	*for each inhabitant*
New South Wales	29,424,008	£19.18s.0d.	36,737,002	£24.17s.2d.
Queensland	6,699,345	£12.14s.10d.	11,939,594	£22.14s.3d.
South Australia	8,439,609	£22.6s.4d.	9,490,667	£25.1s.10d.
Tasmania	2,651,754	£14.15s.10d.	3,711,616	£20.14s.1d.
Victoria	22,337,886	£18.8s.6d.	22,758,828	£18.15s.5d.
Western Australia	6,481,874	£25.18s.1d.	9,871,019	£39.9s.1d.
New Zealand	12,828,857	£14.14s.11d.	15,665,947	£17.19s.11d.
Total	£88,863,333	£18.3s.2d.	£110,184,673	£22.10s.4d.

As can be seen, Western Australia, in proportion to its population, heads the list of Australian states in terms of its imports and exports per capita.

I will now give some comparative figures (in ounces) regarding gold, the main product of the different Australian states.

	Ounces
Western Australia	1,983,230
Victoria	765,596
Queensland	639,140
New South Wales	269,817
Tasmania	65,921
South Australia	29,110
New Zealand	467,897
Total	4,220,711

In the same year the United States produced 4,090,532 (ounces) and the Transvaal 3,773,316; from this it can be seen that Australia holds first place in world production and Western Australia by itself holds third place.

The export of wool from Western Australia in 1905 was worth £494,872. In the same year, again in Western Australia, the total number of sheep was 3,120,703. Each sheep would, therefore, be worth 4.80 lire in terms of its wool (a sheep is worth about £1).

The figures below show the number of sheep in each state in 1905.

Western Australia	3,120,703
New South Wales	39,506,764
Queensland	12,535,231
South Australia	6,202,330
Tasmania	1,583,561
Victoria	11,455,115
New Zealand	19,130,875

It would not be out of place to have a glance at shipping movements, including arrivals and departures, for 1905.

	Ships
New South Wales	5,419
Queensland	1,660
South Australia	2,537
Tasmania	1,916
Victoria	4,650
Western Australia	1,318
New Zealand	1,254
Total	18,754

The main steamship companies who ply regularly between Australia and Europe are as follows (all stop at either Fremantle or Albany in Western Australia).

Peninsular and Oriental (English). Originates in London and sails every two weeks; connects in Port Said with fast steamships, belonging to the same line, which takes the luggage for India from and to Brindisi; stops in Marseilles.

Oriental Line (English). Originates in London and sails every two weeks; stops in Naples.

Messageries Maritimes. Originates in Marseilles and sails every four weeks.

Norddeutscher Lloyd (German). Originates in Bremen and sails every four weeks; stops at Genoa and Naples.

The above lines travel via the Suez Canal. The following lines sail via the Cape of Good Hope.

German Australian. Originates in Hamburg, irregular sailings, cargo only.

Lund's Line (English). Originates in London and sails every four weeks.

White Star Line (English). Originates in Liverpool and sails every four weeks.

Aberdeen White Star (English). Originates in London and sails every four weeks.

The lines that offer a direct route between Italy and Australia are, therefore, the Oriental Line and the Norddeutscher Lloyd. The first stops in Naples and the second in Genoa and Naples. Allow me, at this point, to make a few observations. The adverse effect on our position in Australia, arising from the absence of a shipping line of our own, cannot be overestimated. Unfortunately, beyond the Suez Canal the Italian flag is a myth. It is said it is not worth while there; nevertheless other nations find it so. Certainly, at the outset, one must be resigned to some sacrifices, and a government subsidy would be necessary. Nevertheless, the German Australian Line recently paid 11 per cent interest and the Norddeutscher Lloyd 8 per cent.[2] Obviously there is a certain profit to be had. The Norddeutscher Lloyd line, which began many years ago with very small steamers, now has a huge fleet on the Australian run. Recently (1906) it has replaced its existing ships with new vessels built especially for the purpose.

We have no regular lines. I would say that, in my four years in Australia, I never saw an Italian steamer, only a few sailing ships. Yet we have a tremendous advantage in having an unsurpassable geographical and commercial position in the Mediterranean.

It could be claimed that the foreign companies, which undertake transoceanic voyages that call in to Italy, have Genoa as their terminus.

---

2   The above figures have recently experienced a sharp decline (and there have been actual losses) because of the crisis in maritime transport. This fact does not, however, negate my idea which is that Italy should have a merchant navy worthy of the position it occupies in the world. The crisis will certainly pass and we must, in every way possible, ensure that we do not always occupy last place at the mercy of others.

I have often travelled on German steamers which, when they arrive in Genoa, unload most of their cargo and disembark nearly all their passengers. We Italians rejoice when we see foreigners saving us the trouble and cost of building new ships. We forget, however, the damage that such a system does both in financial terms and to our reputation overseas. However, I must quickly add that it is much better to have no line serving Australia than one consisting of our usual hulks. Australia already has a pretty poor opinion of us. Imagine if they were to see the *Washington, City of Milan, Duke of Genoa* etc.

The rates between Australia and Italy are very variable; from 15 to 18 shillings via the Cape of Good Hope and more via the Suez Canal. A serious problem, that of having to change ships, exists for those of us who want to use the regular lines which ply the Cape route. And, as one knows, this route is the most convenient for the transport of cheap bulk goods.

As I have already noted above, the regular lines sailing between Fremantle and Genoa take 25 to 26 days. The price of a ticket is between £65 and £75 for First Class, £36 to £40 for Second Class, and £13 to £15 for Third Class. From London to Fremantle via the Cape always takes 45 days by the regular lines. The prices are somewhat less.

Conclusion

It can be seen that Great Britain occupies a predominant position in Australian trade. This position is, however, now threatened by foreign countries, especially Germany, who, with daring, perseverance and adequate means, has been able to enter every market. Italy, by contrast, keeps itself apart and pays no attention whatsoever to an important commerce from which it could reap significant profit. Yet Australia is an enormous continent which, with New Zealand, measures almost 8 million square kilometres. Even though the population of 5 million is not in proportion to this vast area, one must not forget that, as we have seen, the import and export trade amounts to £199,048,006, that is, 5000 million francs.

As I have already said, Italy, because it possesses cheap labour, could compete successfully in many areas. It is true that the wages of the Italian worker are rapidly approaching those of their English and German colleagues, but a difference, which could be a vital factor in our effort to be competitive, still exists. To succeed, however, the necessary ways and means must be found.

WESTERN AUSTRALIA AS IT IS TODAY, 1906

It is essential that our businessmen be persuaded that they must negotiate with complete honesty. Dishonesty in business is, unfortunately, punished in this world. The first casualty of shady dealing is the loss of clientele; the second, and certainly the greatest, is the damage done to the good name of Italy and to the ranks of its businessmen. If I speak in this way it is because I have, unfortunately, often witnessed some deplorable incidents. It is, for example, common practice to despatch goods of inferior, if not totally rotten, quality to those ordered. If only that it was limited to fraud! Not so long ago, I recall, several boxes which came from Naples contained lava from Vesuvius instead of pasta! Moreover, both merchants and industrialists should abandon the idea, dreamed up by some of them, to get the addresses of local business firms from the Consulate and make contact with them by letter. I can say from my experience of four years that this sort of approach will achieve nothing.

The Australian businessmen, for whom, since they are Anglo-Saxons, 'time is money,' do not like to get involved in lengthy, tiresome correspondence, which often comes to nothing. What they prefer is to conclude business as quickly as possible and, at the same time, to be assured of the integrity of the person with whom they deal. In other words, it is essential that able and intelligent commercial travellers, equipped with complete catalogues, be sent from Italy. Only in this way can we hope for practical results.

I will not hide the fact that it is very difficult to introduce our products, and other non-British goods. Many Australian firms are branches of English companies and are unwilling to buy goods from overseas producers which might compromise their usual business activities. Some goods, which come into the country as English goods, are actually of Italian origin. It would be much better for our sake if these goods were introduced directly from Italy.

The Germans have overcome this difficulty by establishing some of their better-known firms here and they do a huge amount of business. Italy should follow this example, otherwise the momentum of our trade will always be slight. That is why considerable capital is needed and why, perhaps, the initiative in this field can only be undertaken by an established company.

Having our own shipping line would provide a big boost to our trade. We need to recognise that our steamers, with the exception of the latest, are of poor quality both in terms of speed and comfort. Compared to the magnificent English and German liners our ships cut a poor figure. As I have already observed, up to the present there has been no Italian shipping line sailing between Italy and Australia.

Perhaps with good sense prevailing things will improve. There is a need, however, to change the system and, what is more important, make this change as soon as possible. I suggest a passenger and cargo service via the Suez Canal and another for cargo only, via the Cape of Good Hope.

The establishment of communities of our fellow countrymen on the Australian continent would also be very useful for the expansion of our trade. The commercial links would thus be established naturally, as has occurred in South America and the United States where trade with Italy owes its origin and later growth to emigration.

It would also be very useful to invest some of our capital in Australia. There are a good many enterprises down there which would certainly return handsome profits. Until now Italy has only known how to export work in the shape of its emigrants, who (unless they are of an excellent type) are becoming unwanted all over the world. A judicious investment of capital, even in small amounts, could be a priceless base for further development of our trade.

Australia in general, and Western Australia in particular, possess inexhaustible agricultural and mineral resources, for the most part untouched. The pastoral industry, especially if directed to the pro-duction of wool, returns fabulous profits now. Suffice to say that, in all the nations of the world with the exception of Argentina and Australia, the number of sheep has tended to diminish, whereas the consumption of wool has increased.

It really is time that Italians took a bit more action and learned how to achieve their rightful place in the world. In Italy they do nothing but speak in admiration of the English, the Americans and the Germans, and envy their success. It would be better for us to chat less and act more, not to lose ourselves in cloudy metaphysics but be more practical; admire less and imitate more those who appear to be superior to us; superior up to a certain point, because we lack nothing in talent, nor in spirit of initiative, nor in capital. Only we must be more practical and steadfast.

If individual firms lack the courage and the capacity to meet the heavy expenses required to develop trade with the southern continent, why not consider the idea of combining activity? An Italo–Australian commercial company, even if not endowed with ample means, could certainly produce magnificent results. Its members could come to an agreement about establishing shops to stock and sell our goods in the main cities of Australia, something that would be almost impossible for a private individual. Then, for many articles, direct contact between local firms and their counterparts in Italy could be established. For many other items, especially those sold in small quantities (cotton, wool and silk fabric, clothing, shoes, hats, foodstuffs, objets d'art etc.), such shops would be of great advantage and would lead on to the conquest of further markets. There are several such establishments or 'bazaars' in Australia (Boan Brothers, Foy and Gibson etc.) and they all do extremely well.

The head offices should be in Perth (Western Australia), very close to the port of Fremantle, which now, in most senses, forms one city; Adelaide (South Australia); Melbourne (Victoria); Sydney (New South Wales); Brisbane (Queensland) and Wellington in New Zealand.

The scheme could begin in Perth, the Australian commercial centre closest to Europe and, in terms of the country at large, an almost independent market, since its railway is not yet linked to those in the eastern states. Such a company would have the chance to take into its hands the importation of wool to Italy, a trade presently controlled by foreigners, to whom we pay high commissions. With our own agents and representatives spread about the southern continent, it would be possible to investigate more precisely the immense resources of a country still largely virgin. At the right time we could increase the scope of our activity in particular areas, undertaking the exploitation of certain industries, such as the production of wool, fishing for pearls and mother-of-pearl, the excavation of opal mines, the transportation of copper etc.

The company, if ably directed and administered, could easily rise to great heights. The world famous Dalgety Company is a good example, having some fifty branches throughout Australia. If our investors and industrialists decided thus, they would not only serve their own interests but they would also make a worthwhile contribution to Italy's position in the wider world.

Bibliography

Other works by Leopoldo Zunini on emigration and commerce

Emigrazione, Savona, 1890.

'Dell'importanza comparativa di Fremantle ed Albany con alcune notizie sull'Australia occidentale in genere e sulla navigazione, il commercio, e la colonia italiana in quella regione', *Bollettino Ufficiale del Ministero d'Agricultura, Industria e Commercio* (MAIC), Anno II, Vol. IV, folio 18, 10 November 1903.

'La colonia italiana nell'Australia occidentale', *Emigrazione e Colonie Vol. II, Asia, Africa, Oceania*, Rome, Ministero degli affari esteri, 1906.

'Il commercio dell'Australia, per gli anni 1901–1905, con speciale riguardo all'Italia e ai prodotti che vi potrebbe importare', *Bollettino MAIC*, Anno VI, Vol. VI, folio 5, 1907.

Other works about Zunini and the immigration scheme

G. Ricci, 'Note di un viaggio nell'Australia Occidentale', *Bollettino dell'Emigrazione*, 9, 1907, pp. 1–67.

Margot Melia, 'The Zunini Scheme—A Plan for Italian Group Settlement in Western Australia, 1906–1908', in R. Bosworth & M. Melia (eds), *Aspects of Ethnicity, Studies in Western Australian History*, Vol. XII, April 1991, pp. 71–84.